THE WORLD OF
THE ANCIENT MAYA

Stelae B and C, Great Plaza, Copán

THE WORLD OF
THE ANCIENT MAYA

BY JOHN S. HENDERSON

CORNELL UNIVERSITY PRESS   *Ithaca, New York*

Library of Congress Cataloging in Publication Data

HENDERSON, JOHN S.
  The world of the ancient Maya.

  Bibliography: p.
  Includes index.
  1. Mayas.   I. Title
F1435.H46   972'.01   81-3148
ISBN 0-8014-1232-3   AACR2

First published 1981 by Cornell University Press.

International Standard Book Number 0-8014-1232-3
Library of Congress Catalog Card Number 81-3148
Printed in the United States of America

For my parents,
Kinley K. Henderson
and Louise F. Henderson

CONTENTS

MAPS

Color plates follow page 144.

Here we shall write then,
   We shall start out then, the former words,
The beginnings
   And the taproots...

So this is what we shall collect then,
   The decipherment,
The clarification,
   And the explanation
Of the mysteries
   and the illumination...

We shall save it
   Because there is no longer
A sight of the Book of Counsel,
   A sight of the bright things come from beside the sea,
The description of our shadows,
   A sight of the bright life, as it is called.
There was once the manuscript of it,
   And it was written long ago,
Only hiding his face is the reader of it,
   The mediator of it.
Great was its account
   And its description
Of when there was finished
   The birth
Of all heaven
   and earth...

—From Munro S. Edmonson, *The Book of Counsel:*
The Popol Vuh of the Quiché Maya of Guatemala

PREFACE

The World of the Ancient Maya is a survey of the Maya cultural tradition: an introduction to the societies that make it up and an exploration
of their contrasts, connections, and linked historical development. In
fashioning an overview of this remarkable array of local societies and
regional cultures that evolved together, I have tried to give due weight
to common cultural themes and to the myriad variations on them. To
this end, I have permitted myself a modest degree of repetition in the
pages that follow.

The Introduction places ancient Maya civilization and my approach
to it in the context of larger issues in archaeological thought. Chapter 1,
a sketch of outsiders' views of Maya civilization, describes the discovery and conquest of the Maya world by the Spaniards and traces the
development of modern Maya studies. Chapter 2 is an introduction to
the environments and peoples of the Maya world and their place in the
wider Mesoamerican scene. It includes a précis of the histories of the
various Maya regions, a preview of the fuller discussion in Chapters 5
through 8. Chapter 3 provides an overview of Maya societies in the
sixteenth century, when the Spaniards arrived. Chapter 4 synthesizes
basic Maya religion and philosophy; it is an introduction to the Maya
view of Maya civilization.

Chapters 5 through 8 describe the development of Maya societies
from the earliest peopling of the Maya world to the European conquest. The basic framework here is chronological, in contrast to the
regional approach of Chapter 2. The treatment of early foraging bands

and the evolution of farming in Chapter 5 relies on information from beyond the Maya world, as the archaeological record of these very ancient periods is nearly blank. With the rise of village life and of Mesoamerica's first complex societies, the discussion progressively focuses on the Maya world proper. Chapters 6 through 8 describe Maya societies and their development in the Preclassic, Classic, and Postclassic periods respectively. Chapter 8 recapitulates some of the material on the societies of the conquest period in Chapter 3, placing them in the context of late precolumbian history. Chapter 9 returns to the broader archaeological issues and theoretical concerns of the Introduction, with a less abstract discussion of the problem of explaining Maya civilization and its development in light of the information presented in the intervening pages.

The entries in the Bibliography provide a good guide to my intellectual debts to Maya scholars living and dead. All who share an interest in things Maya owe these men and women enormous gratitude. The special influence of particular scholars and points of view on my thinking is obvious, so I shall not indulge in invidious distinctions here except to extend my thanks to those who read and commented on various parts of the manuscript: Robert Ascher, Carol Greenhouse, David M. Jones, Barbara J. Lantz, Philip S. Lewis, Thomas F. Lynch, Lauris McKee, John V. Murra, David Rindos, and Robert J. Smith, all of Cornell University, and David H. Kelley of the University of Calgary. Despite the universally gentle and persuasive manner in which they expressed their criticisms, I have not accepted all of their suggestions. Three anonymous reviewers contributed marvelously disparate views of the manuscript; their efforts have improved it and clarified my thinking in unexpected ways. In addition to their many contributions to the organization and style of the book, Barbara Burnham and Barbara Salazar of Cornell University Press have been astonishingly patient with my procrastination and futile perfectionism. Jeanne J. Henderson has provided crucial advice and moral support; she originally persuaded me to do the book. George E. Stuart of the National Geographic Society provided the photographs for Figure 94 and for Color Plate 10; Anthony Aveni of Colgate University supplied Figure 102; and Anthony Wonderley of Cornell University provided Figure 118. Marjorie L. Ciaschi, Barbara Donnell, Denise Everhart, and Beverly J. Phillips cheerfully coped with my idiosyncratic hand to produce a legible manuscript. I am enormously grateful to them.

JOHN S. HENDERSON

Ithaca, New York

GUIDE TO PRONUNCIATION

Vowels are pronounced as they are in Spanish:

a as in *father*
e as in *grey*
i as *ee* in *knee*
o as in *most*
u as *oo* in *fool*

When *u* precedes another vowel, it is pronounced as English *w* (except that it is silent after *q*). A quick closing of the glottis occurs between doubled vowels, producing a short, sharp sound.

Consonants are pronounced as in Spanish, except that:

c is always hard
x is pronounced as English *sh*
k is glottalized *c*
q' is a glottalized consonant similar to *k*, but produced in the back of the mouth (in Quiché words)
ch' is glottalized *ch*
dz is glottalized *tz*
h is gently aspirated (in Maya words; silent in Spanish)
tl is voiceless—almost silent, with no buzzing of the vocal cords (at the ends of Nahuatl words)

In Maya, the stress is generally on the final syllable. In Nahuatl, it is often on the penultimate, though Spanish influence has shifted the stress to the final syllable in many cases.

Examples:

Maya:	Chichén Itzá	chee-*chain* ee-*tsah*
	Holmul	hohl-*mool*
	Iximché	ee-sheem-*chay*
	Uaxactún	wah-shahk-*toon*
	Yaxchilán	yahsh-chee-*lahn*
Nahuatl:	Quetzalcoatl	kay-tsahl-*koh*-ahtl
	Teotihuacán	now usually tay-oh-tee-wah-*kahn*
Spanish:	Palenque	pah-*lain*-kay

As the names of Mesoamerican places and peoples have entered our language through the tongue of the first Europeans to learn of their existence, such names are customarily written with the accents that are used in Spanish. That practice is followed here. Accents that normally do not appear in English-language contexts (as in Mexico and Yucatan) are omitted.

CHRONOLOGICAL CHART

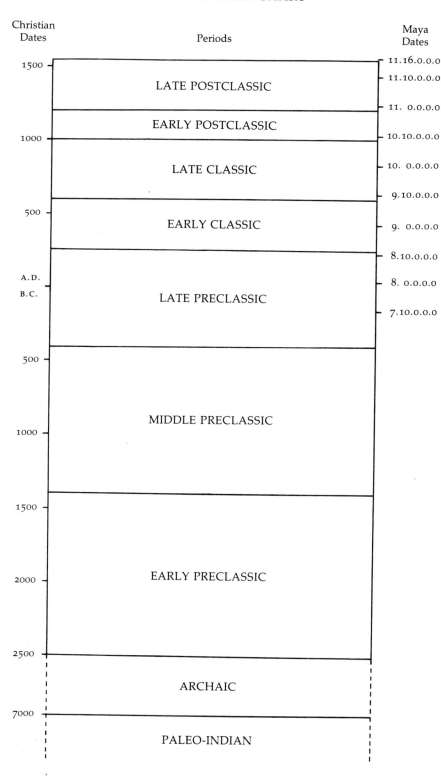

Christian Dates

Periods

Maya Dates

Christian Dates	Periods	Maya Dates
1500	LATE POSTCLASSIC	11.16.0.0.0
		11.10.0.0.0
	EARLY POSTCLASSIC	11. 0.0.0.0
1000		10.10.0.0.0
	LATE CLASSIC	10. 0.0.0.0
		9.10.0.0.0
500	EARLY CLASSIC	
		9. 0.0.0.0
		8.10.0.0.0
A.D.		8. 0.0.0.0
B.C.	LATE PRECLASSIC	
		7.10.0.0.0
500		
	MIDDLE PRECLASSIC	
1000		
1500		
	EARLY PRECLASSIC	
2000		
2500		
	ARCHAIC	
7000		
	PALEO-INDIAN	

Christian dates mentioned here and in the text represent calendar years. Radiocarbon dates have been converted to calendar dates by means of the calibration curves and tables in Ralph et al. 1973. This conversion places some events, particularly in the Early and Middle Preclassic periods, at earlier dates than in traditional chronologies. The end of the Early Preclassic period is set at 1400 B.C. so that the Middle Preclassic period corresponds to the centuries when Olmec civilization flourished in Mesoamerica; many traditional chronologies set the beginning of the Middle Preclassic after 1000 B.C., near the midpoint of Olmec history. Most traditional chronologies also recognize a Protoclassic period between the advent of the Floral Park pottery style in the southern Maya lowlands (about 50 B.C.) and the beginning of the Classic period (about A.D. 250). Because this new style was a regional phenomenon, not a reflection of cultural change throughout the Maya world or even newly developed local cultural complexity, the chart shows the Late Preclassic period continuing until A.D. 250. The chronology of the Classic and Postclassic periods depends heavily on the Maya Long Count. The Maya dates at the right of the chart reflect the 11.16 or Goodman-Martínez-Thompson correlation of the Long Count with the Christian calendar (see Chapter 4).

THE WORLD OF
THE ANCIENT MAYA

INTRODUCTION

All remnants of the distant past are romantic, but ancient Maya civilization has a special fascination. It is a "lost" civilization, whose secrets lie deep in the mysterious tropical forest. The style of Maya architecture and sculpture seems alien and bizarre. An undeciphered writing system, the repository of so many tantalizing secrets of the past, completes the effect. John Lloyd Stephens, a nineteenth-century visitor to the Maya area, was particularly sensitive to the aura of mystery clinging to the monuments of the ancient Maya:

> Of the moral effect of the monuments themselves, standing as they do in the depths of a tropical forest, silent and solemn, strange in design, excellent in sculpture, rich in ornament, different from the works of any other people, their uses and purposes and whole history so entirely unknown with hieroglyphics explaining all, but being perfectly unintelligible, I shall not pretend to convey any idea. Often the imagination was pained in gazing at them.[1]

Stephens was enchanted by Copán, a ruined Maya center in Honduras (Color Plate 1). He called it "a valley of romance and wonder where . . . the genii who attended on King Solomon seem to have been the artists,"[2] and bought the site for $50.

In some ways modern archaeology—with its endless catalogs of artifacts, meticulous descriptions of excavated buildings, prosaic discussions of environmental resources, and brash reconstructions of ancient ways of life—has dispelled this romantic aura. In other respects archaeology has deepened the mystery surrounding the Maya. It has posed the most profound Maya puzzle: that of the Classic Maya collapse. In the ninth century a spectacular cultural decline overtook the Maya of the southern part of Yucatan at what was in many ways the pinnacle of their development. Elsewhere the development of Maya civilization continued, but the southern area never recovered. In many ways the achievements of its Classic period were never duplicated. The causes of this cultural disaster, unprecedented in world history, are still not fully understood.

In a deeper sense, the fuller our understanding of the ancient Maya becomes, the more we can appreciate the enormous gulf that separates their culture from any of those in our own tradition. Nowhere is this gulf more apparent than in Maya philosophy and world view, in which time and space, the physical world and the supernatural universe, are continuous—interconnected facets of the same reality. Maya reality is not ours. It would be difficult to invent a belief system more profoundly different from our own. Similar contrasts appear, less strikingly perhaps, in every other facet of Maya civilization.

If something beyond romantic fascination were required to give Maya civilization a claim on our attention, these differences provide a powerful intellectual stimulus. If most of us are familiar today with any aspect of the ancient world, it is with the cultural heritage of European civilization, stretching back through the Classical world to the ancient Near East. The implicit feeling is that these cultures are the norm, perhaps even the highest possible stage of development, for early civilizations. A proper appreciation of their nature and their achievement can come only with the perspective of a different tradition of civilization. Maya civilization, with its totally different styles, institutions, organizations, and developmental history, provides just such a counterbalance. Even the briefest examination of Maya civilization and its history cannot fail to improve our understanding of other early civilizations.

The problems of defining civilization and explaining its rise have preoccupied some of the best minds in archaeology. Maya civilization, unusual in its setting and its form, makes a crucial contribution to our understanding of the general processes involved in the origins of civilizations. The general public and theorists alike almost universally view civilizations as urban phenomena and focus on cities as their most prominent feature.[3] Theories that purport to account for the origins of civilization are often in fact explanations for the beginnings of urban life. Maya civilization was organized around great civic centers that were seats of power and hubs of social, religious, economic, and political affairs, but they were quite different from cities as they are usually defined. Only a few Maya civic centers ever approached the density of population usually associated with cities, and then only centuries after the essential features of Maya civilization had emerged. No theory that focuses on the rise of cities can account for its development.

With few exceptions, the earliest civilizations arose and flourished in great temperate or semiarid river valleys and in environmentally varied highland regions. Only in Mesoamerica and Southeast Asia were lowland tropical forests their cradles. Most explanations for the rise of civilization are tailored to fit very different environmental circumstances and are of dubious relevance to the Maya case. The ideas of Karl Wittfogel illustrate the problem well.[4] Wittfogel, among the most influential of the theorists to consider the beginnings of civilization, was most familiar with the river-valley civilizations of China and the Near East. Reduced to its most simplistic form, his argument finds the stimulus for civilization in the development of large-scale irrigation facilities needed to feed expanding populations. Such facilities, he claims, have heavy and continuous managerial requirements that can be met only by a highly organized bureaucracy. The need for complex hydraulic works calls centralized, often despotic, states into existence. Without substantial modification, the theory of hydraulic civilization, or Oriental despotism, cannot account for the appearance and florescence of civilization in the tropical lowlands of Mesoamerica, where irrigation makes little sense as a farming strategy. The theory is also open to criticism when it is applied to the areas from which Wittfogel derived the data for its initial formulation, but it has been extremely influential.

Derivative constructs have been used to explain the rise of civilization in the highlands of central Mexico.[5] Most proponents of this school of thought also tie civilization to cities, and much of their discussion is directed toward the beginnings of urbanism. Some scholars simply do not recognize the complex cultures of lowland Mesoamerica—the Maya and the earlier Olmec—as civilizations. A related approach classifies Maya culture as a civilization, but a derivative one. In this view the Maya achieved civilization only under the heavy influence of highland urban civilizations, to whose impact they somehow owe most of their cultural complexity. The most extreme solution to the problems posed by lowland Mesoamerican civilizations must be credited to V. Gordon Childe, probably the most influential of all archaeological theorists. Childe simply eliminated the entire New World as an important arena of ancient cultural development, remarking, "Never been there—peripheral and highly suspect."[6]

For reasons that should become increasingly evident as we explore the problem, these approaches are not satisfactory. There are no rational grounds for excluding the Maya from a comparative view of early civilizations. Civilizations are, in the first place, simply very complex cultures. Adopting a definition of civilization that excludes the Maya cannot obscure the fact that in many ways Maya culture is the most complex ever to arise in the New World. The Maya are, for example, the only native American people to develop a full writing system. The origin and development of a culture of this scale and complexity can hardly be irrelevant to the problem of the origins of civilization.

The question of an appropriate definition of civilization might easily occupy a volume. A simple working definition recognizes civilization as a complex variety of culture, with considerable elaboration in many areas, involving full-time specialists of various sorts. Civilizations occupy substantial geographical areas, and their political organizations are particularly complex, reaching the state level. Institutionalized specialist leadership positions exercise effective control over substantial numbers of people. This definition leaves much unspecified: What kinds of cultural elaboration? How many specialists, of what sorts? How large an area? What kinds of political offices, controlling how many people? The strength of such a definition lies in its vagueness, which makes for flexibility, inclusiveness, and adaptability to archaeological data. Definitions of civilization that emphasize exclusiveness are of questionable value. If we wish to understand the development of complex cultures, it makes little sense to exclude some from consideration. Because early civilizations and the processes by which they came into being are not uniform, trait-list definitions do not work well. The more specific the traits, the more quickly the definition breaks down, so that exceptions are required to include some obviously relevant culture. The Olmec and Maya had no true cities; the Inca of Peru had no writing system; early Sumer had no single political state. Quantitative criteria fare even worse in the face of archaeological evidence, from which it is extraordinarily difficult to wring reliable estimates of population or of the geographical limits of political units.

Specifics are most profitably left for empirical determination and description. The best criteria are the most general, merely pointing to the most important dimensions of civilizations. Within these parameters considerable variation must be accommodated. Cultural elaboration may be found in any or all of a variety of cultural realms—technology, subsistence, economics, commerce, religion, politics. The lack of a particular development, such as bronze metallurgy, is interesting but has no effect on the status of a culture as a civilization. Civilizations are regional, not local, in scale, but the cultural ties that bind localities together may be economic or religious or social as well as political. State-level political organization must embrace a substantial population—considerably more people than would normally engage in face-to-face interaction—but they may be widely dispersed across the landscape rather than packed densely into cities. The definition is elastic enough to embrace the enormous empires of the Inca and ancient Egypt, the city-states of early Mesopotamia, and the regional states of the Classic Maya.

Maya culture, with its monumental art and architecture, variety of occupational specialists, writing system, elaborate body of astrological science, and regional-state political organization, qualifies by any reasonable set of criteria as a civilization. All indications are that it is a primary civilization. There is no convincing evidence that its development depended to a significant degree on influence from the highland civilizations of central Mexico. The tropical-forest setting of Maya civilization and its lack of true cities make it particularly interesting. Its sudden, unprecedented collapse lends Maya civilization additional importance for general theories of cultural development.

Maya civilization also makes a particularly fascinating case study in culture-historical reconstruction on other grounds. A multifaceted and multidisciplinary approach is appropriate for any investigation of culture history, particularly for a complex prehistoric culture. Because of the variety of types and sources of information, Maya civilization lends itself exceptionally well to such an approach.

The creators of Maya civilization did not disappear without issue. Their descendants today occupy vast areas of Guatemala and eastern Mexico.[7] In the face of heavy pressures toward change, now in their fifth century, they cling tenaciously to their own cultural tradition. Mayas have accommodated themselves to the dominant Spanish-American culture in a variety of ways that permit the preservation of traditional patterns. Millions of people still grow up speaking Maya languages as their first tongues and wrest a living from the land principally by means of the ancient traditional methods of slash-and-burn farming. In some regions the old gods still command primary allegiance, and everywhere Christianity is tempered with a strong admixture of native beliefs and practices.

Careful study of the Maya of today can be a priceless source of information about the Maya of precolumbian times. A simple projection of modern Maya culture into the past, though, is useless, for no culture is static. Cultures exist in a dynamic equilibrium with their environments, both natural and cultural. No modern Maya group is a living relic of its ancestry. Such a view ignores one of the most striking aspects of postconquest Maya history: the remarkable flexibility that has allowed Maya cultures to adapt to European domination without losing their distinctiveness. Other bars to a simple backward projection are equally obvious. Which modern Maya society should be the model for ancient Maya culture? Even the briefest survey of the dozens of Maya groups produces one impression above all: that of a cultural kaleidoscope, in which variations of the same elements are combined and recombined to produce an array of related cultural groups whose multifaceted contrasts represent variations on a theme. This variation reflects differences in the ways Maya groups have adapted to the European conquest as well as a complex cultural heritage from precolumbian times. It is not even a simple matter to sort out borrowings from Spanish culture, so subtle are the ways in which they are altered, recombined, and reworked into the fabric of the native tradition.

So many and complex are the contrasts among the Maya of today that it is in some ways difficult to recognize what all hold in common—to specify the essential features of a Maya culture. The only really obvious common denominator is language: all Maya groups speak related tongues. That is in fact how they are defined: in an ethnographic context, that is what one means by a Maya group. In the realm of language, too, Maya groups vary strikingly. Some linguists recognize more than two dozen distinct languages, many of them mutually unintelligible, within the Maya family. The precise relationships among them are a matter of some dispute among linguists. All are recognizably Maya, though, either because language reflects cultural relationships particularly clearly or, more likely, because linguists are more adept at detecting relationships among languages than other cultural anthropologists are at assessing connections among economic systems, political institutions, social organizations, religious beliefs, or art styles.

An enormous quantity of written documents records information, from snippets to treatises, about the Maya between the arrival of Europeans and the present day. The works of early historians, both Europeans and natives interested in recording aspects of their own tradition, preserve not only traditional Maya history, but also literature, poetry, song, myth, and ritual. Precious nuggets of information may be gleaned from *conquistadores'* memoirs and from travelers' journals. Administrative records of state and church complete the list. These records range from general summary descriptions of regions and peoples for the information of distant officials to accounts of court proceedings, dispute settlements, investigations of officials, and all of the minutiae with which bureaucracies concern themselves. Together they constitute a rich fund of information about the Maya. Having been accumulated through such a diversity of intents, it is not a particularly coherent body of information, and much of it remains scattered in dusty archives, unpublished and even unexamined. Still, taken together, these sources can be used, along with reconstructions of the history of Maya languages, to extend the ethnographic record backward in time. The historical ethnography of the conquest period, sketchy though it is, shows no less variation than the modern Maya scene. The sixteenth-century Maya, of course, were no more fossilized representatives of their precolumbian ancestors than are their modern descendants.

Working back into the preconquest period, for which no eyewitness accounts exist, is still more difficult. For the late prehispanic period in northern Yucatan and the central Maya highlands, the native historical traditions set down after the conquest are primary sources. They must be used with extreme caution, for they are not free from bias; nor do they pretend to be objective accounts. Like all histories, they adopt particular points of view, serving particular political ends. These ends may be apparent, as in the case of Spanish churchmen who described the history of a people whose pagan religion was to be obliterated. Native Maya biases are much less transparent, and much more misleading. Though recorded in European script, sometimes by Spaniards and sometimes by reeducated Mayas, the early colonial histories belong at least in part to the Maya tradition of history. Maya history has its own set of goals and assumptions, which give it an entirely different character from European history. Later ethnographic observations and historical linguistics may also contribute to general reconstructions of the precolumbian Maya, but inferences based on these sources seldom provide specific insights.

The farther into preconquest Maya culture we try to penetrate, the more our reconstructions depend on archaeological evidence. Archaeologists draw inferences about people from patterns in the material traces they have left behind: tools and utensils, food remains, remnants of buildings, layouts of settlements, distributions of settlements across the landscape. Such traces are in many areas the only available evidence with which prehistory can be reconstructed. There are other lines of evidence for the Maya, but for periods earlier than the latest preconquest era, archaeology will remain the principal source of information, at least until decipherment of the Maya writing system has advanced considerably beyond its present state.

The archaeological record of the Maya area is by no means uniform. The vagaries of preservation and accessibility of archaeological remains ensure that some regions and time periods are less well represented than others. Large zones are virtually untouched. Even in the most thoroughly investigated regions, research has emphasized certain sites, usually the largest, richest, and most impressive, to the neglect or even exclusion of others. Archaeologists have investigated few small settlements without major public architecture or sculpture. Within the large centers, excavations have usually focused on the impressive buildings and monuments. Few projects have set out to discover the full range of variation within a site in house types, or subsistence strategies, or artifact inventories. Not even the most intensively excavated Maya center is fully understood either in terms of its internal formal and functional variation or in terms of its regional context, its functional role within the region, and its relationships with other settlements.

Nevertheless, enough data have accumulated from various regions and time periods to indicate a very great deal of regional variation among the preconquest Maya. Such variations existed in every period for which data are available. They tended to increase through time, and were particularly pronounced in some periods.

The most productive approach to understanding Maya culture history, then, demands the use of all available sources of information: archaeology, history, linguistics, and ethnography. Few other ancient civilizations have such a wealth of available material. The value and the potential of this approach is particularly apparent in the investigation of ancient Maya thought and symbols. An approach to the Maya hieroglyphic texts in isolation, in terms of their own pattern and structure, yields minimal understanding. Broadening the scope of inquiry to include insights into Maya religion from ethnography, modern analyses of Maya languages, and documents of the colonial period touching on Maya writing, ritual, and belief sets the stage for a multifaceted approach that can lead to a reasonably full understanding of at least some texts and some aspects of Maya thought. Ultimately there is a tremendously exciting potential for actually entering, albeit partially and hesitantly, the symbolic world of the precolumbian Maya. This is a rare opportunity in any area and absolutely unique for the preconquest Americas. It adds considerably to the interest and importance of the Maya as a case study in culture-historical reconstruction.

The chapters that follow examine the history of Maya culture from the earliest archaeological traces of settlement in the Maya region through the great florescence of the first millennium of the Christian era down to the period of the Spanish conquest. The enormous amount of cultural variation within the Maya world at any given time does not lighten the task of understanding the complex processes by which the Maya cultural tradition evolved. Yet this regional diversity is itself a crucial fact of Maya culture history. It can hardly be ignored.

The Classic Maya collapse is a case in point. While it was a spectacular episode in the culture history of the southern lowlands, it did not embrace all of Classic Maya civilization. Farther north, great centers continued to flourish for half a millennium. The common tendency to view all of Maya culture history in terms of the southern lowlands can be seriously misleading.

To consider the growth and development of the Maya cultural tradition and its internal variation at many time levels is a complex task. To examine such regional and developmental complexity through the lens of archaeological evidence, with its all too apparent biases and lacunae, compounds the difficulties. Whenever possible, the evidence of linguistics, ethnography, and history will be brought to bear on the problems at hand, but archaeology is the principal source of data. Too often it is the only source.

It is important to try to examine the great Maya centers as varied functional entities, not simply as collections of monuments and buildings. Insofar as the data permit, each must be placed in its regional context, as a part of a functioning system. This approach dictates a concern with the relationships among contemporary settlements as well as with their similarities and contrasts. At a higher level, the focus shifts to the discovery of contrasts among the many regions of the Maya area and to identification of the relationships that linked them.

Though it is interesting to point to some of the crucial factors and processes involved in the growth and development of the Maya cultural tradition, I shall not attempt to isolate governing causal factors. It would be naive to expect to understand the evolution of a phenomenon as complex and multifaceted as Maya civilization by reference to one or a few causal factors. An understanding of the evolution of Maya culture is more readily achieved, with much less distortion, through detailed culture history: the most precise possible reconstruction of the regional variants of Maya culture and their functional interrelations during as many periods as possible. When these factors are woven into a descriptive historical narrative of a set of related cultures within a single tradition, it may be possible to recognize the cultural processes that connect the stages. If not, at least no violence will have been done to the historical complexity of the Maya cultural tradition.

Myriad threads intertwine in the tapestry of the Maya cultural tradition; their colors blend subtly to represent many themes. We cannot achieve a full understanding of the processes by which Maya civilization came into being by pulling out a few bright threads. True insight depends on the laborious unraveling of many historical strands.

CHAPTER ONE

THE DISCOVERY OF THE MAYA

THE SPANISH CONQUEST

In 1502, during his final voyage of discovery, Columbus met an impressive native vessel in the Gulf of Honduras, near the Bay Islands (Map 1). This was the first encounter between Europeans and the Maya.[1] Commanded by a merchant from the "province called Maia," the canoe bore his entourage and a rich and varied cargo of trade goods: metal tools and ornaments, metalworking paraphernalia, clubs edged with stone blades, pottery, cotton garments with multicolored designs, and a wealth of other items. No one, apparently, attached particular interest to this episode, later cataloged without emphasis among the events of the voyage. Nor was there a special reason to do otherwise. Though plainly prosperous, these traders did not seem to differ much from other native groups the Spaniards had met. Certainly they did not display the anticipated wealth and splendor of the Orient. In any case, the encounter produced no immediate impulse to locate the homeland of the traders. Even when more intensive and sustained contact with the Maya came about in the following decades, it occasioned no special comment, for the impressive achievements of Maya civilization were then centuries and more in the past. No sixteenth-century Maya settlement could compare with Tenochtitlán, the splendid island capital of the Aztecs, and the size and wealth of the Aztec state were unmatched north of Peru. Naturally, the Maya at-

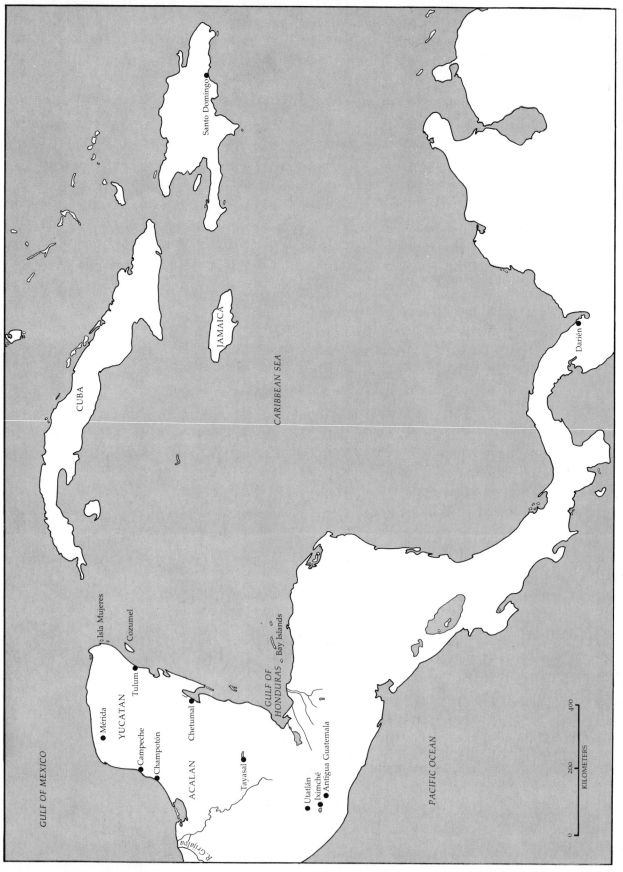

Map 1. The Spanish Main: the Maya world and the Caribbean

tracted corrspondingly less attention from early chroniclers and historians, so that innumerable aspects of their native tradition passed quickly into oblivion following the conquest.

The greater part of the coast of Yucatan was officially discovered in 1508, though again no immediate attempt was made to explore or conquer it.[2] In 1511 a caravel bound from Darien in Panama to Santo Domingo went aground on the shoals off Jamaica. The dozen survivors who drifted ashore on the east coast of Yucatan two weeks later became the first Europeans to have extended contact with the Maya. Juan de Valdivia, the commander, and four companions met quick deaths on the sacrificial altar. Their bodies were consumed in a cannibalistic ritual. Gerónimo de Aguilar, one of the two castaways still living when Spanish exploration of Yucatan began in earnest, recalled, "I, together with six others, remained in a coop, in order that for another festival that was approaching, being fatter, we might solemnize their banquet with our flesh. Understanding that the end of our days was drawing near, we decided to venture our lives in another way, so we broke the cage in which we had been placed, and [fled] through the bush."[3] The European diseases they and the Spaniards who came after them carried, principally measles and smallpox, quickly touched off virulent epidemics that took a devastating toll of Maya populations that had had no opportunity to develop immunity to them.[4]

Aguilar eventually rejoined his countrymen, bringing valuable reports about Maya culture as well as a knowledge of Maya speech. Gonzalo Guerrero, the other survivor, refused to be repatriated, preferring to remain with his Maya wife and children among her people in Chetumal.[5] Guerrero maintained his position as a prominent military commander in the service of the lord of Chetumal for some twenty years. He died in 1536 in Honduras, in command of a flotilla of war canoes, defending the commercial interests of Chetumal against the Spaniards. After the battle, his horrified countrymen found him among the slain—hair worn long, body tattooed, nose, lips, and ears pierced for jewels.

Juan Ponce de León paused briefly along the coast of Yucatan on his return from Florida in 1513.[6] The first protracted exploration came in 1517, when a vessel commanded by Francisco Hernández de Córdoba skirted the coast of Yucatan.[7] His first landfall was Isla Mujeres (Isle of Women), named after the many statues of Maya goddesses found in a local shrine. Taking with them several gold objects, the Spaniards continued west along the coast and then south to the native town of Campeche. Farther south, at Champotón, Hernández's luck ran out. Wounded thirty-three times in a skirmish with the fierce local Maya, he "sadly returned to Cuba."[8] Within two weeks Hernández was dead, but his exaggerated reports of the golden wealth of Yucatan aroused the cupidity of several adventurous countrymen. Thus began the tradition of misunderstanding and violence that the Spaniards, bent on exploration, conquest, and colonization, brought to their interaction with the Maya.

The following year, Juan de Grijalva made a similar voyage along the coast of Yucatan, making note of substantial native settlements.[9] Grijalva landed first at Cozumel, a Maya pilgrimage center off the east coast. He claimed the island in the name of the crown and proceeded south. The Spaniards were particularly taken with Tulum, overlooking the sea. "Towards sunset," wrote the expedition chaplain, "we saw from afar off a town or village so large that the city of Seville could not appear greater or better; and in it was seen a very great tower."[10] Doubling back around Yucatan, Grijalva continued west and north as far as what is now Tampico. From these northern lands, dominions of the Aztec empire, Grijalva brought back gold and silver along with precious stones, colorful textiles, and exotic native ornaments of all kinds.

Word of these discoveries came quickly to the ears of Hernán Cortés in Cuba, nursing his ambitions for conquest, power, wealth, and glory.[11] In 1519 he was at last able to mount the expedition that would result in the conquest of the Aztec empire and the destruction of the native civilizations of central Mexico. His first landfall was Cozumel, where he found deserted villages and shrines. Here Gerónimo de Aguilar, one of the surviving castaways, joined Cortés, providing the Spaniards their first real intelligence about Maya culture.

Leaving Cozumel, Cortés followed the coast, landing again near the Río Grijalva, on the western edge of the Maya area. Here he acquired the invaluable Doña Marina, the daughter of a high-ranking native merchant, who spoke both Maya and Nahuatl (the language of the Aztecs). Through Marina and Aguilar, who spoke both Maya and Spanish, Cortés was now able to communicate more easily with the native groups he encountered. He moved north along the coast and shortly began the march inland that culminated in the conquest of Tenochtitlán, island capital of the Aztecs.

The following decades brought repeated forays into northern Yucatan and the western fringe of the Maya region along the base of the Gulf of Mexico. Though exploration and attempts at settlements were practically continuous, conquest and colonization proceeded very slowly. The Spaniards found themselves in a very different situation here from the one in central Mexico. Yucatan had no single extensive highly centralized state that could be toppled at a blow. Political organization was fragmented, and each local polity had to be dealt with separately. Even when a town had been defeated, its inhabitants were likely to melt into the forest rather than remain to serve European masters. In 1542, with the founding of Mérida, the Spaniards finally established a permanent base in Yucatan, but full, effective control of the peninsula was still many years in the future.

Europeans found it particularly difficult to establish effective transportation and communication facilities in the forested lowlands of the Maya area, and many zones remain isolated today. Though the Spaniards achieved formal sovereignty over Yucatan with relative ease, many local Maya groups successfully resisted effective domination and assimilation for centuries. Substantial numbers of Maya in eastern Yucatan still refused to acknowledge the authority of the Mexican government in the 1920s.

The southern sector of the Maya lowlands, at the base of the Yucatan peninsula, was even more resistant to Spanish domination than the northern zone. With its heavier rainfall and high, lush tropical forest, the environment seemed particularly forbidding to European eyes. Accounts of Cortés's march across the heart of the Yucatan peninsula to Honduras in 1524–25 dwell at length on the suffering occasioned by the Spaniards' inability to cope with the environment. Cortés's description of the approach to the province of Acalán conveys something of his growing distaste for the Maya lowlands:

> After having marched for three days through dense forest along a very narrow track, we reached a great lagoon more than five hundred paces wide, and though I searched up and down for a way across I could find none. Moreover, the guides told me that it was a useless search unless I marched for twenty days toward the mountain.... To turn back was . . . impossible, for it meant certain death for all, not only because of the bad roads we would have to travel, and the great rains which had fallen, swelling the rivers . . . but also because we had consumed all our provisions and could find nothing else to eat.... I determined, therefore, that as there was no other solution I would build a bridge, and at once set about having some timbers cut, from nine to ten fathoms in length.... No one believed that such a task could ever be accomplished, and some even whispered that it would be better to return before everyone was too exhausted and weak with hunger to be able to.... When I saw how discouraged they were, and truly they had cause to be, for . . . they were demoralized and lethargic, having eaten nothing but the roots of plants, I told them that . . . I would complete it with the Indians alone.... So hard did they work, and so skilfully, that in four days they had finished the bridge.... When all the men and horses had finally crossed this lagoon, we came upon a great marsh which lasted for two crossbowshots, the most frightful thing the men had ever seen, where the unsaddled horses sank in up to their girths until nothing else could be seen; and in struggling to get out they only sank in deeper, so that we lost all hope of being able to bring a single horse out safely. But still we determined to attempt it, and by placing bundles of reeds and twigs beneath them to support them and prevent them from sinking, they were somewhat better off.... Thus it pleased our Lord that they should all emerge without loss, though so exhausted they could barely stand up. [12]

These accounts also provide the first picture, albeit a confused one, of the native peoples of the region. Settlement was relatively sparse and ethnic variation considerable. Complex economic, political, and social ties formed links across a mosaic of small, independent political units.

After Cortés's march, this interior sector of the Yucatan Peninsula remained almost totally isolated for centuries, though not entirely untouched by Spanish culture. The Itzá of Tayasal remained unsubjugated until 1697, though Cortés's brief sojourn did result in a remarkable episode in the annals of acculturation. An ailing horse, abandoned by Cortés, achieved lasting fame among the people of Tayasal. [13] Missionaries who arrived there at the end of the seventeenth century found them making offerings of flowers and turkeys to the horse's image, which they called Tizimín Chac. It had become a minor deity associated with thunder and lightning.

The central sector of the Maya highlands succumbed to the Spaniards much more rapidly than did lowland zones.[14] Pedro de Alvarado and his cohorts arrived from Mexico in 1524. His conquest of the most prominent of the native states, the Quiché and the Cakchiquel, along with most of their neighbors, was swift and brutal. The traditional history of the Cakchiquel, transcribed shortly after the conquest, paints a terrifying portrait of the blond Alvarado, called Tonatiuh or Tunatiuh, after the sun god:

> On the day 1 Ganel [February 20, 1524] the Quichés were destroyed by the Spaniards. Their chief, he who was called Tunatiuh Avilantaro, conquered all the people.... Then [the Spaniards] went forth to the city of Gumarcaah [Utatlán, the Quiché capital], where they were received by the kings, the Ahpop and the Ahpop Qamahay, and the Quichés paid them tribute. Soon the kings were tortured by Tunatiuh. On the day 4 Qat [March 7, 1524] the kings Ahpop and Ahpop Qamahay were burned by Tunatiuh. The heart of Tunatiuh was without compassion for the people.... On the day 1 Hunahpu [April 12, 1524] the Spaniards came to the city of Yximché;... Tunatiuh then asked for one of the daughters of the king and the lords gave her to Tunatiuh. Then Tunatiuh asked the kings for money. He wished them to give him piles of metal, their vessels and crowns. And as they did not bring them to him immediately, Tunatiuh became angry with the kings and said to them: "Why have you not brought me the metal? If you do not bring with you all of the money of the tribes, I will burn you and I will hang you," he said to the lords. Next Tunatiuh ordered them to pay twelve hundred pesos of gold. The kings tried to have the amount reduced and they began to weep, but Tunatiuh did not consent, and he said to them: "Get the metal and bring it within five days. Woe to you if you do not bring it! I know my heart!" Thus he said to the lords.... Then we abandoned the city of Yximché.... Ten days after we fled from the city, Tunatiuh began to make war upon us. On the day 4 Camey [September 5, 1524] they began to make us suffer. We scattered ourselves under the trees, under the vines, oh, my sons![15]

A functioning colonial capital, established almost at once near Iximché and later transferred to the site now known as Antigua Guatemala, provided a base for the conquest of the highlands and of the adjacent piedmont and Pacific Coast. Surprisingly, cultural assimilation did not automatically follow in the wake of the swift early conquest and rapid establishment of Spanish administrative control. On the contrary, Maya groups in the highlands still retain their languages and much of the native cultural tradition.

Northern and western sectors of the highlands and the slopes descending to the southern Maya lowlands were not so easily brought within the Spanish colonial orbit. Spanish penetration of these areas was haphazard and retarded. Like the southern lowlands of Yucatan, these zones remained beyond effective Spanish administrative control for a considerable time, and many sectors are still remote and difficult to reach.

The conquest of the eastern fringe of the Maya area, at the base of the Gulf of Honduras, began early and was contested by a variety of

Spanish parties that proceeded independently from Mexico, lower Central America, the Caribbean islands, and later Guatemala and Yucatan. Full administrative control was achieved relatively quickly, under the jurisdiction of Guatemala. Here the native cultural tradition was almost entirely obliterated at an early stage under the combined effects of ferocious competition among Spanish factions and the subsequent single-minded exploitation of native labor in mining operations.

REDISCOVERY

Dazzled by the architectural grandeur of Tenochtitlán and by the material wealth and power of its Aztec rulers, the Spaniards found the sixteenth-century Maya unimpressive. They had little reason to suppose that the Maya past was more spectacular, particularly when even native historical traditions traced the ancestry of the elite, ruling groups to the Toltecs of central Mexico. Only in northern Yucatan, where native tradition documented the historical continuity from the heyday of Chichén Itzá to the Spanish conquest, could the sixteenth-century Maya be linked with impressive archaeological remains. Even here the connection was quickly forgotten. Bishop Diego de Landa's encyclopedic treatise on the Maya of Yucatan—so fascinating to the modern reader—attracted little attention.[16] It was unearthed and published only in the nineteenth century.

The achievements of the Classic period of Maya civilization were more than half a millennium in the past when Spaniards first came to Mesoamerica. Most of its greatest architectural and sculptural monuments were lost in the remote forests of southern Yucatan, and they remained so for centuries. Small wonder, then, that the Maya were so long in claiming their rightful place among the great civilizations of antiquity. In the eighteenth and early nineteenth centuries, occasional explorers came across the ruins of the great Maya centers.[17] Almost without exception, they attributed the monuments to ancient migrants from the Mediterranean—Egyptians, Chaldeans, Israelites, anyone other than the Maya. Fortunately, perhaps, their reports received scant notice.

Between 1839 and 1842, John Lloyd Stephens, an American traveler, lawyer, and sometime diplomat, visited the Maya area in the company of the English artist Frederick Catherwood.[18] Stephens's descriptions of Maya archaeological monuments, magnificently illustrated by Catherwood, became immensely popular. The absorbing accounts of their journeys first brought the remnants of a vanished civilization to the attention of the Western world. Fortunately, Stephens brought caution and reason to interpretation and was a careful observer. He rightly concluded that the ancestors of the Maya—not wandering Near Easterners—were responsible for the monuments. Stephens's careful approach largely set the tone for Maya archaeology during the following century. Such pioneer Maya archaeologists as Alfred P. Maudslay and Teobert Maler concerned themselves mainly with discovery and careful description.[19] They preferred to augment the scanty corpus of information on Maya civilization rather than to indulge in fanciful interpretation.

Meanwhile, of course, the old tradition of untrammeled speculation had not died without issue. The most bizarre interpretations of the ancient Maya came from the pen of Augustus Le Plongeon, a poseur of epic stature who turned to Maya archaeology late in the nineteenth century. Among the tamest of his beliefs was the notion that Maya civilization had been imported to Mesoamerica fully formed from Atlantis. His conclusions about the subsequent spread of Maya culture to the Mediterranean neatly reversed the common diffusionist position, and had the added advantage of making possible startling new interpretations of familiar events. Jesus, on the cross, had spoken Maya, not Hebrew, saying, "Now, now, sinking black ink over nose."[20] Surely a classic in the annals of revisionist history. Fortunately, though the experience embittered him terribly, Le Plongeon's theories attracted little attention in the emergent field of Maya studies.

Around the turn of the nineteenth century, a second major avenue of research into ancient Maya civilization opened with investigations of Maya hieroglyphic writing.[21] Maya writing is not fully readable even today, but a series of brilliant early studies—above all the work of Ernst Förstemann—clarified much of the calendrical and mathematical portion of the Maya script. This basic understanding of the Maya system of time reckoning laid the groundwork for a realistic chronological framework for Maya civilization.

At almost the same time, major excavations of ancient Maya centers began with the work of the Peabody Museum of Harvard at Copán, in Honduras.[22] Large-scale excavations of major Maya centers sponsored by the Carnegie Institution of Washington during the middle decades of the twentieth century set the tone for Maya archaeology until about 1960.[23] Projects were data-oriented, seeking information that could be used for a description of Maya culture and its history in terms of its greatest monumental achievements. Nonelite and geographically marginal facets of ancient Maya civilization generally got short shrift. Problems of explanation—accounting for the rise of Maya civilization, or for its collapse—were secondary goals, suitable subjects for speculation only when sufficient information had been amassed.

Interests have broadened in recent years, with more attention being paid to nonelite aspects of Maya civilization and to its geographical variation beyond the core area of major centers. Investigations are more often directly problem-oriented, with excavations designed to answer particular questions about the ancient Maya as well as to produce more examples of architectural and sculptural monuments. Today's Maya archaeologists tend to be more interested than their predecessors in causation and explanation, and they are more likely to take explicit theoretical stances. Nevertheless, Maya archaeology today is a logical outgrowth of the Carnegie tradition. Large-scale excavation projects continue, with much the same elite-monumental orientation. The differences are primarily in emphasis.

The chief modern breakthrough in Maya studies came in investigations of the writing system. Following Förstemann's lead, Mayanists continued to emphasize the numerical and calendrical aspects of the script. This focus was logical, since the pervasive importance of time in Maya thought and religion was apparent in historical sources of the colonial period and among the modern Maya. Because the reckoning of time occupies such a prominent place in most Maya texts, this was a productive approach. Despite the stubborn resistance of noncalendrical glyphs to decipherment, the content of the few surviving painted books was plain: astronomy, astrology, divination, and other ritual matters predominated. The ubiquitous calendrical dates in the carved inscriptions yielded a precise chronological framework for the great Maya centers of the Classic period. It was not unreasonable to infer, as most Mayanists did, that the undeciphered portions of these texts dealt, like the painted manuscripts, with matters religious and ritual. Tatiana Proskouriakoff led the way to a radically new understanding of these monumental texts in 1960, with the brilliant demonstration that the inscriptions record mainly historical matters.[24] Recent investigations in this tradition have opened a whole new avenue to the understanding of ancient Maya civilization, with a wealth of new insights into the relationships among centers and the careers of individual rulers gleaned from references to genealogical ties, marriages, conquests, and alliances. At roughly the same time Yurii Knorozov revived the moribund theory that Maya writing was partly phonetic.[25] Subsequent investigations following his leads have made giant strides toward actual decipherment of ancient Maya texts.

CHAPTER TWO

THE MAYA WORLD

THE MAYA AND THEIR NEIGHBORS

The descendants of the ancient Maya today occupy the lowland expanse of the Yucatan Peninsula and the mountain valleys of the great highland massif along its southern flank. Here much of the native Maya cultural tradition, including several distinct Maya languages, still persists, after nearly half a millennium of European dominance.[1] In the sixteenth century the area was almost solidly Maya-speaking. The archaeological remains dotting the area are the remnants of the ancient Maya—the material record of the cultural tradition created by Maya peoples over the course of three millennia and more. Maya speakers were probably the first settlers of the area, occupants of the earliest small farming villages. All indications—from archaeology, history, ethnography, and linguistic reconstructions alike—point to essential cultural continuity. There is no evidence that any other people was ever dominant in the Maya area.

Beyond the eastern frontiers of the Maya area, native cultures have not resisted the impact of European culture so successfully. In prehispanic times this zone of upper Central America was the home of peoples with languages and cultural traditions very different from those of the Maya. The Maya also differ from the native cultures to their west and north, though here the contrasts are much less prominent and shared cultural features more evident. Stretching from north-central Mexico to upper Central America, Mesoamerica (Map 2)

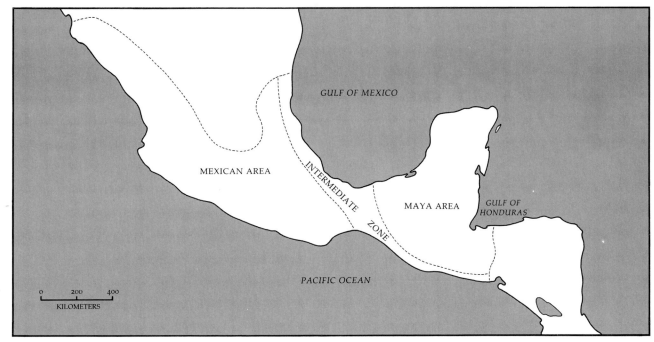

Map 2. Mesoamerica

embraces these related peoples along with the Maya. Their cultural commonality has considerable time depth, stretching back far into the pre-Christian era. Collectively, these peoples and their ancestors represent a cultural tradition as well as a culture area.[2]

The features shared by Mesoamerican cultures are varied. Some are distinctively Mesoamerican, setting its peoples clearly apart from their non-Mesoamerican neighbors. Ceramic lip plugs, wooden swords edged with stone flakes, quilted cotton armor, sandals with heels—these things are distinctive indeed, but they reveal little of the nature of Mesoamerican cultures. Some of the most basic Mesoamerican cultural traits, however, occur widely in the Americas. Farming systems featuring *milpa* or slash-and-burn cultivation of maize, along with beans, squash, and chile peppers, are by no means peculiar to Mesoamerican peoples.

The most interesting features of the Mesoamerican cultural pattern are those that are both basic and distinctive. Perhaps the most fundamental is the full constellation of traits involved in the production and preparation of food. Equally important and far more distinctive are Mesoamerican religion and cosmology. The gods of rain and maize, the death god, the gods of the sun, moon, and morning star, though they bear various names and titles, appear in similar guises in pantheons all over Mesoamerica. Color-coded cardinal directions are the foci of the Mesoamerican universe, which is also layered, with many-tiered heavens and hells. Elaborate calendars kept track of the passage of time and the changing astrological omens. Details vary—the east was red or yellow or blue-green for Mesoamericans in different regions at different times—but all Mesoamerican peoples shared a cosmology in which the universe and the calendar had the same basic structure. Whatever its ultimate origins, this common world view demonstrates the fundamental unity of the diverse peoples of Mesoamerica and the reality of a Mesoamerican cultural tradition.

A ball game played with a solid rubber ball in a formal court was both a ceremonial event and a form of recreation throughout Mesoamerica.[3] The game was often played as a divinatory act, to determine the shape of the future, and losers frequently met death on the sacrificial altar. On other occasions it was simply a spectator sport, with avid wagering on the outcome. Some ball courts have rings on the side walls, through which players had to propel the ball in order to score; others have markers along the sides or along the center of the court floor; others still are perfectly plain.

Specifying precise geographical limits for Mesoamerica is as fruitless a task as trying to pinpoint the time of its emergence as a distinct cultural area. Even for the conquest period, information is not uniform for all regions, and coverage of some of the frontier areas is particularly poor. For earlier prehispanic periods the difficulties are much greater, for many distinctive Mesoamerican cultural features reflected in historical documents, including some of the key traits, are not easily detected in archaeological evidence. In any case, Mesoamerica never had the sharply defined boundaries of a modern political state. The frontiers of Mesoamerica are better conceptualized as regions where Mesoamerican and non-Mesoamerican peoples mingled at many levels, from individual households to entire communities. The transitions of frontier zones were gradual but not uniform, resulting in complex mosaics of groups of contrasting cultural affiliations.[4] Nor is there any reason to suppose that Mesoamerica's frontiers were static. On the contrary, every indication is that they underwent constant, often considerable, shifts through time as political, economic, social, and even climatic and environmental patterns changed.

Mesoamerica had certainly emerged as a culture area before 1000 B.C. for the Olmec civilization that appeared by then is recognizably Mesoamerican. The Mesoamerican cultural tradition presumably did not spring into existence fully formed with the appearance of the Olmec. Rather, it must have emerged as a coherent cultural pattern gradually, over the course of many preceding centuries almost unrepresented in the archaeological record.

Beneath the unity of Mesoamerican culture lies a wealth of diversity—in language, social organization, economics, politics, religion, art, and every other facet of culture. Basic Mesoamerican patterns are expressed in many ways among its various peoples. A focus on this variation dissolves the area into regions with contrasting cultural patterns. Some regions are very homogeneous, with long, stable cultural traditions; others are diverse, showing considerable cultural change through time. All can be subdivided on the basis of still finer cultural variation.

They can also be combined. Cultural and environmental contrasts between southeastern and northwestern Mesoamerica are easily recognized. The Maya area, largely lowland tropical forest, comprises most of the southeastern zone. The drier highlands of central Mexico form the heart of the northwestern area. These regions can be viewed as the hearths of distinct Maya and Mexican cultural traditions. The contrast of the two cultural patterns is not stark. Both are fundamentally Mesoamerican, and their histories are linked at many points. The differences are better conceived as a continuum of variation. An intermediate zone stretching from the Gulf Coast plain south across the Isthmus of Tehuantepec and east along the Pacific coast and piedmont (Map 2) forms an environmental and cultural bridge between idealized Mexican and Maya poles of contrast.[5] The contrast is especially clear in political organization and settlement pattern. Central Mexico was the seat of large political states, even empires, with great urban capitals. In the Maya area, political units were normally much smaller and populations were not densely packed into urban cores, but dispersed in the hinterlands surrounding great centers.

Until the middle of the first millennium B.C., a single cultural pattern, the Olmec, dominated Mesoamerica. The northwest/southeast contrast developed after the decline of Olmec civilization. In the last centuries of the pre-Christian era, Teotihuacán, in the heart of the central Mexican highlands, was emerging as Mesoamerica's first urban civilization. At the same time Maya societies began to take on the complexity that would culminate in Classic Maya civilization. The existence of a Maya/Mexican polarity and the interaction of cultures representing the two patterns are important factors in Mesoamerican culture history from this time on. Maya culture history, as the story of the development of one end of a continuum, cannot be written without continual reference to Mexican Mesoamerica.

THE MAYA AREA

The Maya area is by no means uniform, environmentally or culturally. With environments ranging from steamy lowland tropical forest to near-desert interior valleys to cool, pine-clad highlands, Maya country is remarkably varied. Even the vast tracts of lowland forest, seemingly unbroken and homogeneous, dissolve on closer inspection into a patchwork of regions differing in climate, topography, flora, and fauna.[6]

A massive chain of volcanic mountains curves south and east from southern Mexico to form the spine of Central America. From its base the Yucatan Peninsula juts into the Caribbean like a great limestone shelf. From the coast to the foothills of the cordillera, only the low Puuc hills in the northwest and the Maya Mountains in the east interrupt the expanse of tropical lowlands that is Yucatan (Color Plates 5, 6). Northern Yucatan is much like central and southern Florida. Rainfall is not heavy, and the thin soil supports a low, thorny scrub forest of palms, scrub pine, live oak, and palmetto. Surface water is rare except where the limestone crust has fallen through to expose the water table, forming *cenotes* or sinkholes. To the south, rainfall becomes heavier, up to 3,000 millimeters per year along the southern fringe of the lowlands. Soils are deeper and vegetation grows progressively more lush and less familiar.

The high, canopied rain forest of the southern lowlands boasts mahogany, wild fig, and ceiba trees that soar 50 meters and more (Fig. 1). Sapodilla, cedar, logwood, palms, avocado, mamey, and *ramón* (breadnut), along with a host of other trees and vines, provide a wide range of useful products, including edible fruits and nuts. The high forest is closed above. Little sunlight reaches the forest floor, which remains relatively open, except where a great tree has fallen or where men have cleared the forest. Wherever the canopy is broken, ferocious secondary growth forms a temporary niche of very different aspect—dense, tangled, almost impenetrable. Patches of savannah-like

1. Temples at Tikal, in the heart of the southern lowland tropical forest. Temple II, in the foreground, is about 38 m. tall.

THE WORLD OF THE ANCIENT MAYA

grassland with only occasional stunted trees form open oases throughout the forest. Animal life in the lowlands is rich and varied as well. There are few large mammals: deer, peccary, tapir, and jaguar. Exotic smaller mammals abound, particularly in the higher forests of the south. Agouti and coatimundi roam the forest along with rabbits, foxes, and spider and howler monkeys. The boa joins the rattlesnake, coral snake, fer-de-lance, and a host of less spectacular snakes, lizards, toads, and frogs to fill out the roster of reptiles and amphibians. In the air are hundreds of species of birds, from the curassow, guan, gaudy parrots, and toucans to the more familiar wild turkey and quail. Everywhere insects abound.

Terrain is more varied in the southern lowlands than in the north, with as much as 60 meters of relief between ridges and intervening lower stretches, which support rather different plant communities. The low-lying areas become swamps during the rainy months, so that well-drained slopes and relatively level ridge tops are best for habitation. The heart of the Maya lowlands has no surface streams. Some clay-lined water holes hold collected rain throughout the year, and in a few areas shallow lakes provide fresh water and fish. Along the western edge of the lowlands flow the great Usumacinta and its tributaries. These rivers are major arteries of communication, and they provide hundreds of kilometers of riverine environment where fresh water, fish, and other aquatic resources are available. To the east, the pine-clad slopes of the Maya Mountains rise to elevations of about 1,000 meters. The streams that flow east, emptying into the Caribbean, create another series of riverine niches in the forest. To the southeast are the great inland gulf of Lake Izabal and the lower course of the Río Motagua, which drains much of the highland region. Beyond, the Chamelecón and Ulua drain the foothills at the southeastern edge of the Maya lowlands. This diversity adds up to a remarkable array of distinct local environments within the seemingly uniform tropical forest.

Stretching in a great arc along the western and southern flank of the lowlands, the foothills of the cordillera mark the transition to a region of steep slopes and broken terrain. This is a land of numberless pocket valleys, ravines, steep gorges, and chasms amid mountain peaks (Fig. 2). Millennia of erosion have left little level land in the mountain massif, except in a few great basins. With the highest volcanic peaks reaching elevations above 4,000 meters, the highlands generally are clothed in pine and oak forest, with occasional grassy alpine meadows. Dense cloud forests dominated by oak and laurel, draped with moss and mixed with tree ferns, occupy the highest slopes (above 2,000 meters). In a few regions of intermediate elevation, as along the middle course of the Río Motagua, are stretches of near desert. Animal life is much less abundant than in the lowlands, perhaps because of today's much denser highland population. Numerous mountain streams feed the two great highland lakes, or join the Usumacinta and Motagua river systems to empty ultimately into the Gulf of Mexico and the Gulf of Honduras. South of the continental divide, the rivers of the slopes

2. Hilly terrain with terraced farm plots in the western Maya highlands.

drain into the Pacific. Descending, the piedmont becomes progressively more tropical. Thorn forest gives way along the coast to tidal lagoons, estuaries, and mangrove swamp rich in fish, molluscs, crabs, caymans, and other marine animals.

Throughout the area, the alternation of wet and dry seasons dominates weather patterns and the farming cycle. In May the rains begin, continuing almost daily until October or November. In some years the rains slacken during the midsummer dog days, but not always. During the dry season, beginning in November or December, there is little or no rain, and milpa farmers turn to clearing new fields. By April the cut vegetation is dry. Now is the time for burning, to release nutrients into the soil, and for planting. The traditional farmer has only to poke holes

3. Making milpa. In the cleared and burned fields the farmers drop maize seeds, carried in the pouches at their belts, into individual holes made with pointed digging sticks.

THE WORLD OF THE ANCIENT MAYA

in the ash with his digging stick, drop in the seeds—commonly maize, along with beans, squash, and chile peppers—and wait for the rain (Fig. 3). Timing is important, for burning and planting should be completed before the rains set in. At the same time, too early a start may court disaster, for the nutrients in the ashes may be scattered by the wind, and the seeds may die before moisture reaches them. There is some margin for error, though. If the rains are delayed, it is often possible to make a second planting and salvage a crop. Harvesttime is in the autumn, though in favored areas two crops are sometimes possible. Fallowing varies enormously with local soil, moisture, and vegetation conditions. In some highland regions with deep fertile soils, plots may be cultivated for a decade or longer, requiring only a few years to regain fertility. In many lowland zones, by contrast, a plot may produce reasonable yields for only two seasons, after which it must lie fallow for as long as a generation. Native domestic animals are few: dogs are ubiquitous, turkeys common, and in some regions bees are kept for honey and wax.

In much of the Maya world, milpa farming is still the cornerstone of local economies and maize the staff of life, as it has been for three thousand years and more. Tzotzil *milperos* of Zinacantan are not fossilized prehistoric Maya farmers, but their techniques for wresting a living from the land draw mainly on their traditional Maya heritage.[7] Prehispanic Maya farming systems were not utterly different.

Zinacantecos cultivate milpas locally in the highlands and they also journey into adjacent lowland regions to work rented lands. The best highland plots may be cultivated continuously for decades. In the lowlands the agricultural cycle is shorter and fields must be prepared more often. Here the farmer must fell trees in December to allow sufficient time for drying. Brush and other secondary growth can be cut at any time before March, and the dried vegetation is burned in April. Planting takes place in May (earlier in the highlands), following ceremonies designed to placate the Earth Owner, who controls the clouds, the rains, and the wind. A man knowledgeable in ritual matters, often with a special relationship to the Earth Owner and other gods, will join his kinsmen in a special meal and lead them in a ritual procession to shrines set up at the corners and in the center of their fields. Here the farmers will offer prayers, candles, flowers, and pine boughs in the hope of steady rains and a fine crop.

A pointed digging stick and an armadillo shell or net bag to carry the carefully selected seeds are the only planting tools. The milpero moves through his plot row by row. Into the small hole made with his digging stick he drops several seeds of maize, covers them over with his sandal, and moves on. Bean and squash seeds may be planted in the same hole with maize, most often in highland plots. Here the milpero's wife usually follows along the rows, adding the complementary seeds to each hole. Squash is more often planted on the fringe of the milpa.

Every milpa must be weeded at least once, after another ceremony to propitiate the Earth Owner. Fields in use for a few years require two

4. Milpa with dried maize cobs left on the dead stalks to await harvest.

or more weedings, usually in mid-June and mid-July. The maize ripens by September. The farmer again moves through his milpa, bending each stalk double, allowing the maize to dry and harden without being ruined by the rain (Fig. 4). Now the milpero sows another bean crop between the bent rows of maize in lowland plots. October is harvesttime in the highlands, but the drying lowland maize can be left on the dead stalks until December or January.

Most farmers plant chiles, *chayotes,* gourds, and other minor crops separately. They cultivate a variety of fruit trees, mainly in or near their house compounds. Hunting is now a casual activity for Zinacantecos, though it was surely more important before dense populations decimated the local fauna. Today beans are the chief source of protein. Meat provides only a minor dietary supplement. Zinacantecos still occasionally shoot deer and rabbits. They trap birds, rats, and mice and collect wasp larvae, other insects, river snails, and some land snails. Chicken, the principal meat for ceremonial occasions, has supplanted the indigenous turkey. Today as in the past, iguanas sometimes replace fowl for ritual use.

Wild plants, by contrast, are very important. Zinacantecos collect more than a dozen varieties of edible mushrooms, several plants cooked as greens, coriander and other condiments, a special plant to chew when one is working to reduce thirst, and many plants for medicinal and ritual use. This sketch barely indicates the importance of noncrop plants to Zinacantecos, for it is all too easy for outside observers to overlook interactions with plants that do not conform to familiar agricultural patterns.

The Lacandón Maya, occupying the remote forests west of the Río Usumacinta and least affected by European cultural patterns, make extensive use of the exuberant natural flora. Alfred Tozzer, who lived among the Lacandón in 1901 and 1903, remarked that "the native makes use of practically every tree, plant, and shrub for food, medicine, or in the practice of some of his arts."[8] The plants and their uses are listed in Table 1.

Lacandón farmers cultivate several fruit trees, along with maize, beans, chiles, tomato, manioc, sweet potato, chayote, gourds, cotton, and tobacco. Deer, peccary, armadillo, monkey, agouti, iguana, wild turkey, curassow, partridge, quail, and snails are only the most important of the many animals the Lacandones hunt, trap, and collect. They take fish with lines, nets, and arrows. Beekeeping—involving hollow logs placed in temples—is primarily a ceremonial activity.

The distribution of natural resources is far from uniform, and the exchange of commodities among the diverse regions has always been important. The Maya area has never been without networks of exchange linking its parts. Limestone is readily available for construction throughout the lowlands. In many areas it contains deposits of chert that can be fashioned into cutting tools, though highland obsidian is much superior. Hard volcanic stone, used for grinding tools, and volcanic mineral pigments occur only in the Maya Mountains and in the highlands. Jade, the most precious of all materials, can be found only

Table 1. Plants and plant products of southeastern Mexico and uses to which they are put by the Lacandón Maya

Plant or plant product	Use
Mahogany	Canoes
Logwood	Arrow shafts, dye
Lignum vitae	Bows
Protium heptaphyllum resin (*pom*, copal)	Incense
Rubber tree sap	Incense
Pitch pine	Torches
Lonchocarpus longistylus bark	*Balche*, a fermented intoxicating beverage for ceremonial occasions
Vines, many varieties	Tying thatch and house frames; wicker-work house doors; baskets; source of water for travelers; general use as rope or twine
Palm leaves	Thatch
Guava (*guayaba, Psidium guajava*)	Food
Tamarind (*Tamarindus indica*)	Food
Avocado (*Persea gratissima*)	Food
Mango (*Mangifera indica*)	Food
Cocoanut (*Cocos nucifera*)	Food
Papaya (*Papaya carica*)	Food
Sweetsop (*Anona squamosa*)	Food
Soursop (*guanabana, Anona muricata*)	Food
Chicosapote (*Achras sapota*)	Food
Mamey (*Lucuma mammosa*)	Food
Cocoyol palm (*Acrocomia mexicana*)	Food
Cacao	Chocolate, ceremonial drink (important source of fat; conquest-period Yucatecs extracted from it "a grease which resembles butter," used to make another drink)

in the Motagua Valley. Salt is readily available in the coastal regions of Yucatan, along the Pacific Coast, and from deposits along the northern fringes of the highlands, but it is not to be found in the central lowland region. Tropical-forest products include resins from various trees (used as incense), hardwoods, and the plumage of brightly feathered birds, as well as drug and spice plants. A variety of marine products are vital to Maya ritual: shell, coral, pearls, stingray spines. Add to this array a thriving trade in local agricultural specialties and manufactured products—cacao, honey, wax, pottery, textiles, lapidary work, and the like—and exchange emerges as a major force in Maya culture history, balancing regional diversification with elaborate networks of communication and interaction.

Culturally the Maya world is less variable than the natural environment. In the sixteenth century, except for a few groups along the Pacific piedmont and in the northwest along the Gulf of Mexico, the entire area was solidly Maya-speaking. Today, of course, the Hispanic-American national cultures of Mexico, Guatemala, Belize, Honduras, and El Salvador are dominant. Those groups that have not lost their native heritage entirely are increasingly reduced to the status of marginal peasant subcultures. They face an often hostile tradition that surrounds and threatens to overwhelm them. Even allowing for the homogenizing pressures of modern Latin American societies, Maya groups are by no means uniform. On the contrary, no two have ever been exactly alike, and the overall picture is one of endless variation on the same fundamental themes.

The distribution of Maya peoples follows the main lines of natural regions (Map 3). There are no sharp boundaries; the shift from one Maya group to the next is even more gradual and complex than the transition between adjacent environmental provinces. In the same way, the external frontiers of the Maya area are zones where contrasting cultural patterns and the people who carry them mingle in complex mosaic arrangements. Reconstructions of the history of the Maya family of languages (Fig. 5) call for a more or less homogeneous ancestral Maya stock centered in the highland region.[9] Before 2000 B.C. the ancestors of today's Maya groups began a long, slow process of progressive differentiation and dispersal. The result is the present distribution of distinct Maya tongues, comparable in their variability to the Romance languages.

The Northern Lowlands

Northern Yucatan is the home of the Yucatec, the most numerous and widespread modern Maya group.[10] Among the first to separate from the ancestral Maya stock, the Yucatec have occupied the northern lowlands for many centuries. Here the Spaniards found them in the sixteenth century, with traditional histories linking them to ruins already hundreds of years old. Cultural upheavals apparent in the archaeological record of the area late in the first millennium of the Christian era reflect the influx of other peoples rather than the arrival of the Yucatec.

Small farming villages, composed of a few one- and two-room houses, appeared in northern Yucatan midway through the Preclassic period (2500 B.C.–A.D. 250; see Chronological Chart). These first known occupants of the region may have been the ancestral Yucatec, who had emerged as a distinct language group before 1000 B.C. During the following centuries settlements grew larger and more complex. By the beginning of the Christian era, public buildings of masonry construction graced several northern centers. The small houses and plain bu-

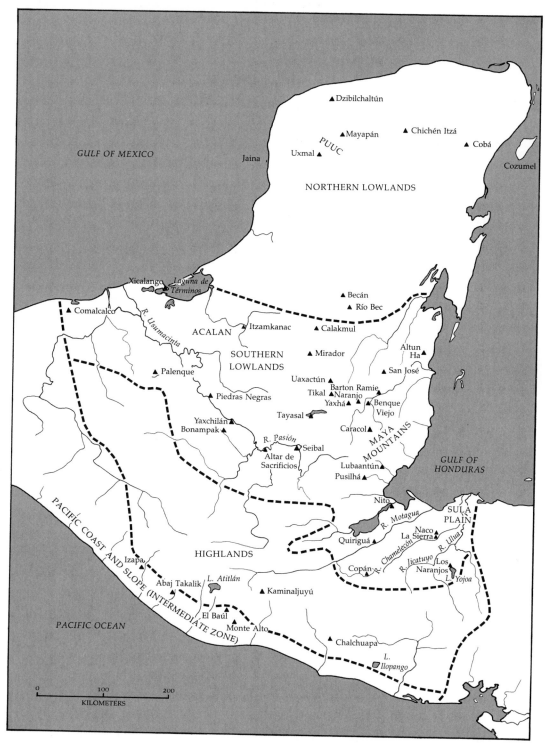

Map 3. The Maya world

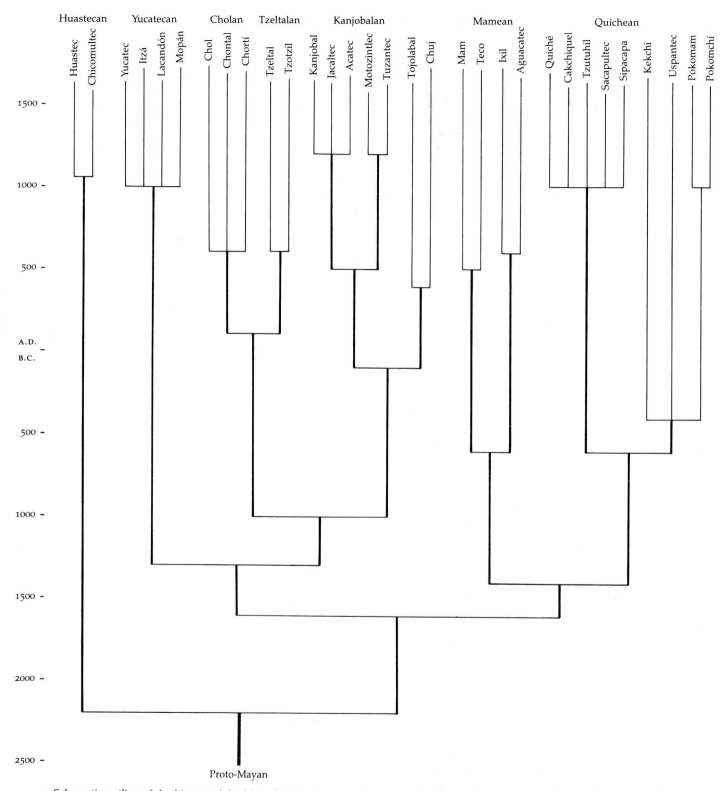

5. Schematic outline of the history of the Maya family of languages (based primarily on Kaufman 1976). The absolute time scale is a rough approximation.

rials of ordinary farmers contrast with large dwellings with plaster-coated stone walls and tombs stocked with rich funerary offerings. Distinct social groups marked by differences in wealth and rank were emerging within communities. Eventually, powerful aristocratic families dominated each local society.

Growth and development continued during the Classic period (A.D. 250–1000). Dzibilchaltún, Uxmal, Río Bec, Becán, Chichén Itzá, Cobá, and many other communities became powerful civic centers. Elaborately decorated masonry palaces, administrative buildings, and temples on tall platforms dominated large and diverse communities. Regional differences became apparent, with related but distinctive cultural spheres along the east coast, on the northern plains, in the hilly western Puuc region, and in central Yucatan. Central Yucatan was in many ways culturally intermediate between the northern and southern lowlands. Eastern centers also maintained especially close ties with their southern lowland counterparts.

The beginning of the Postclassic period (A.D. 1000–1525) brought a cultural upheaval. Most older centers declined, and northern Maya societies came under foreign tutelage. For several centuries Mexicans and Mexican-influenced Mayas from the Gulf Coast, on the western fringe of the Maya lowlands, had extended their influence to the north and east. After A.D 1000, Mexican aristocrats and their western Maya allies, the Itzá, dominated the northern lowlands from the refurbished center of Chichén Itzá. With the waning of Mexican power, the Itzá held sway until Chichén fell to an uprising of subject towns about A.D. 1200. Remnants of the Itzá fled south, while the newly dominant Cocom, a noble Yucatec family, established a capital at Mayapán. Another revolt brought an end to the rule of Mayapán in the mid-fifteenth century. Three-quarters of a century later, the Spaniards found northern Yucatan politically fragmented, with more than a dozen petty states vying for local dominance. Long-distance trade, particularly maritime networks, linked the towns of Yucatan with the Gulf Coast and with commercial centers at the base of the Gulf of Honduras.

Today the Yucatec share the northern lowlands with Spanish-speaking Mexicans. Native Yucatec and modern Mexican culture coexist in varying blends: from urban, Mexican Mérida to very traditional rural villages. Life in the more remote hinterlands of eastern and central Yucatan has a very definite Maya character.

The Southern Lowlands

The southern part of the Yucatan Peninsula has undergone considerable population flux during the last thousand years. Historical information is scarce, for the southern lowland zone has been remote from colonial and modern seats of bureaucracy. It is a difficult region to characterize culturally and linguistically. Allowing for relatively recent shifts, the southern lowland area is fundamentally the homeland of the Cholan branch of the Maya language family: the Chol, Chontal, and

Chortí.[11] Before A.D. 1000 the region may have been solidly Cholan-speaking.

THE WESTERN LOWLANDS AND FRONTIER ZONE   The western margin of the lowlands, along the southern Gulf Coast of Mexico, is a frontier zone between the Maya area and the Mexican region stretching to the west and north. Environmentally the area is one: the tropical forest continues unbroken along the entire coastal plain. Culturally, too, there is no sharp boundary. At the time of the conquest this was a complex zone where speakers of Nahuatl, the language of the Aztecs of central Mexico, mingled with the Chol and Chontal Maya. Far to the north on the Gulf Coast are the Huastec, now isolated from all other Maya speakers.[12] Linguistically and culturally very different from other Maya peoples, the Huastec were probably first to separate from the ancestral stock.

The southern Gulf Coast just west of the Maya area was the cradle of Mesoamerica's first truly complex culture, the Olmec. Olmec civilization emerged not long after 1500 B.C. and soon spread far beyond the heartland to dominate most of Mesoamerica. In some ways the heritage of Maya civilization can be traced to the Olmec, and there are even some grounds for entertaining the possibility that the Olmec may have been Maya speakers. If so, it is surprising that the Maya lowlands are one region of Mesoamerica where Olmec civilization made few inroads.

The earliest known occupants of the western Maya lowlands are village farmers of the late second millennium B.C. Their pottery and other material equipment show the impact of Olmec styles, but they did not adopt the monumental art and architecture of heartland Olmec centers. Community growth and development followed much the same course as in the northern lowlands, reaching their height in the Classic period. Comalcalco, near the coast, is the westernmost Classic Maya center. Its varied styles of architecture, arts, and crafts plainly reflect its frontier status. Palenque, farther east and inland, near the foothills of the western highlands, is more squarely within the Classic Maya stylistic tradition in art and architecture, though it has its own distinct regional cast.

The west was in the vanguard at the time the forces of decline swept the southern lowlands, at the close of the Classic period, and the peoples of the region may have been involved in the spread of the collapse. Palenque was the first of the great centers to fail, about A.D. 800. Village societies persisted until the conquest, but no Postclassic community matched Palenque in size or influence. At the end of the prehispanic era, the Chol were the native inhabitants. They continue to occupy the region today, though traditional Chol culture is increasingly giving way before the inroads of modern Mexico. The people who inhabited the region in the Classic period probably spoke the Chol language. The hieroglyphic inscriptions of Palenque seem to reflect grammatical peculiarities of Chol speech. The ruins of Palenque figure prominently in the myths of today's Palencano Chol.[13]

North and east of Palenque is the homeland of another Cholan group, the Chontal. Though poorly known archaeologically, Chontal country figures prominently in historical documents of the colonial period. In the last centuries of the prehispanic era, this was Acalán, a region dotted with mercantile centers, dominated by Itzamkanac. The traders of Acalán carried on a thriving and far-flung commerce, maintaining economic links with Maya groups far to the south and east as well as with northern Yucatan and with Mexican peoples of the Gulf Coast to the north and west. Nahuatl-speaking merchants affiliated with the Aztec empire maintained a commercial outpost at Xicalango, a center on the Laguna de Términos which was rather like a free-trade zone. Acalán and Chontal culture had a decidedly international flavor.

THE SOUTHERN LOWLAND CORE   The heart of the southern lowland region, to the south and east, is often considered a cultural core zone—the hearth of Maya civilization. Here are some of the largest, most impressive, and most thoroughly investigated centers of the Classic period. Tikal is only the foremost of many. In consequence, this region has had an impact on conceptions of Maya civilization out of all proportion to its actual prominence.

In the eastern lowlands, farming villages were established by 2500 B.C., many centuries before the first known settlements elsewhere in the Maya world. Two thousand years of community growth and development led to the emergence of the first southern lowland civic centers.

At Tikal, Uaxactún, and a few other communities, large-scale construction projects were under way by the closing centuries of the pre-Christian era. Temples rose above all other buildings. Dwellings and burials of wealthy aristocrats contrast sharply with those of the bulk of the populace.

The history of the Classic period in the southern lowlands is a story of progressive growth and elaboration. Communities multiplied. Many grew into powerful civic centers with imposing public architecture. Monumental art and hieroglyphic inscriptions became increasingly prominent. True palaces and enormously rich burials marked widening social gaps. Occupational specialists held positions of intermediate status between small ruling groups and masses of ordinary farmers. The great centers of the southern lowland core reflect distinctive regional cultural spheres: Piedras Negras, Yaxchilán, and its tributary, Bonampak, in the Usumacinta region; Altar de Sacrificios and Seibal, along the Pasión; Tikal, Mirador, Calakmul, Naranjo, Uaxactún, and Yaxhá, in the central zone; San José, Barton Ramie, Benque Viejo, Altún Ha, Caracol, and Lubaantún, in the east. These are only the most prominent among hundreds of communities.

In the ninth century, a process of decline overtook the great civic centers and brought about the collapse of Classic Maya civilization throughout the southern lowlands. First along the Usumacinta, then along the Pasión, finally in the heart of the southern lowlands, center after center stopped constructing buildings and erecting monuments.

Seibal held on for nearly a century, its art and architecture colored by the impact of a heavy cultural intrusion from the north. Even here, however, survival was temporary. By the early decades of the tenth century, all major centers had effectively ceased to function, though occupation did not end entirely at every one. A remnant population lived on at Altar de Sacrificios until about A.D. 950. Squatter groups camped in the ruins of other centers even later, but most were actually abandoned. The southern lowlands suffered an overall population decline from which it has still not recovered.

During the Postclassic period, most southern lowland communities were small villages. Occasional settlements grew to the size of towns, but no great civic center rivaled those of the Classic period. These societies hold less interest for most archaeologists than their splendid predecessors of the Classic period, and the archaeological record for the late prehispanic period is correspondingly sketchy.

Documents of the colonial period have little to say about the native cultures of the region. Then, as now, they were largely isolated from the workings of government. All indications are that in colonial times the basic population of the region was Chol. The sector around Lake Petén Itzá is a partial exception. The Itzá, refugees from the overthrow of Chichén Itzá, established a new capital on an island in the lake. From Tayasal they exercised hegemony over the immediate area. Here they were established, an enclave in Chol territory, when Cortés passed through on his march to Honduras in 1524–25. Here they remained, independent and isolated, beyond the reach of Spanish colonial government, until the end of the seventeenth century.

Even today, most of the southern lowlands are only lightly populated. In the remote country south and west of the middle Usumacinta live the wild and enigmatic Lacandón.[14] Reduced to a few hundred souls by the pressure of encroaching modern Mexico, the Lacandón have retreated progressively deeper into the forest. Their ancestry is mysterious, though linguistically they are closely related to the Yucatec. Almost entirely isolated from the modern world, the Lacandón differ from all other Maya peoples in their peripatetic lifestyle and in the corresponding simplicity of their material culture. In the east are the Mopán, also linguistic relatives of the Yucatec.

Elsewhere in the southern lowlands, recent immigrants, mainly of non-Maya culture, make up the bulk of the population. Individuals, families, and small groups, attracted by the wilderness and frontier quality of life, continue to move into the underpopulated forests. The Kekchi, traditionally a highland people, have been the most prominent Maya colonists. Kekchi settlers, moving down from their homeland along the northern slopes of the highlands, are progressively colonizing the sparsely inhabited southern fringe of the lowlands.

THE SOUTHEASTERN LOWLANDS AND FRONTIER ZONE Little is known of the earliest inhabitants of the southeastern region, though there are scattered traces of occupations during the Preclassic period along the eastern margin of the Maya lowlands. To judge by early pottery from the northeast coast of Honduras, Mesoamerican cultures extended farther east before 1000 B.C. than in later centuries. [15] Olmec civilization had a recognizable stylistic impact in the Sula plain and the area to the south. Los Naranjos, on the shores of Lake Yojoa, even has monumental architecture comparable to that of contemporary great centers in the Olmec heartland, on the Gulf Coast.

Copán, on a tributary of the Río Motagua near the headwaters of the Río Chamelecón, was the greatest center in the southeast during the Classic period. Like Palenque, Copán had its own very distinctive regional style. Quiriguá, to the north along the lower Motagua, was, at least at times, a political dependency of Copán and shared many of its stylistic peculiarities. Farther north, beyond Lake Izabal, the regional style fades, though Quiriguá's political dominion may once have reached as far as Pusilhá. To the south, Copán's stylistic affinities stretched into the eastern highlands. Smaller centers along the Chamelecón and Jicatuyo, at least as far east as La Sierra, were under the sway of Copán. Beyond, the Sula plain and the Lake Yojoa region fell within a frontier zone in which Maya cultural patterns mingled with those of non-Mesoamerican peoples.

The collapse reached the southeast too. Copán succumbed early in the ninth century, and its dependent centers not long after. Late in prehispanic times, trade centers grew up at Nito, near the mouth of the Río Dulce; in the Sula plain; and at Naco, on the middle Chamelecón. These and other towns maintained active commercial links with eastern and northern Yucatan, with the great trade ports of the Gulf of Mexico, and with Central America, to the east and south. The thriving international trade involved extensive maritime networks as well as overland routes.

By the time of the conquest, the southeastern lowlands were an area of remarkable cultural diversity. A variety of foreign mercantile enclaves further complicated the region's heterogeneous makeup. The area of Lake Izabal and the lower Río Motagua, along with the coastal zone as far east as the Sula plain, were Chol territory. The Chortí occupied the inland region stretching east from Copán. In the Sula plain (Figs. 6, 7) and adjacent sectors of the Maya frontier, Maya groups mingled with Jicaque, Paya, Lenca, and other Central American peoples to form a complex cultural mosaic. Southeastern Maya peoples, like their eastern Central American neighbors, suffered greatly at the hands of colonial administrations. Much of the region's native cultural tradition has been destroyed. Only the Chortí retain substantial portions of their Maya heritage.

The Highlands

The mountains of the volcanic cordillera comprise the ancient homeland of other branches of the ancestral Maya stock. More than a dozen distinct Maya languages are still spoken in the highlands. European cultural patterns have made fewer obvious inroads among highland Maya peoples than among most of their lowland relatives.

6. The Sula Valley. The Río Ulua meanders through
the middle distance.

7. Thatched house in the Sula Valley. The walls are
made of adobe with a pole framework.

THE WESTERN HIGHLANDS The western highland zone, north and east of Zoque country, is the home of the Tzeltalan branch of the Maya language family.[16] Tzeltalan peoples became distinct from their Cholan relatives about the time of Christ. Sometime thereafter, the Tzeltal and Tzotzil reached their present location, where the Spaniards found them in the sixteenth century.

The archaeological record for the area is sketchy indeed. Earlier periods are almost entirely blank. In the Classic period, poorly understood regional variants of Maya civilization developed in the western highlands and in the foothills descending toward the Río Usumacinta. These variants may reflect stages in the westward movement of Tzeltalan speakers after their split from the Cholan block. Ancestors of the Kanjobalan speakers, now eastern neighbors of the Tzeltal, might also have been involved in the creation of these cultures.

THE CENTRAL AND EASTERN HIGHLANDS A village farming way of life was established in the central and eastern highlands by 1500 B.C. Not long afterward, the impact of Olmec civilization left its mark on ceramics and portable art objects. After 1000 B.C. Kaminaljuyú and a few other communities grew to great size, boasting large-scale civic architecture. Dwellings and burials reflect sharp differences in wealth and social status between aristocrats and ordinary farmers. By the time of Christ, Kaminaljuyú and many other highland centers were part of the Izapan world, centered in the Intermediate Zone. Maya art and writing evolved in the highlands and piedmont in this period. Izapan art styles and symbols formed a major component of the emergent Maya tradition.

In subsequent centuries, the prominence of Kaminaljuyú waned, to revive again in the Classic period under the powerful stimulus of contact with the urban Mexican civilization of Teotihuacán. From a base at Kaminaljuyú, Teotihuacanos developed economic ties with a few centers in the southern lowlands. The end of direct Teotihuacán involvement in the Maya world about A.D. 600 ushered in a poorly understood period of regionalization in which local cultures vied for prominence. The florescence of Classic Maya civilization evidently did not include central and eastern highland societies. Communities in these areas did not produce the monumental architecture, sculpture, and hieroglyphic inscriptions that are so typical of lowland Classic centers. The nature of the relationship between highland Maya peoples and the better understood lowland variants of Classic Maya civilization remains to be worked out.

In the closing centuries of the prehispanic epoch, a series of relatively small, ethnically and linguistically distinct Maya groups competed for local political hegemony in the central and eastern highlands. The most prominent were the Quiché.

At the western edge of the zone lived the Kanjobalans: Kanjobal, Jacaltec, Acatec, Motozintlec, Tuzantec, Tojolabal, and Chuj.[17] Their role in the region's culture history is obscure. Today they are vastly reduced in numbers, and their native languages and cultural traditions are almost extinct. They cling to a precarious existence at the margins of modern Mexican and Guatemalan society.

The Mamean branch of the Maya language family separated early from their Quichean relations, probably by 1500 B.C., not long after Eastern Mayan became distinct from the Proto-Mayan stock. Mamean languages have remained very archaic. Of all Maya tongues, Mam, Teco, Ixil, and Aguacatec have changed least from the Proto-Mayan language. In late prehispanic times, these peoples were more numerous and more prominent than their western neighbors. The Mam dominated a substantial zone from their capital at Zaculeu. Just before the conquest they came under heavy pressure from their eastern neighbors, the Quiché. In the centuries since the conquest, Mamean speakers have expanded south into the piedmont and coastal regions.[18]

The central highland region around Lake Atitlán is the homeland of Quichean speakers (Color Plate 8).[19] Quichean underwent a late divergence, with Quiché, Cakchiquel, Tzutuhil, Sacapultec, and Sipacapa emerging as distinct languages only about A.D. 1000. In the last centuries of the prehispanic era a parallel process of cultural and political differentiation produced independent Quiché, Cakchiquel, and Tzutuhil states competing for local hegemony. The arrival of the Spaniards interrupted the Quiché's rise to dominance.

The eastern highlands are the home of other Quichean peoples: Kekchi and Uspantec in the north and Pokom in the east.[20] In the last century, the Kekchi have expanded into the southern fringe of the lowlands. On the northeast are the Cholan Chortí, in the foothills descending to the southeastern lowlands.[21] On the east and south, Pokom speakers occupy the frontier of the Maya area and of Mesoamerica. The Pokomam and Pokomchí separated only about A.D. 1000. Their distribution at the time of the conquest may reflect a relatively recent expansion to the east and south into what may formerly have been non-Maya territory. Beyond the Pokomam are non-Mesoamerican peoples: the Paya, Lenca, and Xinca.

The Pacific Coast and Slope

Farming villages appeared in the coast and piedmont sector of the Intermediate Zone before 1500 B.C. They evolved from an earlier tradition of settled communities that exploited the rich wild food resources of the coast. In the centuries after 1500 B.C., the region was an integral part of the Olmec world. Olmec civilization spilled out of the Gulf Coast heartland, crossed the lowland belt spanning the Isthmus of Tehuantepec, and stretched far to the east along the Pacific Coast and piedmont.

During the final centuries of the Preclassic period, the Intermediate Zone was the home of a confusing series of related cultures. Izapa, El Baúl, Abaj Takalik, and Monte Alto, along with such highland communities as Kaminaljuyú and Chalchuapa, grew into prominent civic centers. Monumental architecture and sculpture with hieroglyphic inscriptions burgeoned. An underlying similarity in style and content cuts across the regional differences in these vigorous local cultures. This Izapan artistic tradition shows a plain heritage from Olmec civilization. Equally clear is the contribution of Izapan art and symbols to the emergence of Classic Maya art, calendar systems, and writing.

The piedmont and coastal zone had a complex history during the Classic period. In the east, cultural relationships with lowland Maya civilization, especially its southeastern variant, were strongest. Here, along the southern end of the frontier zone bordering Central America, considerable mingling of peoples created a complicated mosaic of cultural patterns. Farther west were several poorly understood regional cultures, many of them evidently aligned more with the Mexican than with the Maya tradition. Beginning as early as A.D. 800, speakers of Pipil, a branch of Nahua closely related to the language of the Aztecs, filtered southward and eastward from central Mexico, settling in enclaves among local groups. These movements reflect sweeping political and cultural changes that took place in central Mexico after the collapse of Teotihuacán.

At the time of the conquest, the western Pacific Coast and slope was basically Zoque country, with a substantial Pipil component. The Aztec empire had recently incorporated a large portion of the area into the coastal province of Xoconochco (Soconusco), ensuring access to its rich cacao production. To the east, Pipil enclaves were increasingly prominent among speakers of Xinca, Lenca, and other Central American languages. In recent centuries, Maya-speaking groups have spilled down from the highlands into the piedmont and coastal plain.

The uneven quality of available data exaggerates the cultural and historical contrasts among the various regions of the Maya world. The occupation of the eastern lowlands so long before other areas, for example, is probably more apparent than real. Evidence of early settlements, often buried under later construction or obliterated by it, is found more often by chance than by design. Enormous regions remain almost unknown archaeologically, even for later periods. Much of central Yucatan, intermediate between the northern and southern lowlands, has hardly been investigated. Huge tracts of southern forest, especially in the foothills rising to the highlands, are practically unexplored. Copán, in the southeast, and Palenque, in the northwest, seem marginal to central lowland patterns mainly because the intervening territory is nearly blank on the archaeological map. Recent work in central Yucatan has uncovered intermediate forms and styles that dull the contrast between northern and southern lowlands. By the same token, when more is known of the southern margin of the lowlands, transitional variants will bridge the apparent gulf between highland and lowland Maya cultures.

CHAPTER THREE

THE MAYA WORLD ON THE EVE OF THE SPANISH CONQUEST

The Spaniards who conquered and colonized the Maya area were firsthand observers of Maya societies before the demise of their economic and political independence. The picture of sixteenth-century Maya societies that can be pieced together from Spaniards' accounts is spotty. Few groups have thorough documentation, and some have none at all. The conquerors were most interested in native political geography and trade networks, for these institutions could be adapted to Spanish ends. Such cultural spheres as religion, difficult to comprehend and slated to be stamped out, attracted much less attention. Even the best descriptions of Maya groups in early colonial documents are heavily biased toward politics and economics. Uneven and imperfect as they are, these glimpses of native Maya societies just after the conquest are priceless, for they often reflect facets of culture that are all but impossible to reconstruct from archaeological evidence. Though much of the Maya tradition survived to become the subject of modern observation, never again were Maya societies untouched by the political, economic, and social impact of the dominant European culture.

THE STATES OF NORTHERN YUCATAN

The sixteen politically autonomous districts comprising northern Yucatan in the sixteenth century (Map 4) had been provinces under the

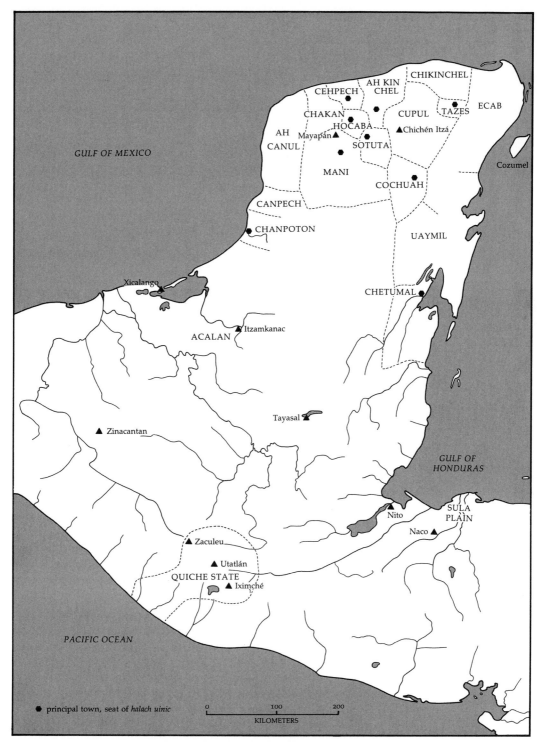

CHIKINCHEL

CEHPECH AH KIN
CHEL

CHAKAN CUPUL TAZES ECAB

HOCABA

AH Mayapán ▲Chichén Itzá
CANUL SOTUTA

Cozumel

MANI COCHUAH

GULF OF MEXICO

CANPECH

CHANPOTON

UAYMIL

Xicalango▲

CHETUMAL

ACALAN ▲Itzamkanac

Tayasal

GULF OF
HONDURAS

▲ Zinacantan

SULA
PLAÌN

Nito▲

▲Naco

▲ Zaculeu

▲ Utatlán

QUICHE STATE ▲ Iximché

PACIFIC OCEAN

● principal town, seat of *halach uinic*

0   100   200
KILOMETERS

Map 4. The Maya world on the eve of the Spanish conquest. The limits indicated for the Quiché state represent its maximum expansion, achieved in the mid-fifteenth century.

sway of Mayapán a century earlier.[1] Though all were culturally and linguistically Yucatec, to some extent they were ethnically distinct, dominated by powerful competing families. Some provinces had shed the old centralized organization entirely. Chakán, in the northwest, and Chikinchel, along the north coast, scarcely constituted political units at all. Casual alliances linking the independent towns shifted frequently. Ah Canul, in the west, maintained a slightly firmer identity. Nobles of the Canul family controlled most of the main centers and generally acted in concert. A similar situation obtained in the east-central plains, where the Cupul family dominated.

Maní was the home of the Tutul Xiu, whose nobles were at the forefront of the revolt that toppled Mayapán. Sotuta had become the refuge of the Cocom family, deposed lords of Mayapán. Here and in Chanpotón, Cehpech, Hocaba, Ah Kin Chel, Tazes, Cochuah, and Chetumal, central political and economic hierarchies persisted. Each of these provinces was, at least nominally, under the authority of a *halach uinic* ("true man"), though his control was not always complete. In some provinces, outlying towns exercised effective local independence, while recognizing the nominal authority of the halach uinic. His functions were mainly political and military, and he was concerned especially with defense of the province and maintenance of its boundaries. At the same time, the halach uinic had important religious roles, and he could be referred to as a "bishop." The office was hereditary, often passing from the incumbent to his younger brother, then to his son. Subject towns provided for the upkeep of the halach uinic and his ménage through tribute, usually in foods.

The *batab* headed municipal organization. The halach uinic himself served as batab of provincial capitals. This office too was principally political and military, charged with general administrative and judicial oversight, particularly of farming and public construction activity. Townspeople provided the batab with food and domestic service. Each ward or municipal subdivision had its local administrative head, the *ah cuch cab*. Collectively these officials formed a sort of town council that served the batab in an advisory capacity. Most towns had, in addition, several lower ranks of municipal officers.

Throughout northern Yucatan, society was organized along much the same lines. At birth each person became a member of a lineage group, comprising kinsmen related through males. Children entered the lineage of their father, taking his surname, which was also the lineage name. Persons with the same lineage surname were scattered throughout the provinces of northern Yucatan. However distant the actual kinship relation, they were forbidden to marry. Common lineage names also implied at least the theoretical obligation of mutual assistance, though conflicting political loyalties often intervened. Locally, lineages constituted functioning corporate groups, with their own council chambers. Local lineages were ranked. Though differences in social and economic status cut across lineage lines, high political offices and wealth tended to concentrate in the hands of male leaders of powerful families in high-ranking lineages. The *ah holpop,* head of the most

THE WORLD OF THE ANCIENT MAYA

prominent local lineage, often served as batab or filled some other powerful office.

Ownership of land, buildings, orchards, beehives, jewels, and other real property passed mainly along male lines, from fathers to sons. Women also held property, sometimes land, in their own right, and daughters inherited from their mothers. Like men, women derived high social rank from family and lineage connections, and they occasionally held important political offices. In addition to the lineage surname, each person took a *naal* ("house name") from his or her mother.

Young men lived in community or barrio dormitories, where they underwent informal social and religious education. Those destined for the priesthood or high political office received more formal training elsewhere. On marriage, typically in late adolescence, a young man moved in with his bride's family for a period of service that might last six years or more. Thereafter the couple went to live with the husband's family or established a new household. Multiple-family dwellings were the norm.

Men of noble or wealthy family and lineage connections gravitated toward careers in politics. Young sons of wealthy houses for whom no offices were available or who were unsuited for political life often turned to commerce. An alternative, probably also open to achieving sons of lesser families, was the priesthood. Assorted religious offices fell into a rough status and authority ranking, but they were not part of a single formal hierarchy. Some priests performed a wide range of ritual duties, while others specialized. *Chilams* interpreted prophecy. More numerous were specialists in heart removal and other methods of human sacrifice.

Sons of lesser families ordinarily become farmers. Agrarian methods were much the same as they are in Yucatan today, but with a much enhanced religious and ritual component. The prehispanic milpa farmer operated not in a world of fixed natural processes, but in a universe filled with supernatural powers of variable disposition. He therefore had not simply to follow mechanical farming methods, but to adopt procedures designed to persuade these beings to confer a bountiful harvest by producing favorable conditions.

Extreme contrasts in wealth and social status separated nobles from ordinary farmers, but only slaves constituted a sharply bounded social class. Craft specialists and minor merchants comprised a loosely defined middle group that ranked below the aristocracy but above the common farmers. Debtors, criminals, and prisoners of war were enslaved. Most slaves performed domestic service or agricultural labor; some provided victims for the sacrificial altar.

Social, economic, and even political ties cut across the fabric of formal political divisions in northern Yucatan. The same lineages were represented everywhere, and common lineage membership promoted a feeling of solidarity that could stimulate cooperation in the economic and political arenas. Economic links connected the districts. Each had a diversified economy with a strong milpa farming component, but emphases differed. A few coastal towns specialized to a high degree in fishing or salt collecting. Chetumal's prosperity flowed from exceptionally productive cacao orchards as well as from its position as an important trading center. Commerce, monopolized by noble merchants, was active and extensive. The island of Cozumel was a major commercial center in the maritime exchange network ringing the coast of Yucatan.[2] As in the days when Chichén Itzá and then Mayapán had held sway, cotton cloth, salt, honey, wax, and slaves moved south to Chetumal and on to Nito and Naco, at the base of the Gulf of Honduras. In return, cacao, precious metals, feathers, and the like were shipped north.

Religion, too, promoted communication. Special regional shrines of wide repute became pilgrimage centers, attracting devotees in large numbers from great distances. The ruins of the old capital of Chichén Itzá retained ritual importance. People from all over northern Yucatan and beyond came to cast offerings into its cenote, sacred to the rain god. The practice has not quite died even yet, for offerings dredged from the cenote's muck include plastic dolls of modern manufacture. Cozumel had special importance for worshipers of Ix Chel, moon goddess and consort of the sun, patroness of weaving, divination, medicine, and childbirth. A steady stream of pilgrims came to Cozumel to consult the oracle at Ix Chel's shrine, where a concealed priest answered questions put to her image.

Despite the many cultural links that bound them together, relations among districts were not always harmonious. Boundaries between provinces, never sharply defined, were often disputed, and disagreement occasionally erupted into armed conflict.

ACALÁN

Exchange networks stretched west and south from northern Yucatan to Gulf Coast ports and the inland trade centers of Acalán. Xicalango, on the Laguna de Términos, was a mercantile nexus of the first importance.[3] Merchants came to Xicalango from Yucatan, from Acalán, and from Mexican towns along the Gulf Coast to the west. Even *pochtecas*, men of the Aztec merchant class, came from distant Tenochtitlán. Xicalango had something of the character of a free-trade zone, a politically neutral town where merchants could conduct business regardless of their cultural and political affiliations. Several cultural groups maintained resident enclaves, trading and managing warehouses and other commercial facilities. Nahuatl was evidently the leading language of Xicalango.

The Candelaria basin, south and east of Xicalango, was the Chontal Maya province of Acalán ("Place of Canoes").[4] Chontal societies were organized along much the same lines as those of northern Yucatan. Noble families controlled politics, commerce, and religion. Ordinary farmers comprised the largest social group. Slaves, lowest in the social hierarchy, probably provided most of the labor for Acalán's great cacao

THE WORLD OF THE ANCIENT MAYA

plantations. Cacao ripens throughout the year, requiring a constant supply of labor. Acalán was one of Mesoamerica's premier cacao-producing regions. The only notable difference from Yucatecan societies is that couples were much more likely to live permanently with the wife's family after marriage.

Itzamkanac, the capital of Acalán, was a large and prosperous town. Early Spanish visitors described hundreds of fine houses. Those of the principal families even boasted masonry walls. Cortés found Itzamkanac much more impressive than Tayasal, the Itzá capital. One administrative building in the town center was spacious enough to accommodate all of the Spaniards who accompanied him, and their horses too. Itzamkanac was divided into four quarters, each with its own administrative head. Collectively they exercised considerable power, but they were formally subordinate to a supreme ruler, *ahau*, equivalent to the Yucatecan halach uinic. In 1525 one Paxbolonacha held this office, ruling Itzamkanac and all of Acalán. There must have been many more levels of the political hierarchy, both within Itzamkanac and in the subordinate towns.

Itzamkanac had many impressive temples, the principal one sacred to Cukulchán, the tutelary god of the ruler. Cukulchán is the equivalent of Yucatec Kukulcán ("quetzal bird–snake"), a god and culture hero identified with the episode of Toltec domination. Each quarter had its own temple, dedicated to especially important deities, including Ix Chel and Ykchaua. The latter, called Ek Chuah in Yucatan, was the patron of merchants and cacao producers, a logical combination, since cacao was a standard of exchange and value—a form of money.

With their strong mercantile orientation, the Chontal towns had a long history of economic interaction with Mexican peoples of the Gulf Coast. Over the centuries their own culture had taken on a decided Mexican cast. Nahua personal names were widespread. Several communities or barrios within communities consisted of enclaves of Nahua-speaking Mexicans.

Acalán's prosperity depended on commerce as well as cacao growing. Acalán's ruler was also its principal merchant. According to Francisco López de Gómara, chaplain and secretary to Cortés:

> In the land of Acalán, so they say, the people have the custom of choosing as their lord the most prosperous merchant, which is why Apoxpalón (Paxbolonacha) had been chosen, for he enjoyed a large land trade in cotton, cacao, slaves, salt, and gold (although this was not plentiful and was mixed with copper and other things); in colored shells, with which they adorn themselves and their idols; in resin and other incense for the temples; in pitch pine for lighting; in pigments and dyes with which they paint themselves for war and festivals, and stain their bodies as a defense against heat and cold; and in many other articles of merchandise, luxuries or necessities. For this purpose he held fairs in many towns, such as Nito, where he had agents and separate districts for his own vassals and traders.[5]

Acalán did not focus its commercial interests exclusively on the Gulf Coast and northern Yucatan. Chontal merchants also traded in markets to the south and east. On his march from the Gulf Coast to Honduras in 1524–25, Cortés followed some of the overland trade routes stretching from Acalán through the southern lowlands, at least as far as the Gulf of Honduras. Paxbolonacha, Acalán's ruler, maintained a commercial enclave at Nito, the Chol trade port on the Gulf of Honduras. His brother governed the Chontal quarter of the town.

TAYASAL

Tayasal dominated the region of Lake Petén Itzá at the time of the Spanish conquest.[6] Refugee Itzá from northern Yucatan had founded the town after the fall of Chichén Itzá (about A.D. 1200). Here they formed an enclave in sparsely populated Chol territory. Remote from centers of colonial administration, they remained independent until the end of the seventeenth century.

Five small islands in the lake comprised the heart of the Tayasal community. The principal island, only 500 meters long and half as wide, housed Tayasal's civic core, with elaborate masonry and stucco temples, palaces, and administrative halls. Clustered together on the high ground at the center of the island, the temples were surrounded by aristocratic dwellings nearer the shore. Evidently only the highest-ranking lords and their retainers lived on the main island. One Spanish estimate put the population of this civic nucleus at 2,000 on the eve of its conquest; an earlier visitor mentioned 200 houses. Island dwellers maintained secondary residences on the mainland for periods of heavy agricultural work. Outlying subordinate settlements on the mainland were quite small. Most ordinary farmers, the bulk of the population, lived dispersed in the surrounding countryside. Tayasal's political sphere embraced some 22,000 souls at the end of the seventeenth century.

Culturally the Itzá of Tayasal were much like their Yucatec relatives to the north. Their language was either an archaic dialect of Yucatec or a related language heavily influenced by Yucatec during their sojourn in northern Yucatan. Most of the Itzá of Tayasal had Yucatec personal names. Lineage organization played a leading role in society and politics. Ahau Canek, the ruler of Tayasal at the time of its fall, bore the same dynastic or lineage name as his predecessor who had greeted Cortés. His first cousin, Kin Canek, was the high priest. *Ahau* and *ah kin* are Yucatec titles of political officials and priests, respectively. Politics and religion were intertwined, for Ahau Canek had religious duties and Kin Canek held political power. Priests and rulers also shared esoteric knowledge, for Ahau Canek could read the books of history and prophecy kept in his house. Officials in charge of outlying communities were often priests as well. The main temples were evidently dedicated to special aristocratic cults and tutelary deities of the nobles, for common folk worshiped elsewhere, mainly at sacred places in the forest.

Four batabs (another Yucatec title) ruled the quarters of Tayasal.

THE WORLD OF THE ANCIENT MAYA

These quarters were subdivided into smaller units that probably corresponded in part to lineage groups, for the name of the official in charge of each district could be applied to all of its inhabitants. Residences accommodated multiple or extended families. The *nacon*, a military officer, bore the same title as his Yucatec counterpart.

Most of the Itzá gods, including the preeminent Itzamná, were also worshiped in northern Yucatan. At the top of the stair before the main entrance to Kin Canek's principal temple was an idol "squatting on its heels." Reclining Chacmool figures were ubiquitous in Yucatec temples. Images of some deities spoke to worshipers, recalling the oracle at Ix Chel's shrine on Cozumel. Human sacrifice, especially by heart removal, was quite common. The music of flutes and drums accompanied the ceremonial dances performed on such occasions. A ritual meal of the victim's flesh often followed. Prisoners of war were the preferred victims, but Itzá boys from Tayasal were also sacrificed and devoured. On one occasion the Itzá impaled the heads of a group of Spaniards on stakes on a low mound, evidently a rustic counterpart of the *tzompantlis* (skull racks) of northern Yucatan and central Mexico. Spanish reports that homosexuality was common recall traditional Yucatec aspersions on the "lewdness" of the Itzá.

Milpa farming, the foundation of the Itzá economy, was exceptionally productive in this region. Milpas ordinarily produced two crops a year, sometimes three, and remained fertile for a decade or more. In addition to maize, milperos cultivated beans, squashes, chiles, maguey, manioc, sweet potatoes, and many other vegetables and root crops. They tended orchards of cacao and fruit trees and kept bees for honey. Fish, shellfish, turtles, deer, wild pigs, rabbits, dogs, turkeys, and many other birds provided protein. Tobacco was the most important of the plants cultivated for ritual and medicinal use.

Cotton was a particularly important crop and luxury textiles were a major export. Salt, hard stone for grinding tools, obsidian for cutting tools, and other vital resources had to be imported, and Tayasal depended on external exchange networks. The Itzá maintained enclaves in foreign territory, where needed commodities could be had. Canek told Cortés of his vassals who lived on the Caribbean coast in order to grow cacao. This outpost was probably at Nito, though Chetumal is another possible site. Both were situated in important cacao-producing regions, and both were prominent ports on the sea routes ringing Yucatan. The Itzá enclave probably had commercial as well as agricultural functions.

NACO AND THE SULA PLAIN

The Sula plain, just southeast of Nito, was another, perhaps even busier, mercantile zone.[7] Here Chetumal and other northern trade centers maintained commercial outposts with storage facilities. Here, in times past, the lords of Chichén Itzá and Mayapán had come to trade

8. Modern Naco. Villagers, who still tell folk tales about the Spanish conquest, take a close interest in archaeological investigations of the ancient trade center beneath their homes and streets.

for gold, other metals, feathers, and particularly the cacao for which the region was famous. The Sula plain was a connecting link, probably a major transshipment point, between the exchange networks of the Maya world and those stretching east and south, beyond Mesoamerica, into the metal-rich regions of Central America. It was part of a frontier zone where peoples of Chortí and Chol speech mingled with Jicaque, Lenca, and possibly Paya and Care. Chontal Maya and Nahua-speaking Pipil with ties to the Pacific Coast may have formed enclaves alongside Yucatec outposts.

Naco, a prosperous town of some 10,000 souls located in the middle Chamelecón Valley (Fig. 8), was the most prominent center in the frontier region when the Spaniards arrived. Its economic and political sphere extended east, down the Río Chamelecón, into the Sula plain itself, but craft styles also link Naco with the highlands to the south and west. Highland obsidian was a major import for local consumption and for resale. During the Classic period Naco's valley fell well within Copán's sphere. In the sixteenth century Naco was probably a Chortí town, but as an important frontier trade center, it surely had a cosmopolitan character. There are hints that a Pipil enclave may have settled there.

THE HIGHLAND STATES

Early colonial documents have little to say of western highland peoples. Tzotzil, Tzeltal, and Kanjobalan groups comprised many small independent political and economic spheres. Farther east, the

THE WORLD OF THE ANCIENT MAYA

Mam capital of Zaculeu controlled a much larger territory. Zinacantan, the Tzotzil trade center, was the most prominent western town. A Spanish conquistador remarked that Zinacantecos were "sensible people and many of them traders." Aztec merchants were vitally interested in regional products, but they regarded Zinacantan's sphere as dangerous territory and donned elaborate disguise when they traveled there. Salt, amber, quetzal feathers, and animal pelts were among the exports reaching central Mexico from Zinacantan. Eventually the Aztecs established a permanent enclave there. Chiapanecs to the west and south disputed Zinacantan's monopoly of valuable natural resources. Competition between them, especially over salt deposits, periodically flared into open conflict.[8]

Early documents describe central highland peoples in considerable detail. The Quiché, the most powerful group, had their capital at Utatlán.[9] In the sixteenth century they were still expanding from their original homeland in the Quiché basin. Their territorial holdings, mainly of very recent acquisition, were imperfectly consolidated. Growth had evidently outstripped the evolution of systems of political control and administration. Quiché society had undergone enormous changes in the last centuries before the Spanish conquest. It was still in a state of flux when the Spaniards arrived.

The Quiché aristocracy monopolized power, filling all important political, military, and religious offices. Quiché nobles based their claims to authority and legitimacy on two grounds: descent from Toltec lords and a special relationship with Toltec gods. Traditional histories even describe ceremonies in which Toltec lords invested Quiché rulers. So firm was the Quiché aristocracy's title to sovereignty that the Quiché ruler formally confirmed the succession of his Cakchiquel and Tzutuhil counterparts. The Quiché sovereign was the only highland Maya lord who wore the nose plug, the emblem of supreme authority among central Mexican peoples. Gold and jade jewelry, quetzal-feather ornaments, and a host of other status symbols reserved to the aristocracy set them visibly apart from common folk. Nobles dwelt in sumptuous palaces in the civic precincts of Quiché communities. Even after death, elaborate funerary rites confirmed the lords' exalted status. Posterity immortalized the greatest nobles, even deified them, preserving their remains as objects of veneration.

Quiché society, economy, and politics revolved around aristocratic kinship organization. At birth every noble child entered the lineage of his or her father. The most prominent lineages traced their ancestry back in the male line to Toltec lords. Marriage regulation was an ancient function of Quiché kin groups: no noble could wed a member of the same lineage. Political considerations created a preference for marriage outside of the community as well, and Quiché rulers often found noble wives among the Cakchiquel, the Tzutuhil, the Mam, and perhaps even among the Itzá of Yucatan. Obligations of mutual assistance linked all members of a lineage, who were expected to act in concert, as a group. Raising the bride price required to conclude a noble marriage was a lineage affair. Lineages were also corporate groups, with their own buildings and land. For some purposes, lineages were grouped into sets, though these "major lineages" and moieties seldom functioned as cohesive groups.

In the course of Quiché history, noble lineages played an ever increasing role in affairs of state. Eventually they became subdivisions of the Quiché political system. Each lineage was linked to an important political office, from which it took its name. The lineage head automatically assumed that office. Lineages were ranked, those of greatest status providing the highest officials. The *ah pop,* or ruler, was the head of the Cawek lineage, while the *ah pop q'am haa* (assistant chief) came from a lower-ranking group in the same major lineage. Lineage members provided the head with a staff of subordinate officers to assist him with lineage affairs and with the duties of his political post. One such set of minor officials included ambassador to foreign peoples, councilman, council debater, council announcer, council diviner, tribute collector, war leader, war dancer, guardian of the wall, guardian of orphans, chief carrier, messenger, blood sacrificer, tormenter, chief of the sweat bath, bracelet keeper, painter, flutist, rattler, banquet servant, saver of fowl, toaster, helper, and several other titles. The number of lineages grew steadily with Quiché expansion and the attendant internal political elaboration. By the sixteenth century there were sixty-four principal lineages, with hundreds of subdivisions. Relations between lineages and the composition of higher-order groupings changed with shifts in political and economic fortune.

Utatlán, the Quiché capital, was a composite community occupying several plateaus separated by deep ravines. Three distinct civic centers, each occupied by different sets of lineages, formed the heart of the community. Q'umaric Ah (also written Gumarcaah or K'umarcaaj), home of the Cawek lineage, was preeminent in the sixteenth century. Within each civic precinct, discrete complexes of temples, palaces, and council chambers corresponded to each lineage.

Ordinary farmers, who made up the largest segment of Quiché society, lived in outlying residential suburbs. The fruits of their labor sustained the aristocracy, to whom they owed allegiance as well as service. Aristocratic status symbols were forbidden them, and they were excluded from rites of the Mexican tutelary gods of the nobles. Commoners had their own lineage groups, which functioned mainly to regulate marriage and family relations. Commoners, too, had to marry outside of their lineages. Unlike nobles, they normally found spouses within the local community.

Several occupational groups ranked somewhere between lords and commoners. Military orders, merchants, and artisans evidently comprised something of an emergent middle class. Warriors were crucial to the political designs of the Quiché state. By the sixteenth century military leaders had acquired titles indicating that they had been elevated to a new lower echelon of the nobility. These warrior nobles gained access to some restricted status symbols, moved into the civic precincts, and took greater roles in state affairs. Formal authority and the balance of political power remained in the hands of the old aristocracy.

Merchants, too, had some attributes and privileges of high rank, including free association with nobles. Artisans also occupied intermediate social positions. Some were actually low-ranking members of noble lineages. In Utatlán, at least, other artisans may have been foreigners, residing in Mexican enclaves.

Below the commoners were landless "serfs," who worked the lands of nobles as sharecroppers. This group, consisting mainly of freed prisoners of war, grew as the Quiché state expanded by military conquest. Other prisoners went directly to the sacrificial altar. Others still became slaves, as did convicted criminals. The very poor could also be sold into slavery by their relatives or their lords. Most slaves were slated for eventual sacrifice on a variety of ceremonial occasions. Some died at once; others performed domestic service or agricultural labor for nobles before accompanying their lords to the afterlife.

The Cakchiquel, close relatives and perennial rivals of the Quiché, were their neighbors on the south and east.[10] From their capital at Iximché (Color Plate 7) the Cakchiquel dominated much of the region around Lake Atitlán. In the years immediately preceding the conquest, the Cakchiquel had thrown off the yoke of the Quiché state. In the sixteenth century they were increasing their own territorial holdings and economic sphere of influence at the expense of the Pokom and other neighboring groups. In political, economic, and social organization, the Cakchiquel closely resembled the Quiché, with whom they also shared much of their mythology and traditional history.

The Tzutuhil, at the time of the conquest, were under pressure from their expansionist near relatives on the west, north, and east.[11] They resisted subjugation, but Quiché and Cakchiquel successes effectively blocked the Tzutuhil on almost every front. All indications are that poorly documented Tzutuhil society was much like that of their better-known relatives. At the same time, their restricted horizons presented a more limited scope for political and economic complexity.

Farther east, the Pokom also had a recent history of territorial and economic expansion, particularly along the frontier facing Central American peoples.[12] In most respects the Pokom were comparable to the Quichean peoples to the west. Naturally, influenced by the foreigners along their eastern flank, they present an eclectic cultural picture. To the south and east, solid Pokom distributions gave way to Pokom enclaves among Pipil, Xinca, Lenca, and other non-Maya peoples. Chalchuapa, in the southeastern highlands, was one such Pokom community, part of the eastern frontier of the Maya world and Mesoamerica.[13] Farther east, in Lenca territory, non-Mesoamerican cultural patterns were dominant.

CHAPTER FOUR

THE MAYA UNIVERSE

The Maya world described in the last chapter makes little sense in the terms of Maya thought. It would be unfamiliar, perhaps unrecognizable, to a Maya. The emphasis is entirely misplaced. In the Maya ethos, the world cannot be defined in the cold terms of natural environment—climate, topography, flora, fauna, and so forth. This is no definition at all, merely an overly detailed consideration of one facet among many. Artificially divorced from its position in the universe, without context, the physical world is bereft of real meaning.

In the Maya conceptual system, the universe is a unity.[1] The physical world is inextricably intertwined with other realms. The province of the supernatural, of the incorporeal, and of extrasensory experience is a part of everyday Maya experience, an ordinary aspect of reality. Maya space is not bounded by the limits of the terrestrial world. It embraces the heavens and the underworlds as well. One set of dimensions unifies the natural and supernatural worlds. Space and time are inseparable complementary components of the Maya universe.

A host of supernatural entities inhabits the Maya universe. Along with ordinary humans, animals, and plants, it harbors the deities of the Maya pantheon, the symbolic flora and fauna of Maya thought, and legions of minor spirits. Each of these beings has special associations with one or more regions of the universe—with a particular cardinal direction or a specific unit of time. They do not occupy their sectors exclusively, for all of the universe is continuous. Its denizens constantly move through the space-time continuum. But special relationships do exist. In this sense, the Maya supernaturals are also dimensions of the universe, facets of time and space.

Maya reality, then, differs radically from most others. Reduced to these bald abstractions, the Maya concept of the universe sounds like mystical foolishness. The pages that follow describe a few aspects of Maya reality in greater detail, to clothe the skeletal framework with enough flesh to lend it meaning. It is difficult for the outsider to appreciate these seemingly bizarre notions as a coherent, functional system of integrated beliefs. Every society believes that its own version of reality is "real" and classes other realities as fantasy—charming, perhaps, but surely distorted. To escape this trap one must suspend disbelief to a degree that strains the rationalist mind. Yet only so is it possible to begin to achieve the empathy necessary to enter at least a little way into the Maya universe.

There is no single Maya world view, any more than one Maya group can be made to stand for the entire Maya cultural tradition. As in all facets of Maya culture, beliefs vary from region to region, and they have changed through time. Yet the several Maya cosmologies and symbol systems are particularly coherent. In this sphere, Maya cultures share many elements and most major themes. In this realm, more than in any other, the Maya resemble other Mesoamerican peoples. In a broad sense, there is one Maya, and even Mesoamerican, conception of the universe. Names, details, the minor elaborations vary from group to group. Much has changed during the course of Maya culture history as well, but the basic patterns are remarkably stable. In fact, possession of a variant of this cosmology may be the best criterion for defining both Maya and Mesoamerican cultural traditions.

Naturally, evidence about symbols in the earlier prehistoric periods is often sketchy. It is not certain exactly when this complex of beliefs developed. Presumably it did not spring into being full-blown, but emerged gradually, over many centuries. Many of the basic features were present in the last centuries of the pre-Christian era. From that time until the Spanish conquest, all Maya groups shared its fundamental patterns. Intensive suppression of native belief systems during the last few centuries has left some modern Maya groups bereft of a substantial portion of this heritage.

The description of the Maya universe presented here is a composite sketch put together from archaeological, historical, and ethnographic information. It is not specific to any particular time period or region of the Maya world. It relies heavily on belief systems of the last centuries of the preconquest era reflected in precolumbian native books and documents of the early colonial period. Archaeological evidence, particularly from the Classic period in the southern lowlands, confirms and extends the reconstruction. Information from modern Maya ethnography and occasionally from observation of other Mesoamerican peoples can be used sparingly to clarify or expand certain points. The Aztecs are particularly illuminating. Early Spanish churchmen scrutinized their belief systems intensively and recorded their observations in detail.

Not every Maya group always possessed every element described here. Some elaborations of the calendar system did not survive the Classic period. Some features of the pantheon reconstructed from later prehispanic sources no doubt represent considerable change from the situation in the Classic period. This composite cosmology is not an exhaustive catalog of Maya beliefs about the universe. Still, it is distinctively Maya. Every well-documented prehispanic Maya group possessed a recognizable variant of it.

TIME

Time is the most thoroughly understood dimension of the Maya universe.[2] Precolumbian hieroglyphic texts, colonial documents, and modern ethnographic observations all reflect Maya concepts of time. This wealth of source material leaves no doubt that beliefs about time are central to Maya thought. They permeate every aspect of daily life.

Some facets of the Maya conception of time are familiar: time is not static; it has a direction; it is measurable. Time can be divided into hierarchical units that can be manipulated mathematically—to calculate amounts of elapsed time, to make projections into the future, or simply to locate events at specific points in the stream of time. Other Maya notions about time seem bizarre. Maya time is cyclical, not linear. Points in time and the events assigned to them are not unique. As named units of time recur, so the events linked to them in the past are likely to be duplicated. This conception follows from the structure of the Maya universe. Supernatural beings gain special influence over events from their association with particular segments of time. The past is a clue to the present and both can be used to project the future. This cyclical notion naturally adds a divinatory or astrological quality to the Maya concept of time.

Mathematical and calendrical notation is the most straightforward part of the Maya symbol system. It is not difficult to work out the mechanics of the time references that fill preconquest hieroglyphic texts. An outsider can easily comprehend the basic structure of the Maya calendar and can even begin to understand the larger principles governing its operation. The subtleties of the Maya philosophy of time, the nuances that lend real meaning to the whole, are elusive. Still, a full understanding of the mechanics of Maya time is the best approach to the conceptual world that lies behind it.

The Calendar

The Maya calendar is a complex synthesis of many discrete parts.[3] A series of cycles, all proceeding concurrently, keeps track of the passage of time in a variety of ways. Each cycle performs unique functions, but they are not separable. Overlapping associations with the same deities and quarters of the universe connect the cycles. The calendar as a whole is an intricate mechanism in which each part can influence all others. Divination—calculating the omens for a given time or determining the suitability of a particular action—becomes a marvelously complex operation.

THE RITUAL ALMANAC   The most basic part of the Maya calendar is a cycle of 260 days. Primarily religious and divinatory in function, it serves to schedule ceremonial activity and is the chief guide to the auguries. It is usually called the ritual almanac. An alternate designation bestowed by modern scholars is *tzolkin*, literally "count of the days" in Yucatec Maya. The actual Maya name is not known.

The day, *kin* in Yucatec, is the elementary unit of the ritual almanac and of all calendar cycles. Each day has a designation produced by the combination of two elements: a number between 1 and 13 (Fig. 9) and one of a set of twenty names (Fig. 10). The numbers and names form repeating cycles, so that the first day is 1 Imix, the second 2 Ik, the fourteenth 1 Ix, the twenty-first 8 Imix, and so on. The permutation of the two rounds creates a cycle of 260 combinations. The designation 1 Imix does not reappear until the 261st day.

Each of the twenty names is associated with a deity, who assumes particular importance on days bearing the corresponding name. Numbers are commonly written with bars and dots, but there are alternate glyphs that feature heads of deities (Fig. 11). The thirteen numbers probably also designate patrons of particular days. These deities, along with additional associations stemming from other cycles and from the assignment of days to quarters of the world, determine the omens of each day.

Attempts to explain the ritual almanac as a reflection of some natural phenomenon—the length of the rainy season, the period of time between zenith passages of the sun, even the term of human pregnancy—are not convincing.[4] The ritual almanac repeats continuously, with no breaks; the proposed models do not. The 260-day period may simply be an artifact of the permutation of its two subcycles. Thirteen and 20 are numbers of considerable ritual and symbolic importance throughout Mesoamerica. There is no compelling reason to suppose that 260 is significant in its own right.

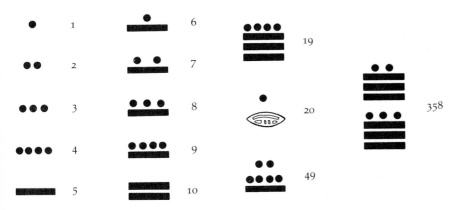

9. Maya numbers. The commonest method of writing numbers features a dot for 1 and a bar for 5. For numbers greater than 19, Maya place notation employs a stylized shell for 0. The place system is vigesimal, so that the value of the places increases by 20 (reading up), though for time calculations a special convention sets the third place equal to 360 instead of 400.

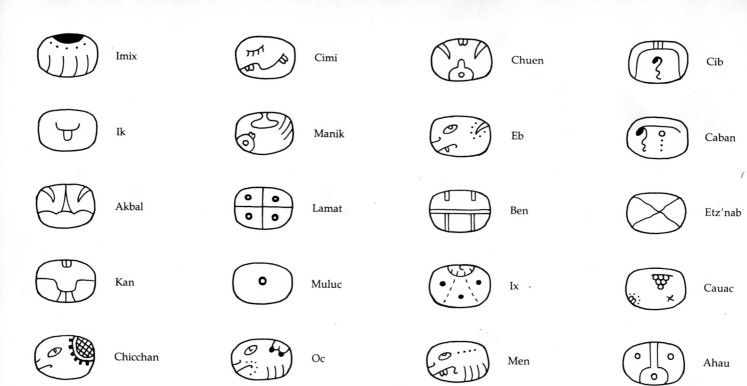

10. Name glyphs of ritual almanac days in the style used in painted books. The names are those of the Yucatec language recorded by Bishop Diego de Landa in the sixteenth century; Maya scholars conventionally use Yucatec terms to refer to calendar glyphs.

The ritual almanac is among the most basic items of the Mesoamerican cultural inventory. Every Mesoamerican people possessed a variant of it, and the correspondence among them in the meanings of the names assigned to the days is remarkably close. The ritual almanac is the oldest attested component of the Mesoamerican calendar, having come into use before 500 B.C., at least in the Valley of Oaxaca.[5] It is also the most tenacious. Though almost every other aspect of the Maya calendar has been lost, the ritual almanac survives today among several highland Maya groups in the face of heavy competition from the Christian calendar.[6]

11. Portrait variants of Maya numbers. Each number from 1 through 12 is represented by a distinctive portrait, while the glyphs for 13 through 19 are composites formed by the addition of part of the sign for 10, the fleshless jaw of a skull, to the heads for 3 through 9.

THE SOLAR YEAR   A second calendar cycle, called *haab* in Yucatec, corresponds to the solar year. Eighteen months of 20 days each, along with an additional 5-day period, make up this cycle of 365 days (Fig.

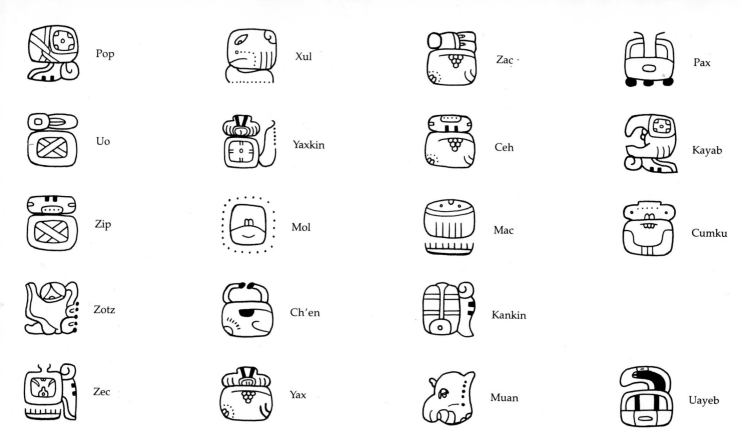

Pop	Xul	Zac	Pax
Uo	Yaxkin	Ceh	Kayab
Zip	Mol	Mac	Cumku
Zotz	Ch'en	Kankin	
Zec	Yax	Muan	Uayeb

12). Though the solar year is actually slightly longer than 365 days, the Maya calendar makes no provision for added "leap" days. Each month is named, and the days are designated by numbers. The first day of the first month is 0 Pop, better transcribed as "the seating of Pop"; the second day is 1 Pop, the third 2 Pop, and so on through the twentieth day, 19 Pop. The following day is the beginning of the second month, "the seating of Uo." An alternate way of writing "the seating of Uo" also designates it the twentieth and final day of the preceding month, Pop. Though time periods may be discrete in reckoning, in another sense they overlap. This method of timekeeping may reflect a belief that the influences of a time period and its deities extend slightly beyond the official span.

Like the days of the ritual almanac, the months have specific patron deities, who exert influence over persons and events. For purposes of divination, the solar year must be taken into account along with the ritual almanac. Though many activities scheduled with reference to the solar year are ritual, its overall function is probably more along the lines of a civil-agricultural calendar.

Like the ritual almanac, the 365-day cycle is a basic feature of Mesoamerican cultures. It may be equally ancient, though its first documented appearance, also in the Valley of Oaxaca, is slightly later. All precolumbian Mesoamerican groups used some version of the 365-day cycle, but there is not nearly the same degree of corre-

12. Name glyphs of solar-year months in the style used in painted books. The names are Yucatec. The first 18 months are of 20 days each; the final Uayeb period represents the remaining 5 days of the year.

spondence in month names as in day names of the ritual almanac. The Maya 365-day cycle, confronted with direct competition from the solar year of the Christian calendar survives today only among a few groups.

THE CALENDAR ROUND   The ritual almanac and the solar year are simultaneous cycles. Each day can be designated by reference to either system or to both. In practice, the solar-year designation never appears alone in hieroglyphic texts or in historical documents. Days are referred to by ritual almanac designations alone or, more often, by these designations in combination with solar-year positions. Just as the 13 numbers and 20 names combine to produce a cycle of 260 days, so the permutation of the 260-day ritual almanac against the 365-day solar year creates a larger cycle of 18,980 days (Fig. 13). That is, a given pair of positions—1 Ik o Pop, for example—recurs only on the 18,981st day. Thus the dual designation specifies a unique day within a period of 52 solar years (18,980 ÷ 365), called the calendar round.

Naturally, the calendar round has the same Pan-Mesoamerican distribution as its constituent cycles. The earliest known calendar-round date is also the first evidence for the solar year. For most Mesoamerican peoples, the calendar round offered sufficient precision in specifying a day's position in time. For modern interpreters, though, the repetition of the same calendar-round position every 52 years leaves considerable ambiguity in some traditional native histories. Only the Maya calendar includes a much more precise mechanism for fixing events in the stream of time.

THE LONG COUNT   Days are the elementary units of the Long Count, but its basic component is the *tun*, a period of 360 days (Fig. 14). A tun consists of 18 *uinals*, each of which contains 20 kins, or days. Twenty tuns comprise a *katun*. Twenty katuns in turn make up a *baktun*, the largest unit of the Long Count. The Long Count uses these units to record the number of days elapsed since the beginning of the current "Great Cycle."

Though there were earlier "Great Cycles," each covered a span of thousands of years. On this scale there is no ambiguity in placing historical events, though the Maya did not limit their calculations to what we would call the span of historical time. The Maya concept of time does not call for a distinction between the historical and the mythical. Large numbers in some texts stretch back through millions of years to reach vastly remote epochs. The Long Count and the calendar round are complementary systems of time reckoning. A Long Count date always specifies the position in the calendar round reached by the indicated number of elapsed days. The portrait of the patron deity of the corresponding solar-year month forms part of the sign that opens a Long Count date.

A Long Count, or Initial Series, date typically begins Classic period inscriptions (Fig. 15). Opening with the oversized Initial Series Introducing Glyph, the date goes on to specify the number of elapsed days in terms of each of the units. An Initial Series is, in effect, a 5-digit

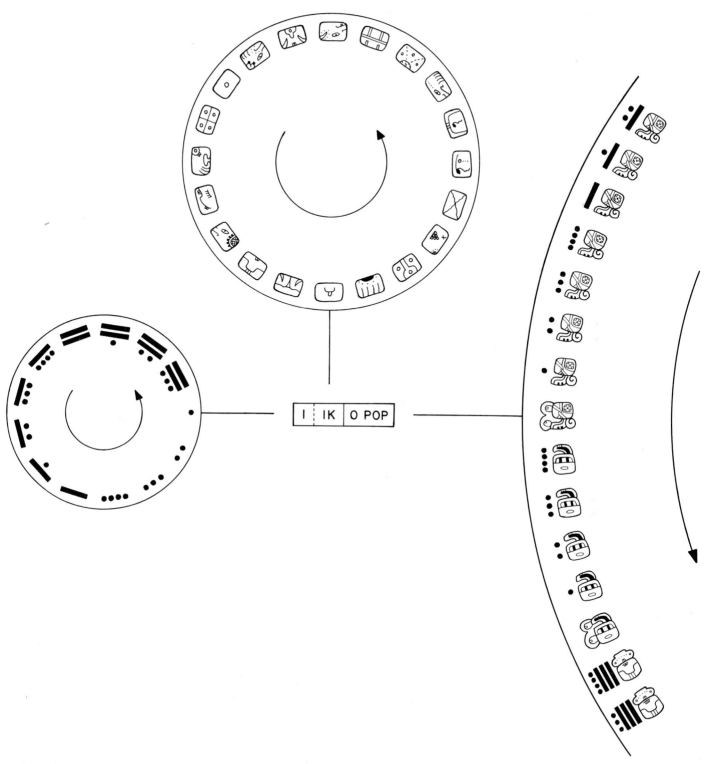

| I | IK | 0 POP |

13. The calendar round. Repeating cycles of 13 numbers (*left*) and 20 names (*top*) create the 260-day ritual almanac. The permutation of the ritual almanac against the 365-day solar year (*right*) creates the calendar round of 18,980 days, or 52 solar years.

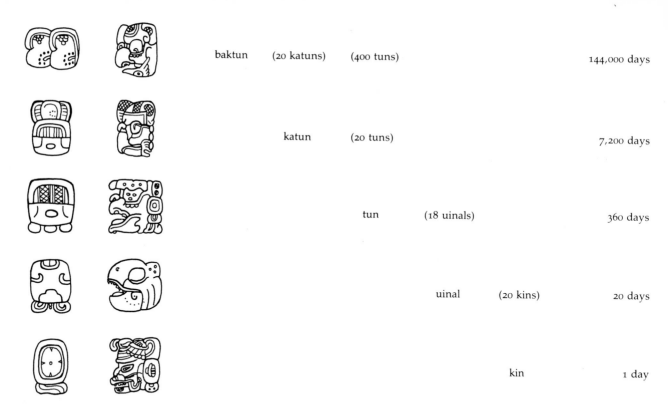

baktun	(20 katuns)	(400 tuns)	144,000 days
katun	(20 tuns)		7,200 days
tun	(18 uinals)		360 days
uinal	(20 kins)		20 days
kin			1 day

14. Symbolic and portrait variants of the glyphs for the units of the Long Count in the style used in carved inscriptions.

number in a modified vigesimal (20-base) system. The ritual almanac position follows the elapsed time tally. Then, after a series of additional glyphs, the date ends with the solar-year position. One intervening glyph names the current lord of the night, one of a series of nine underworld deities who come repeatedly into prominence in another perpetual cycle. Others record information about the moon—its age on the day in question and the length of the current lunar period.

Like the numbers, the glyphs for the units of the Long Count have both abstract and portrait forms. They are personified, not inanimate parts of a mechanical device. In a few Initial Series dates the numbers appear as full figures of deities, each bearing the sign for the corresponding unit of the Long Count on his back (Fig. 16). Here is another insight into Maya philosophy: time is not so much a force in its own right as a series of burdens moved through the universe by the gods.

Initial Series dates appear in so many hieroglyphic texts of the Classic period, particularly in the southern lowlands, that they provide a wonderfully precise chronological framework for this phase of Maya civilization. Unfortunately the Long Count went out of general use in the tenth century, creating ambiguity in the dating of later developments.

Had the Long Count survived until the Spanish conquest, correlating it with the Christian calendar would be a simple matter. It did not, and the correlation problem is complex.[7] Many lines of evidence are relevant. All are indirect and some are mutually inconsistent. No correlation can accommodate every scrap of data. The most satisfactory

THE WORLD OF THE ANCIENT MAYA

solution places the Spanish conquest of Yucatan at about 11.16.0.0.0 in the Long Count. The 11.16 correlation, sometimes called the Goodman-Martinez-Thompson correlation after its principal architects and exponents, fits best with the archaeological picture in the southern lowlands, where the majority of Long Count dates are found. It does create some apparent anomalies, particularly in the chronology of events in northern Yucatan. For this reason, until very recently some specialists preferred an alternate correlation (the Spinden or 12.9 correlation) which places all Long Count dates 260 years earlier in the Christian calendar.

The 11.16 correlation, followed here, places the beginning of the current "Great Cycle" in the year 3114 B.C. This date is more than three thousand years earlier than the earliest contemporary Long Count record. It must have been determined in later centuries by calculation backward into the time range of mythical events and creations. Texts at Palenque incorporate dates near the beginning of the current Great Cycle into a discussion of the birth of the gods.

The earliest contemporary Long Count dates were inscribed during baktun 7, in the first century B.C.[8] Though the Long Count became a

15. Initial Series: the opening of the hieroglyphic text on Lintel 21 at Yaxchilán. The first seven glyphs and the final glyph comprise the date proper, conventionally transcribed 9.0.19.2.4 2 Kan 2 Yax. The intervening glyphs name the reigning lord of the night and record information about the moon, including its age (7 days) and the length of the current lunar period (29 days). The Initial Series Introducing Glyph (ISIG) contains the head of the patron deity of the month Yax. (Adapted from I. Graham and Von Euw 1977:49.)

ISIG with head of patron deity of Yax	9 baktuns	(9 × 144,000)
0 katuns	19 tuns	+ (0 × 7,200) + (19 × 360)
2 uinals	4 kins	+ (2 × 20) + (4 × 1)
2 Kan	Lord of the Night (deity name)	= 1,302,884 days elapsed since the beginning of the current "Great Cycle" (on a day 4 Ahau 8 Cumku in the year 3114 B.C.), reaching a day 2 Kan 2 Yax in the year A.D. 454.
lunar glyph	lunar glyph (moon age: 7 days)	
lunar glyph (incorporating head of deity)	lunar glyph (length of current period: 29 days)	
2 Yax		

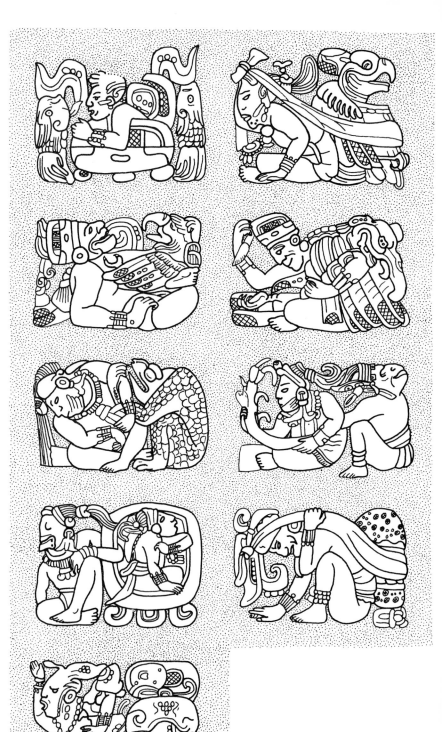

16. Initial Series: the opening of the hieroglyphic text on Stela D at Copán, transcribed 9.15.5.0.0 10 Ahau 8 Ch'en. Glyphs for numbers and Long Count units are full portrait figures (compare heads with portrait variants in Figs. 11 and 14). The Initial Series Introducing Glyph features the portrait of the moon goddess, patron of the month Ch'en. The sun god, carrying a jaguar-skin bundle, is the lord of the night, appearing between the ritual almanac day (10 Ahau) and the solar year day (8 Ch'en). (Adapted from C. Thomas 1904:Pls. 76, 77.)

hallmark of lowland Classic Maya civilization, particularly in the south, these early baktun 7 dates come from the highlands and from the Intermediate Zone. The Long Count may have been in use in the Maya lowlands in baktun 7, but the earliest dates found there so far are some three centuries later. The development of the Long Count, like that of Classic Maya civilization itself, involved areas outside of what became the Maya world, though Mayas may once have lived there. A few Long Count dates of the Classic period have been found beyond the Maya frontiers as well, though they may have been produced under Maya influence. The vast majority of Long Count dates are from Classic Maya centers. In the strictist sense, the Long Count may not be peculiarly Maya, but it was certainly of the greatest importance to the Maya of the Classic period.

THE SHORT COUNT   Though the carving of Initial Series dates came to an end with the decline of Classic Maya civilization, the Long Count itself survived in part. The native histories of northern Yucatan set down after the conquest use a system of time reckoning that is essentially a broken-down version of the Long Count. This Short Count, called the *u kahlay katunob*, "count of the katuns," measured the passage of time in terms of katuns, the 7,200-day periods of the Long Count. A katun is named after the ritual almanac position of the day on which it ends. The final day is always Ahau, with one of the thirteen numbers as coefficient. This reckoning creates a cycle of thirteen katuns, lasting approximately 256 years. The Short Count is more precise than the calendar round, but it still leaves room for ambiguity in the interpretation of native histories.

SPACE

The four cardinal directions are the foci of the flat earth.[9] A great tree supports each quarter of the heavens. Each quarter has its special color, which typifies the gods assigned to it as well as its tree. Time is likewise assigned to the directions. The days of the ritual almanac move continuously through vividly colored space in a counterclockwise circuit: east-red, north-white, west-black, south-yellow (Fig. 17). In some respects the center, or the up–down dimension, with its green ceiba tree (*yaxche*, "green tree"), constitutes a fifth direction.

The heavens are layered, with specific deities and celestial bodies occupying each of its thirteen tiers. In another sense, the dominant feature of the sky is a two-headed dragon whose body bears the symbols of the sun, the moon, Venus, and other celestial bodies (Fig. 18). Its terrestrial counterpart is a monstrous saurian floating in a great pool, its back forming the surface of the earth. The underworld occupies the maw of this beast, whose jaws emit the gods at birth and swallow up the dead. The underworld has nine levels, each with its own lord of the night. These deities rule the days (or nights) of the Long Count in succession.

17. The four quarters of the universe: a section of pages 30 and 31 of the Dresden Codex, a prehispanic painted book. Each of the four sections shows Chac, the rain god, in the world direction tree that supports one quarter of the universe. The text above each picture consists of four glyphs; the upper pair—an introductory glyph and Chac's name glyph—is repeated over each section. The lower pair specifies the color of the tree and the direction associated with each quarter: red tree, east; white tree, north; black tree, west; yellow tree, south. The Chacs themselves differ as well: the Chac associated with the west is himself black, like the tree of the west. This section of the codex is actually the beginning of a shorthand almanac. The day signs and numbers link certain days of the 260-day cycle with each section and therefore with the world quarters and their associated trees, colors, and gods. Note the "bumps" on the *te* glyph and on the tree trunks. (Adapted from Codex Dresdensis 1975:30, 31.)

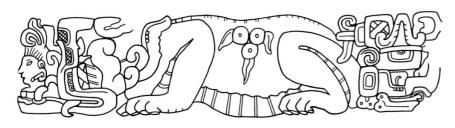

 Chac   *chac*, red   *zac*, white   *ek*, black   *kan*, yellow

 te, wood, tree   *likin*, east   *xaman*, north   *chikin*, west   *nohol*, so

18. Two-headed dragon (Altar 41, Copán). (Adapted from Spinden 1913, Fig. 52.)

GODS

19. (*Opposite page*) Maya deities: portraits and name glyphs taken from the prehispanic painted books. Note the similarity between the name glyphs and the elements of the headdresses in a, c, and g. (a) Itzamná; (b) death god; (c) sun god with *kin* ("day," "sun") sign on his forehead; (d) moon goddess; (e) Venus god with Venus glyph in his headdress; (f) maize god with an ear of maize in his headdress; (g) one of the four bacabs; (h) Ek Chuah, patron of merchants and cacao producers, carrying a traveler's pack with a tumpline. (Adapted from Codex Dresdensis 1975:7, 9, 13, 26, 47–49 and Codex Tro-Cortesianus 1967:52.)

The Maya pantheon is remarkably complex.[10] Deities may appear in a host of guises, with many names and titles. Most Maya deities are not one, but four: one aspect associated with each cardinal direction. The appropriate colors are incorporated into their regalia, their names, or both. At the same time, a dualistic conception invests each deity with diametrically opposed qualities and roles: male/female, old/young, good/evil, celestial/underworld. It is no simple matter to sort the dozens of divine aspects into clusters corresponding to discrete deities, nor is it certain that Maya theologians and artists thought of their pantheon as a collection of easily distinguishable gods with invariable attributes. It is still more difficult to match precolumbian visual representations with names and epithets recorded in postconquest documents. In place of a massive inventory of gods of uncertain function and affiliation, a few relatively well-known deities, or common combinations of attributes, can represent the richness of the Maya pantheon.

Chief among the gods is Itzamná (Fig. 19a), who is both celestial

THE WORLD OF THE ANCIENT MAYA

and terrestrial, a creator and patron of knowledge. He has supreme importance for every facet of Maya life. Equally powerful, but with a contrasting character, is the many-faceted death god (Fig. 19b), ruler of the underworld. The important celestial bodies are deities: the sun, the moon, and Venus are the most prominent. Each has numerous separately named aspects. Sometimes young but often old, the sun, Ah Kin (Fig. 19c), is hard to distinguish from Itzamná, whose aspect he may be. In the sky he is the familiar sun, who may bring warmth or drought. In the underworld he becomes the night sun, with features of the jaguar. The moon goddess (Fig. 19d) is Ah Kin's consort. She may be an aspect of Ix Chel, a lunar goddess who presides over weaving, divination, childbirth, and medicine. Ix Chel, or another older goddess, is the consort of Itzamná. Venus (Fig. 19e), sometimes the sun's brother, has a plethora of named aspects. Most are malevolent and dangerous, particularly when the planet first rises as the morning star.

Terrestrial phenomena are equally represented in the pantheon. Notable among the benevolent gods in this class are the maize god (Fig. 19f) and the multifaceted Chacs, bringers of rain, thunder, and lightning. The Chacs are four, one associated with each world quarter (Fig. 17). There are also four Atlantean bacabs (Fig. 19g), who support the heavens at the corners of the universe.

Patrons of the various occupational and social groups form yet another class of deities. The most prominent are Ek Chuah (Fig. 19h), god of merchants and cacao producers, and Kukulcán, the feathered serpent, special god of the aristocracy. Kukulcán illustrates the difficulty of using later information to reconstruct beliefs of the Classic period. The feathered serpent had many guises and many names throughout Mesoamerica.[11] In northern Yucatan, Kukulcán took on extreme importance and many new features following the Mexican incursions in the Postclassic period. At least one prominent historical personage of the epoch bore his name as a title. Traditional histories confuse this man (or these men), who became a larger-than-life culture hero, with the god. It is particularly difficult to separate the earlier Maya conception of the feathered serpent from later beliefs that grew up in the wake of this historical episode.

DIVINATION AND PROPHECY

Most of these deities, along with a host of others, have calendrical roles as patrons of one or another unit of time. Collectively, they hold sway over human affairs. As the cycles of the calendar are repeated, so the gods come again and again to prominence in endless sequences. Rational action in this universe demands an assessment of the forces in the ascendant at any given time. The omens are of crucial importance in determining the suitability and probable outcome of a proposed action, in predicting the fate of an individual according to the date of his or her birth, and as a general guide to action and preview of des-

(a)

(b)

(c)

(d)

(e)

tiny. Determining the omens, though, is no simple matter. The complexity of the calendar ensures that many deities reign concurrently, and there is no guarantee that their dispositions will be consistent.

The two patrons of the ritual almanac day (one designated by the name, one by the number) exert the preeminent influence, but they do not act alone. The patron of the solar-year month also has a role to play, as does the lord of the night, and probably the gods of the larger units of time—the tun, the katun, and the baktun. Venus and the other celestial bodies also wield influence, as deities in their own right and as the bases for additional cycles that associate gods with segments of time. The connections between time and space bring the associations of the cardinal directions into play as well.

Divination is plainly an esoteric business. For advice about optimal scheduling of important events and about the advisability of contemplated actions, lay Mayas turn to specialists. Precolumbian priests were trained in the complexities of astrological science and were conversant with the books in which the relationships among time, space, and the pantheon were recorded. Even today in isolated parts of the Maya highlands calendar priests use surviving fragments of the traditional calendar to divine the future.

The history of the universe itself is cyclical in the same way. The world has been repeatedly created in past ages, each time to be destroyed in a great cataclysm. The present creation, too, will meet a spectacular end, presumably at the completion of the current Great Cycle. The world and all of its inhabitants will perish in another universal catastrophe.

The same profoundly cyclical quality of time carries over into Maya conceptions of recent historical time. Parallel events should occur in time periods with the same designation. The past is a guide to present action, and the present sheds light on the events of the past; both reflect the future. History and prophecy are one. In the seventeenth century, missionaries reached Tayasal and demanded that the Itzá accept Christianity and Spanish rule. The Itzá declined, but invited the

(f)

(g)

(h)

THE WORLD OF THE ANCIENT MAYA

churchmen to return at a later time. Then, in a katun in which major political change was to be expected, they would submit.[12]

ICONOGRAPHY AND WRITING

Graphic representations—painted in murals, in books, or on pots; carved in stone; incised on portable objects—reflect many aspects of prehispanic Maya belief. Graphic modes range from straightforward pictorial representation to extremely conventionalized sets of abstract symbols. Maya art, like that of other Mesoamerican peoples, involves well-defined and widely understood pictorial conventions and symbols that enhance its information content. A forearm held across the breast, the fingers outstretched toward the opposite shoulder (Fig. 20), is a standard gesture of friendship or submission. Buildings, especially temples, are represented in stylized cross section. Particular items of dress and ornamentation, as well as distinctive physical features, distinguish individual deities (Figs. 17, 19). Symbols for numbers and time periods (Figs. 9, 10, 12) are more abstract. Maya calendar signs and deity emblems are comparable to the symbol systems developed by other Mesoamerican peoples. They are limited, special-purpose systems, not capable of automatic extension to other realms of meaning. In addition to these symbols, the Maya had others that directly represent not units of meaning, but the sounds of language.[13] With these

20. Portraits of captives at Palenque. The first four figures make gestures of submission with their arms across their breasts; the fifth has his arms bound behind his back.

signs they could write any message that could be spoken. With phonetic signs the Maya carried the elaboration of graphic symbols to a degree unmatched elsewhere in the Americas. Maya hieroglyphic writing is just that—a true writing system, capable of expressing an unlimited range of information.

Maya hieroglyphic writing is not a pure phonetic system. Like ancient Egyptian writing, the Maya system also makes use of other principles. The bar-and-dot numbers, the day signs, and many deity name glyphs represent either concepts—"seven," "twentieth day," "sun god"—or the particular words for them in the language recorded by the writing system. The system is mixed, with phonetic and nonphonetic signs.

In practice, distinctions among the types of symbols are blurred. A single sign may represent a word or concept in one context, a sound in another. The Cauac day sign sometimes takes the phonetic value *cu*. Glyphs, or elements of glyphs, appear with emblematic roles in pictorial representations as well as in texts. The sign for "wood" or "tree," *tee* or *chee* in Yucatec Maya, also stands for the numerical classifier *te*. The two bumps that characterize the glyph evidently double as representations of buds, for they adorn trees depicted in the painted books (Fig. 17). The sign with the basic meaning "day" (kin) appears in the glyphs for "east" (*likin*) and "west" (*chikin*), in the glyph for the seventh month (Yaxkin), and as the basic sign in the name glyph of the sun god (Ah Kin, to the Yucatec). It also appears as an element in the sun god's headdress (Figs. 12, 17, 19).

The Maya writing system did not long survive the conquest. The Spaniards quickly recognized that the Maya's writing was inseparable from the fabric of their belief and symbol systems. It became a prime target for extirpation. Whether or not the Maya came to believe that these native symbols endangered their souls, possession of ritual books and other repositories of visual symbols certainly put their bodies in deadly peril of the churchmen. A great portion of Maya thought perished with the native books, most of which the Spaniards destroyed. Diego de Landa, a sixteenth-century bishop of Yucatan, presided over the purge: "We found a large number of books in these characters and, as they contained nothing in which there were not to be seen superstition and lies of the devil, we burned them all, which they regretted to an amazing degree, and which caused them much affliction."[14] Of the thousands of native books—genealogies, biographies, collections of songs, books of science, history, prophecy, astrology, ritual—only four remain. Like the books themselves, knowledge of Maya writing went underground after the conquest, ultimately to be lost. Mayas continued to produce documents recording aspects of the native tradition, but now with Spanish characters. There are no bilingual texts in Maya hieroglyphs and Spanish. The closest thing to a Maya Rosetta Stone comes from the pen of the bibliophobic Bishop Landa. His encyclopedic account of native life in Yucatan includes a discussion of Maya writing. Though he misunderstood the system, his remarks do provide useful leads to dicipherment of the script.

The principal sources of Maya hieroglyphic texts are the surviving books, or codices, and the inscriptions on stelae, lintels, and wall panels in Maya centers. Hieroglyphs may also appear in murals, painted on pottery, and incised on small jade, bone, or shell objects. Fortunately, pictorial representations often accompany hieroglyphic texts, especially in the codices. The glyphs are most profitably analyzed along with the pictorial symbols, which are sometimes more straightforward. Information from historical documents, archaeology, and ethnography is also often useful. It is often possible to interpret a glyph or the sense of a text without being able to read it in the sense of knowing the actual words intended by the scribe. The first day of the ritual almanac (Fig. 13) is conventionally transcribed "1 Imix," using the Yucatec day name recorded by Bishop Landa. There is no certainty that an ancient Maya reader would have pronounced the glyphs *hun* ("one") *Imix*.

A principal bar to decipherment is uncertainty about the language or languages represented by the hieroglyphic texts. Perhaps, like many Chinese characters, Maya glyphs had standard meanings but different sound values for speakers of different Maya languages. It is barely possible that Maya texts actually embody several closely related but distinct writing systems. The similarity among glyphs and texts throughout the Maya world suggests otherwise, though there is sufficient variation to indicate at least regional differences in usage.

No modern Maya language is identical to the language of the texts. Maya languages, along with other facets of Maya cultures, have undergone considerable change since the sixteenth century. More than fifteen hundred years elapsed between the period of the earliest baktun 7 inscriptions and the conquest. During this period the six main branches of the Maya family split into thirty-one distinct languages (Fig. 5). The corpus of Maya texts must reflect an enormous amount of language change. Still, for purposes of discussion, Maya writing may be treated as though it records a single language widely understood, at least among the literate classes, throughout the Maya world.

Internal evidence in the structure of the glyph system indicates some of the properties of the language of the texts. The portrait variants of the numbers (Fig. 11) provide a good illustration. Unique signs represent 1 through 12, while the glyphs for 13 through 19 are formed by the addition of a fleshless lower jaw, part of the sign that stands for 10, to the heads for 3 through 9. The language of the texts must have had unique words for 11 and 12, but constructed the words for 13 through 19 as we do: three + ten, four + ten, and so on. Several lowland Maya languages match known structural aspects of the writing system. Of these languages, Yucatec is by far the best documented, especially in the form in which it was used during the early colonial period. In a few cases, Yucatec words provide highly plausible linguistic readings of surviving texts, another indication that the language of the texts is not utterly different. In any case, the use of Yucatec words as tags for glyphs probably does not lead to undue distortion.

A linguistic approach to decipherment of Maya writing is not new,

21. Bishop Landa's "alphabet," with two of his examples of Maya writing and his version of the month sign Pop. (Adapted from Kelley 1976:Fig. 60.)

22. Syllabic glyphs used in the prehispanic painted books. The glyph under discussion appears in bold line. (a) *ku-k(u)*, "quetzal"; (b) *cu-tz(u)*, "turkey"; (c) *tzu-l(u)*, "dog"; (d) *u-cu-ch(u)*, "her burden"; (e) *chu-ca-h(a)*, "captured" (note that Chac has his arms bound behind his back). (Adapted from Codex Dresdensis 1975:7, 16, 17, 37 and Codex Tro-Cortesianus 1967:91.)

nor is the question of phoneticism in the glyphs a recent issue. Charles-Etienne Brasseur de Bourbourg's rediscovery of Bishop Landa's lost *History of the Things of Yucatan* in the nineteenth century added a concern with Maya writing to the general reawakening of interest in things Maya.[15] Landa understood the Maya calendar reasonably well, and his manuscript provides a lucid account of the system, along with illustrations of the calendrical glyphs. Landa's comprehension of other aspects of Maya writing, however, was less than perfect. He describes the system as though it included a simple modified alphabet. Brasseur was the first of many to go badly astray by using Landa's alphabet to produce a translation of the codices. He "discovered" what he wished to find: an account of the lost civilization of Atlantis.

By the beginning of the twentieth century, linguistic decipherment was in low repute. The only real achievement of the phonetic approach had been the reading of Landa's *U*, common in the codices, as a third person possessive (his, her, its; *u* in Yucatec). Nonlinguistic glyph identification, by contrast, had enjoyed notable success. The greatest breakthrough, interpretation of the basic numerical and calendrical signs, produced considerable insight into the content of hieroglyphic texts. The glyphs for the directions, the colors, several animals, and a few other nouns (burden, capture, sky) were all correctly identified (Fig. 17). Several representations of gods were matched with specific "name" glyphs (Figs. 17, 19), though few could be identified with deity names known from postconquest sources.

The topic of phoneticism became almost taboo for the next half century. The emphasis shifted heavily toward nonlinguistic identification, particularly of calendrical and astronomical glyphs. Such glyphs are now quite well understood. This approach, along with the view that phoneticism was not an important principle of Maya writing, held sway until the 1950s. J. Eric S. Thompson was the foremost practitioner of the nonlinguistic approach. He identified an enormous number of glyphs, and his work constitutes a massive contribution to the understanding of Maya texts.[16] Thompson himself proposed a few linguistic readings. Most were of the rebus type, in which signs that stand for words (such as *tee*, wood, tree) were extended to represent homonyms (such as *te*, a numerical classifier). More often he marshaled evidence against the occasional exponent of phoneticism in the Maya script. His devastating arguments probably delayed recognition of the true nature of Maya writing.

Since 1950, following the lead of the Russian Yurii Knorozov, Maya epigraphers have increasingly returned to the linguistic approach and the phonetic hypothesis.[17] Knorozov suggested a syllabic rather than an alphabetic phonetic principle. That is, some Maya glyphs would stand for consonant-plus-vowel combinations. On close inspection, Landa's alphabet (Fig. 21) does look like a misunderstood syllabary. Several signs are plainly labeled as syllables, and several Spanish letters have more than one corresponding Maya character. Asking his informant for Maya equivalents of Spanish letters, Landa did not

90

realize that he was recording signs corresponding to the *names* of the letters.[18] His first *B*, a footprint, stands for the syllable *be*, "road" or "travel" in Yucatec, and the Spanish name for the letter *B*. Landa's unlikely-looking example of the Maya spelling of the word *le*, "noose," shows two signs repeated. For some, this duplication is sufficient ground for discarding him as a useful source. On closer examination, this example illustrates the nature of the misunderstanding between the bishop and his informant. Conceiving of *le* as a two-symbol word, Landa must have asked for the Maya spelling as generations of elementary schoolteachers have done, naming the letters, then the word: How do you write *L, E: le?* In Spanish he would have said *ele, e: le*. Now thoroughly confused, his informant gave a perfect rendering of the entire utterance—*e-le, e: le*. Landa misunderstood, glossing the first *le* as *L*.

When Landa's alphabet is used as a starting point, a series of plausible readings can be made. Landa's *KU*, doubled, forms the glyph group for "quetzal bird" in the codices (Figs. 21, 22a). In Yucatec, the quetzal bird is called *kuk*. Here is strong support for the syllabic hypothesis. The second vowel, which echoes the first, is suppressed since the word ends with a consonant. Landa's *CU* sign (not the same sound as glottalized *KU*) is the first sign of the pair that stands for "turkey," *cutz* in Yucatec (Figs. 21, 22b). In accordance with the syllabic hypothesis, the second sign should represent *tz-*, perhaps *tzu* to echo the initial vowel. The hypothetical *tz-* is also the first sign in the glyph group for "dog" (Fig. 22c). One Yucatec word for dog is *tzul*, confirming the *tzu* reading and suggesting hypothetical *l-*, possibly *lu*. The same glyph is one of Landa's *L* signs (Fig. 21). A divinatory almanac in one precolumbian book shows a three-sign glyph group (Fig. 23) above the column of day signs, where the mathematical structure of the almanac demands the number 11. The first sign has been destroyed; the second is the hypothetical *l-*; the third is *cu*. The Yucatec word for "eleven" is *buluc*, confirming the *lu* and *cu* readings. Another glyph group featuring *cu* accompanies representations of gods carrying things in the codices (Figs. 22d, 23). This group has long been identified as "burden," *cuch* in Yucatec. The second sign of the group should be *ch-*, possibly *chu*. It is also the first sign of the glyph group that accompanies scenes depicting captives (Figs. 22e, 23). Landa glossed the other two signs of the group as *CA* and *HA* (Fig. 21). *Chucah* would be "captured" in Yucatec. The internal confirmations in this chain of hypotheses (Fig. 23) lend considerable weight to the particular readings. They establish beyond reasonable doubt that Maya writing makes use of the phonetic principle through syllabic signs.

Maya writing is not exclusively syllabic: there are far too many glyphs for a simple syllabary. Most signs must stand for concepts or words. At the present stage of decipherment, it is difficult to distinguish the two. Nonphonetic glyphs may stand alone, or they may be combined with phonetic signs. A good example of this sort of phonetic complement appears in Landa's drawing of the glyph for the month Pop (Fig. 21). The syllabic *po* sign, doubled, gives the phonetic render-

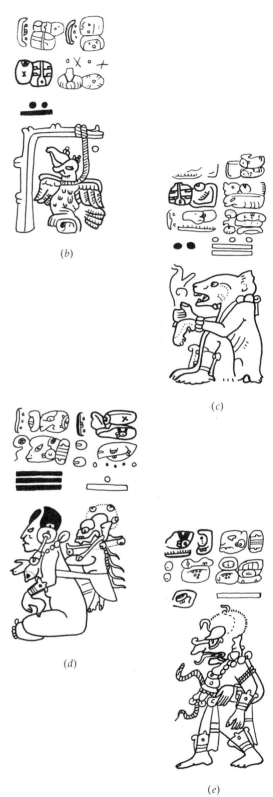

(b)

(c)

(d)

(e)

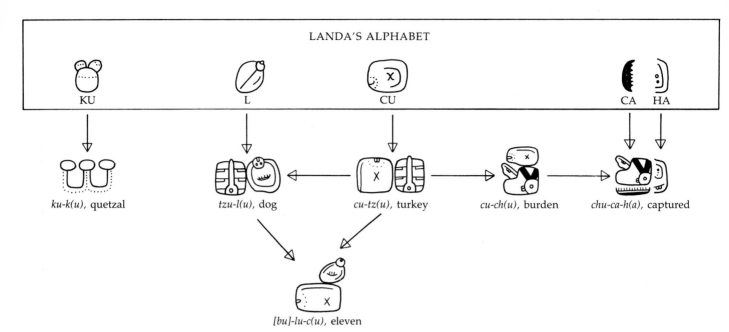

LANDA'S ALPHABET

KU   L   CU   CA   HA

ku-k(u), quetzal   tzu-l(u), dog   cu-tz(u), turkey   cu-ch(u), burden   chu-ca-h(a), captured

[bu]-lu-c(u), eleven

23. The logic of the syllabic hypothesis.

ing alongside the glyph that ordinarily stands for the month in prehispanic texts. By the mid-sixteenth century there may have been some confusion about the name of the month represented by the sign, prompting the scribe to add the complementary phonetic information. Perhaps contemporary Yucatec usage differed from that of the prehispanic texts. In any case, this sort of compound glyph group appears to be common in Maya writing. Along with uncertainty about the language of the texts, the heavy use of nonphonetic signs adds enormously to the difficulties of decipherment.

The two main sources of Maya texts, painted manuscripts and inscriptions on stone monuments, contrast sharply in date, style, and subject matter. Maya books, or codices, are made of paper manufactured from the bark of the fig tree. Each book consists of a single long strip folded like a screen. A thin coating of white plaster on both sides provides finished surfaces for pictorial representations and glyphs. The four surviving books were painted in late prehispanic times, probably in the northern lowlands, though they may incorporate earlier material. All four deal with religious and scientific matters. Most of their content is given over to divinatory almanacs setting out the auguries for various time periods (Fig. 17). Astronomy is represented by a table of the movements of Venus (Color Plate 9), an eclipse table, and a zodiac, and possibly by references to other planets. Here, too, the slant is astrological, with emphasis on the gods and omens associated with heavenly cycles. Other sections contain fairly explicit cosmological statements specifying relations among time, space, and deities. The calendrical structure of these sections is clear, gods are identifiable, some glyph groups can be read, but the nuances of meaning are elusive. Substantial sections of the codices dealing with other facets of astrology and cosmology are even more obscure.

THE WORLD OF THE ANCIENT MAYA

Most known monumental inscriptions come from lowland centers of the Classic period. They deal mainly with historical and political matters. Recognition of the subject matter of the inscriptions is the greatest achievement of the nonlinguistic approach to Maya writing, though initially it was as heretical as Knorozov's phonetic hypothesis. Until 1960, conventional wisdom held that the inscriptions, like the codices, dealt with religious matters. Most epigraphers interpreted the ubiquitous Long Count dates as esoteric astrological and mythological references.

The first departure from orthodoxy was Heinrich Berlin's identification of a class of glyphs designating specific ancient centers.[19] One prefix commonly attached to these "emblem" glyphs seems to mark a title. It is also part of the sun god's name glyph (Fig. 19c). An emblem glyph may refer to the ruler or ruling group rather than to the center as an abstract entity. In any case, emblem glyphs function as though they actually name the centers.

A similar recognition of internal pattern in the texts and associated pictorial representations at Piedras Negras led Tatiana Proskouriakoff to identify references to historical individuals and their careers.[20] She noted that the monuments formed sets. Within each set, texts emphasize the same names and titles, and dates cover a period that might reasonably represent an individual's life span. The earliest monument of each series shows the accession of a ruler to power: a young figure appears in a raised niche and the fancifully named "toothache" glyph (Fig. 24c) accompanies the contemporary date. A date some years in the past, marked by the "upended frog" glyph (Fig. 24b), refers to his birth, or perhaps to a ceremony corresponding to baptism. Later monuments in the series refer to these and other important events in the ruler's life. After his death, a new set of monuments was raised to record the career of his successor. Proskouriakoff's insights have been extended to other centers, and at some it has been possible to work out surprisingly complete dynastic sequences with references to births, accessions, marriages, offspring, alliances, conquests, deaths (Figs. 24, 25).[21] Politics was not divorced from religion, and rulers often sought

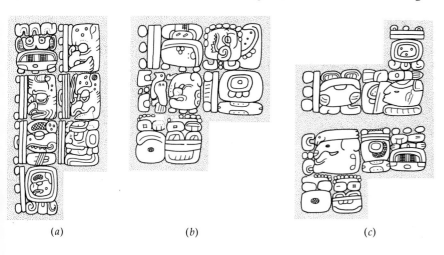

(a)　　　　　　　(b)　　　　　　　(c)

24. Record of Bird Jaguar's birth and accession to rule at Yaxchilán: excerpts from a hieroglyphic text spanning Lintels 29, 30, and 31, all from Structure 10. (a) The text opens with the date 9.13.17.12.10 8 Oc (A.D. 709); (b) 13 Yax (end of Initial Series); "upended frog" glyph, marking this as the birth date of Bird Jaguar, whose name glyphs follow, along with the dual Yaxchilán emblem glyph; (c) a distance number (omitted) leads to the calendar-round day 11 Ahau 8 Zec (corresponding to 9.16.1.10.0, A.D. 752); the "toothache" glyph marks this as the date on which Bird Jaguar came to power. Bird Jaguar's name glyphs, a notation of his age (he was in the third katun of his life), and the Yaxchilán emblem glyphs follow. (Adapted from I. Graham and Von Euw 1979:67–71.)

25. Capture scene at Yaxchilán. Lintel 8 shows Bird Jaguar, ruler of Yaxchilán (on the right), and a noble companion taking prisoners, whose name glyphs appear on their thighs. The main text opens at the upper left with the calendar-round date 7 Imix 14 Zec (corresponding to 9.16.4.1.1, A.D. 755) followed by *chucah*, "captured" (compare Fig. 22e), and Jeweled Skull, the name of Bird Jaguar's captive. It continues in the upper right with a title, Bird Jaguar's name, and the Yaxchilán emblem glyph. A loose translation would be: On the day 7 Imix 14 Zec (in the year A.D. 755) Bird Jaguar, lord of Yaxchilán, captured Jeweled Skull. The secondary text, above the captives, designates Bird Jaguar's companion captor of the second prisoner. (Adapted from I. Graham and Von Euw 1977:27 and Proskouriakoff 1963b, Fig. 1.)

to establish supernatural charters for their reigns. Several texts connect living rulers with divine ancestors and mythical events far in the past.[22]

Not every monumental inscription deals with political events. Those that do, like all political documents, incorporate biases that are difficult to understand clearly. No Maya inscription is an objective historical report. Few texts are fully decipherable. Still, the outlines of prehispanic Maya political and social history are beginning to emerge. Details of the history of particular centers provide insights into the nature of Maya society. When Proskouriakoff identified female names and titles, figures that had often been taken for pudgy priests became immediately recognizable as women.[23] The importance of women in the inscriptions profoundly altered the accepted view of the role of women in Maya aristocracies. These advances, along with new insights into Maya belief systems and new archaeological data, make it possible to begin to write ethnographies of precolumbian Maya societies.

CHAPTER FIVE

ORIGINS

EARLIEST MESOAMERICA

The first Mesoamericans were people of Asian ancestry.[1] During the glacial epochs millions of gallons of sea water were locked up in ice. Grassy tundra studded with shrubs and trees covered much of what is now northeastern Siberia, the Bering Sea, and Alaska. Great herds of game animals grazed these plains. Over the course of many millennia, small groups of people spread east and south from Asia into the Americas. This was no purposeful migration, simply a slow natural expansion into rich new areas with resources untapped by human populations.

People reached the South American Andes before 10,000 B.C.[2] Many thousands of years earlier their ancestors had lived in Mexico and Central America. In the following millennia small bands established themselves throughout Mesoamerica.

Before 7000 B.C. Paleo-Indian bands in Mesoamerica were small and very mobile. When food was plentiful, they temporarily formed larger groups, occasionally remaining together in a single camp for an entire season. More often, bands of a few related families moved about independently in a seasonal foraging cycle that required frequent changes of camp. Their lifestyle put a high premium on simple shelters and portable tools. They left few lasting traces in their wake as they moved about the landscape. Archaeological remains of Paleo-Indian bands are quite limited: a few campsites with discarded stone tools and perhaps bones of game taken in the hunt, and an occasional kill site with stone spearheads or butchering tools associated with remains of the quarry. Paleo-Indian archaeological sites, never conspicuous, are most often found in relatively open highland environments. Where there are no dense forests, archaeologists can easily locate caves and rock shelters, obvious camping places for early bands. Lowland Mesoamerica, particularly the tropical rain forests of the Gulf Coast and Yucatan Peninsula, offer limited prospects for locating early camps. Few have yet been found there. Readily interpretable tools found in early camps, stone spear or dart points, are hunting implements. The most obvious functions of other common tools relate to the processing of carcasses: choppers and knives for skinning and butchering, scrapers for preparing hides. Plant remains rarely survive in very early sites. Animal bones normally provide the only evidence that reflects subsistence directly, and even these do not survive unless soil and other conditions are favorable. When these factors are taken together, it is small wonder that Paleo-Indians, in Mesoamerica and elsewhere, are usually thought of as hunting peoples. Most known Mesoamerican Paleo-Indian bands were adapted to open, lightly forested environments, where group hunting techniques would be effective, particularly in the taking of large herd animals.

Kill sites, with remains of mammoth and other large Pleistocene mammals now extinct, are certainly the most impressive Paleo-Indian remains. Hunting was a major subsistence activity of early Mesoamerican bands, and several sites near modern Mexico City show that some occasionally succeeded in taking a great mammal. These are not sufficient grounds, however, for supposing that they were basically big-game hunters, or even for calling them hunters. Plants have been at least as important as meat in the diets of most later prehistoric and modern peoples. Most often, a great proportion of the animal food comes from activities that are better labeled collecting or foraging than organized hunting: the gathering of insects, larvae, eggs, snails, shellfish, rodents, reptiles, and amphibians; fishing; scavenging; and the opportunistic killing of small and slow game, particularly immature and injured animals. It is easy to recognize, in the abstract, that early bands were foragers, not hunters, but it is another matter to ascertain the relative importance of the variety of food-getting strategies they employed. Paleo-Indians relied on small animals and plants, but these foods have left few archaeological traces.

In the Maya area, as in the rest of Mesoamerica, Paleo-Indian remains have been found mainly in highland regions. The fullest evidence from the Maya highlands comes from temporary campsites high in the Totonicapán mountains, northwest of Guatemala City (Map 5).[3] A few stone points, knives, scrapers, engraving tools, and flakes of indeterminate use are all that remain to provide a glimpse of one aspect of the way of life of one Paleo-Indian band. These camps, along with scattered finds of isolated tools, do at least indicate some occupation of the Maya highlands in early postglacial times. The lowland regions to the

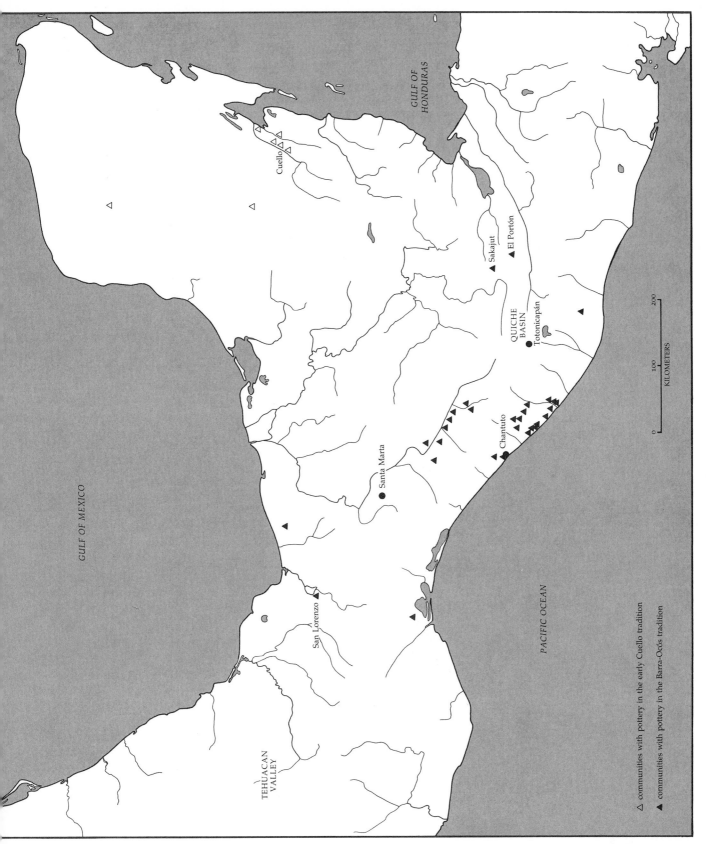

GULF OF MEXICO

GULF OF
HONDURAS

Cuello

Sakajut ▲
El Portón ▲

QUICHE
BASIN
● Totonicapán ▲

Santa Marta ●

Chantuto ▲

PACIFIC OCEAN

San Lorenzo ▲

TEHUACAN
VALLEY

0   100   200
KILOMETERS

△ communities with pottery in the early Cuello tradition

▲ communities with pottery in the Barra-Ocós tradition

Map 5. Early sites in eastern Mesoamerica

north are usually thought to have been unoccupied at this time, and for thousands of years afterward, because they do not offer environments in which open-country hunting would be suitable as a major subsistence strategy. It is true that there are few traces of very early occupations in the lowlands: stone tools found with the bones of Pleistocene animals at Loltún Cave in northern Yucatan, a few undated campsites with similar tools in the eastern lowlands, and an ancient sloth bone with butchering marks supposedly found with stone flakes in the Río Pasión drainage.[4] Given the nature of Paleo-Indian remains, though, negative evidence is hardly compelling. It would be foolish to conclude that Paleo-Indians were incapable of coping with lowland tropical-forest environments even though no sites representing such an adaptation have been found. The odds against finding Paleo-Indian remains in these environments are overwhelming.

THE TRANSITION TO VILLAGE FARMING

The Paleo-Indian way of life—small, seminomadic bands that practiced a wide variety of foraging strategies, with a unique blend of food sources and patterns of seasonal movement in each region—is quite different from that of most later Mesoamerican peoples. Spaniards found Mesoamericans, almost without exception, living in substantial permanent settlements and relying on agriculture as the mainstay of subsistence. Communities ranged in size from tiny hamlets to huge cities. Some groups practiced basic milpa farming, others had intricate agricultural systems featuring *chinampas*,[5] canal irrigation, and other intensive techniques.

Discovering how and when ancient Mesoamericans made the transition from Paleo-Indian "hunting" to "village farming" has preoccupied Mesoamericanists for decades. In this quest, the natural tendency to create simplified categories has combined with an imperfect understanding of historic and modern Mesoamerican subsistence practices to cloud the picture. Mesoamericanists have traditionally thought in terms of three ways of life: nomadic hunting, seminomadic hunting and gathering, and settled farming. They assumed at first that these are neatly separable lifestyles and that they represent stages of Mesoamerica's culture history. The history of subsistence in Mesoamerica is much more complex. In fact, "hunters" do many other kinds of foraging, depending heavily on plant foods. "Farmers" also hunt and collect wild plants.

Much of the problem stems from the supposed link between settled life and agriculture. Earlier generations of archaeologists around the world believed that the relationship was clear-cut and absolute: sedentism is a "better" way of life and one that was naturally adopted everywhere when the development of agriculture increased productivity to such an extent that people could afford to give up nomadic ways. In an alternative formulation: agriculture is an obviously superior mode of subsistence, so that once it developed, people naturally chose the sedentary life it demanded. Recent archaeological and anthropological thought calls these links into question. Clear-cut archaeological and ethnographic cases show that nonagricultural peoples in resource-rich environments have led fully sedentary lives.[6] In some parts of Mesoamerica, varied environmental zones are closely spaced. A wealth of plants, small animals, fish, shellfish, and other wild foods provided the economic foundation for several early village communities. The notion that a settled agricultural way of life is superior and desirable reflects the values of farming societies. Nonfarmers have very different value systems revolving around mobile foraging lifestyles.[7] They have often puzzled Westerners by their "irrational" refusal to convert to settled farming.

A statistical connection certainly exists between agriculture and settled life: nearly all historically known farming peoples have been sedentary. Conversely, few known foraging groups have been so. Well-documented foraging peoples have inhabited environmentally marginal areas. In the past few thousand years farming societies have occupied nearly all of the world's richest environments. In earlier epochs, when foraging groups had access to areas rich in wild food resources, sedentism without agriculture must have been more common. All well-known farming peoples represent highly developed subsistence traditions—for the most part they have had elaborate agricultural systems. Many prehistoric farming peoples were less closely tied to the land than their modern counterparts. Still, the agriculture-sedentism link persists in archaeological thought. Prehistorians are quick to interpret any permanent, settled community as agricultural unless there is obvious evidence to the contrary. There seldom is.

The relationship between settled life and agriculture is by no means a simple one. Nor was it always and everywhere the same. In some instances agriculture and a settled way of life developed very gradually in tandem. The constraints of farming schedules created long-term pressures toward more permanent communities. As growing agricultural yields reduced the comparative advantages of a seminomadic food quest, increasing sedentism made greater investments of time and energy in plant cultivation more practical. In other circumstances, foraging groups adopted settled ways long before they began to incorporate agricultural activities into their subsistence systems. Simple cause-and-effect formulas (agriculture requires sedentism; sedentism requires agriculture; sedentism permits agriculture; agriculture permits sedentism) oversimplify and distort a wide range of very complex developmental processes.[8]

Agriculture is hard to define and harder still to recognize archaeologically. Mesoamerican peoples of the conquest period produced most of their food by means of a complex series of activities: preparing and clearing plots, planting crops, protecting them from other plants and animals, and often more elaborate techniques as well. It is perfectly reasonable to call these practices agriculture. Even today, though, native Mesoamericans do not rely solely on farming for their food: they hunt; they fish; they gather insects, mollusks, and other animals; they acquire plant foods in a variety of ways besides cultivating crops and collecting wild plants. People often protect fruit trees that they regard as their own, though they have not planted them. They may plant trees but not tend them. They may clear unwanted plant competitors from berry patches or from around medicinal herbs. They may alter the distribution of any of these plants by dispersing their seeds—scattering berries near houses, for example—and the new locations may foster more intensive tending. In addition to obvious crops, most groups cultivate or otherwise encourage a wide range of other useful plants. These activities are not agricultural in the strict sense, but they can have similar functions. They provide important foods and medicines and they have similar effects on plant populations. Modern ethnographers, like Spanish colonists and conquistadores before them, have been distracted by those facets of native subsistence most like modern farming. No outsider has produced a truly comprehensive description of native Mesoamerican plant use.

Archaeological remains never include the complete roster of useful plants, and there is seldom any way to judge what proportion they do represent. At best, when preservation is exceptionally good, fragments of some of the plants used by a prehistoric group survive along with some of the tools used in processing them. Such incomplete evidence does not always show whether plants were cultivated. Agriculture may produce physical changes in the crop plants themselves, such as increased seed size, but not in every instance. Simpler kinds of cultivation can also produce similar alterations. Affected plant parts do not always survive. Even if there were some way of determining the relative contribution of strictly agricultural activities to prehistoric diets, what proportion defines an "agricultural" way of life? The data will always be incomplete, and assigning early subsistence systems to such narrow categories as "agriculture" and "hunting and gathering" will always be arbitrary and misleading.

The situation is not hopeless: taken together with other remains, prehistoric plant material often provides considerable insight into subsistence activities. In most of highland Mesoamerica, maguey (agave, the century plant) ranked high among useful plants. The simplest (and probably most common) method of consuming maguey is to chew the leaves after they have been slowly roasted, discarding the fibrous remains when the nourishment has been extracted. In late periods, at least, maguey was also the source of a fermented drink, now called *pulque*. Besides its food value, maguey was an important source of fiber from very early times. In the dry highlands of central Mexico, maguey was a dietary mainstay of early foraging bands, for it could be harvested year-round.[9] During the height of the dry season it was one of the few available plant foods. In the Tehuacán valley, where ancient plant remains have survived unusually well, maguey quids found in early campsites represent the remnants of many prehistoric meals. Fragments of the shoots of maguey plants are common as well. Even in very early times, Tehuacanos harvested maguey at the most opportune point in the plant's life cycle: after the shoot had appeared. By this time the plant had died, so that a natural fermentation process was already under way. This harvest timing minimized the threat to the survival of the maguey population, for plants at this stage had already dispersed their pollen, yet did not interfere with continuous use of maguey, since a plant may produce its shoot at any time of the year. The archaeological remains do not show whether maguey plants were tended, nor do they indicate how conscious early maguey users were of the ecological implications of their harvesting activities. In terms of its *effects*, though, this food-getting system is comparable to knowledgeable management of an important food resource. Other subsistence activities had equally subtle ramifications.

Attempting to pinpoint the beginnings of agriculture is a hopeless task. Reconstructing particular prehistoric food-getting systems in as much detail as possible is much more productive. Collectively, many scattered bits of evidence do indicate trends of change in subsistence patterns.

THE ARCHAIC PERIOD (7000–2500 B.C.)

Standard syntheses of Mesoamerican culture history recognize a very long transitional Archaic period between the earliest Paleo-Indian "big-game hunters" and the settled farming societies of the Preclassic period. The usual view holds that about 7000 B.C. Paleo-Indian hunting gave way to more generalized hunting-and-gathering subsistence strategies, in which plants played a larger dietary role. There were subtle shifts involving changes in scheduling, in specific food resources, and in the relative importance of plant and animal food, but the same basic pattern of broad-range foraging continued.

The Archaic period itself is often called a stage of "incipient agriculture" in Mesoamerica. It is said to be characterized by (1) a progressive increase in the importance of plants in the diet, with a corresponding decrease in the contribution of animal foods; (2) the appearance of the first domesticated plants and a continuous increase in their relative importance; (3) accelerating population growth; and (4) attendant changes in technology, settlement patterns, and other aspects of the overall way of life. By the end of the Archaic period incipient agriculture had supposedly given way to true settled agriculture in much of Mesoamerica. The Archaic/Preclassic boundary has been set at many dates, mostly falling between 2500 and 1000 B.C.

This standard characterization of the Archaic period is arbitrary and potentially very misleading, though it does include some elements of validity. It is convenient to retain an Archaic period, redefined in strictly chronological terms: the time between the end of the Pleistocene glacial period, about 7000 B.C., and the first appearance of pottery in the Maya area, about 2500 B.C. Eliminating the implication that the Archaic period represents a subsistence stage on the evolutionary route from hunting to farming contributes to a more realistic understanding of the ways of life followed by Mesoamerican peoples during these millennia. A less biased look at available data on early Mesoamerican subsistence makes it easier to identify trends of change in them.

The Archaic period is not well represented in the Maya area. Good archaeological evidence on the earlier part of the period has been found only in dry areas to the north and west, especially in the Tehuacán Valley, in the central Mexican highlands.[10] Data from these regions, of course, reflect specific adaptations to the environments and natural resources of semiarid highland zones. In the very different environments of lowland Mesoamerica, specific plant and animal foods, procurement activities, and scheduling practices would have been quite different. Reconstructions of early highland ways of life are not simply transferable to lowland settings, but they do provide very general insights into some of the processes involved in the evolution of Mesoamerican settlement patterns and subsistence systems.

In the most general terms, the early Archaic period was a time of slowly changing subsistence adaptations. The end of the Pleistocene epoch, with the withdrawal of massive ice sheets in northern latitudes, did bring noticeable environmental changes to Mesoamerica. Climates, previously a bit drier and cooler, shifted toward modern patterns. The combined effects of climatic changes and hunting drove some of the larger game animals, notably mammoth and horse, to extinction. Others, such as pronghorn antelopes and jackrabbits, moved into new territories. Plant distributions underwent comparable, even less dramatic adjustments. These environmental changes inevitably had an important impact on human adaptations, particularly on food procurement. New plant and animal foods came into use. Hunters now concentrated on small game almost exclusively, and plants were more prominent. There was no radical shift in subsistence pattern, for Paleo-Indians always relied heavily on plants and small animals. In large part, new adaptations involved the gradual replacement of old food sources by comparable new ones, with corresponding shifts in procurement activities and scheduling. The same fundamental pattern of broad-spectrum foraging continued.

Within each region, food-procurement systems became a bit more standardized, with more regular scheduling of food-getting activities and more systematic seasonal rounds. Conflicting harvesttimes required choices among food resources, leading to greater reliance on certain foods, especially certain plants. In this limited sense, subsistence adaptations became more specialized, with increased dependence on a narrower range of food resources, but overall subsistence strategies certainly continued to involve a wide variety of food sources.

Many food plants important in the Archaic period were ancestral to the crop plants of later Mesoamerican agricultural systems. There is little doubt that cultivation was an increasingly important facet of human exploitation of many useful plants. An increasing number of plants represented in archaeological remains show morphological changes that resulted from human activities. In this sense, the Archaic period was a time of accelerating plant domestication. This trend is a part of the historical background of later Mesoamerican agriculture, but it would be misleading to speak of a stage of incipient agriculture. Subsistence continued to be quite varied throughout the Archaic period, with hunting and collecting remaining the major food-getting activities. Analytically, it is useful to recognize a process of domestication at work in a set of changes in one aspect of subsistence. It is a convenient way of summarizing certain comparable trends in the few regions represented in the archaeological record. Human groups did not recognize domestication or cultivation as a separate component of their plant procurement, though, and they certainly did not consciously choose to increase these activities to improve their diets.

When one looks at the regions of Mesoamerica individually, in terms of actual lifeways of specific human groups, the homogeneity dissolves. In these more localized terms, there was no single process of domestication at all, just as there was no one subsistence adaptation common to all of Mesoamerica. Each region had its own specific food resources, scheduling patterns, and seasonal rounds. Different plants came under cultivation in each region, and at different times. The various domesticated plants played different roles in each local economy. There was interaction between regions, however, so that plants cultivated in one region were transferred to other areas, sometimes even beyond their normal ranges. The "process of domestication" in Archaic Mesoamerica dissolves into a mosaic of roughly comparable but quite varied local processes. The highland regions where archaeological work has uncovered unusually complete remains of the early Archaic period cannot fully represent the history of domestication in Mesoamerica. Even for Tehuacán, the best-understood area, it is impossible to list all of the plants that were cultivated in any given period. Most of the details of the domestication process are lost. In view of the fact that the Archaic period is a blank in most regions of Mesoamerica, especially the lowlands, it is likely that (1) nothing is known of most of the plants that were cultivated because they never became widespread agricultural crops; (2) many plants were domesticated independently in various areas at various times; and (3) none of the known cases of early cultivation actually represents the first or only domestication of the plants in question.

During the last thousand years of the Archaic period, plant cultivation was quite extensive in Tehuacán and at least a few other regions of western Mesoamerica. Domesticated plants included, in one region or another, maize, beans, squashes, and chile peppers, the basic crops of later Mesoamerica. These plants made important contributions to the diets of human groups, but cultivation was not the dominant subsistence activity of any Archaic society. Nowhere is there direct evidence of the kind of elaborate cultivation techniques that characterized later agricultural systems. It would be very misleading to call even the late Archaic period a time of incipient agriculture.

Though the archaeological record of other zones is much sketchier than that of Tehuacán, there is some evidence of Archaic adaptations from a few environments of the Intermediate Zone along the western fringe of Maya country. Remains of early (ca. 7000–3500 B.C.) temporary camps in the Santa Marta cave, in the central depression of Chiapas, indicate that Archaic groups in this region were small bands of seminomadic foragers who followed extensive seasonal rounds.[11] The surviving material culture is limited almost entirely to stone tools, many of which could be used in processing animal and plant foods: grinding stones, nut-cracking stones, hammers, choppers, knives, scrapers, awls, gouges, and points. Collecting and trapping small animals (ocelots, armadillos, agoutis, tepescuintlis, squirrels, monkeys, birds, land crabs, snakes, snails) was evidently more important than hunting larger ones (deer, peccaries). Unidentifiable charred plant remains in the refuse and the low density of animal bones indicate the probable importance of plant foods in the diet. Some plants may even have been cultivated, though the absence of maize pollen suggests that the later Mesoamerican staple was not among them. Traces of larger and more permanent Archaic-period camps in the Quiché Basin, to the east, suggest that the richer environments of the Maya highlands supported some larger bands with less extensive seasonal rounds. More than two hundred poorly dated campsites along the eastern margin of the Maya lowlands probably span the entire Archaic period, but they have not yet yielded detailed information on the lifestyles of early lowland bands.[12]

Slightly later occupations (3000–2000 B.C.) along the Pacific coast of Chiapas reflect the very different human adaptations in lowland Mesoamerica more fully.[13] Five shell mounds in the Chantuto estuary represent many years' accumulation of refuse left by shellfish eaters. Living in the mangrove swamps just inland from the beach, these early coastal people relied heavily on the rich animal protein resources of the estuary-lagoon system. Marsh clams provided the bulk of their meat, supplemented by fish, turtles, iguanas, snakes, amphibians, birds, and occasionally mammals (deer, racoons). Although they left no archaeological trace, shrimp probably comprised an important part of the diet. There is no direct evidence of plant use, though *metates* and *manos* (grinding stones later widely used to grind maize and other plants) suggest the processing of plant foods. Some people evidently lived year-round in the mangrove-lagoon-estuary environment, for a clay house floor indicates permanent dwellings there—either isolated homesteads or tiny hamlets. Others may have come from inland regions in the spring, when shrimp and other protein sources are especially abundant. The Chantuto people possessed a very simple material culture: mainly grinding stones and simple tools, useful for a variety of cutting, scraping, chopping, and pounding tasks. Some tools are made of obsidian, which occurs naturally only in the highlands, indicating that these coastal groups acquired raw materials from distant regions. Obsidian trade is probably only one facet of flourishing exchange systems that brought inland products to coastal environments in exchange for fish and shellfish. This trade provides only the barest hint of the ties that must have linked many varied late-Archaic societies.

Occupation of the Chantuto region continued, evidently with little change, at least until 2000 B.C.—500 years after the end of the Archaic period. Pottery had already come into use elsewhere in Mesoamerica but it would make no appearance on the Chiapas coast for several centuries. The appearance of pottery-using villages on the eastern edge of the Maya lowlands about 2500 B.C. marks the beginning of the Preclassic period, but this date signaled no change in the way of life of Archaic peoples living in coastal Chiapas.

Linguistic reconstructions suggest that Proto-Mayan, the ancestral Maya tongue, constituted a separate, undifferentiated language stock during the late Archaic period (Fig. 5).[14] Most hypotheses about the history of the Maya family of languages call for an expansion from a "homeland" region in the west-central Maya highlands. Late Archaic populations in this area probably did speak Proto-Mayan, but the language was not necessarily restricted to a small highland core zone. Reconstructions of the Proto-Mayan vocabulary include words for lowland plants and animals as well as their highland counterparts. The ancestral Maya language may have been quite widely spoken, but there is no way to plot its geographic distribution in detail, for the archaeological record of the Maya world is a blank before 2500 B.C.

Proto-Mayan began to diversify not long after the end of the Archaic period with the development of a distinct Proto-Huastecan language. Huastecan, isolated from the rest of the Maya world on the northern Gulf Coast, has no special relationship with any other Maya language. This early fission may have marked an actual separation of ancestral Huastecans from the main body of Maya speakers and the beginning of a northward and westward movement to their historic homeland.

THE PRECLASSIC PERIOD (2500 B.C.–A.D. 250)

The appearance of the earliest pottery now known in the Maya area (and Mesoamerica) about 2500 B.C. marks the beginning of the Preclassic period. By A.D. 250 Maya societies had evolved the basic institutions of a great civilization. These are logical points at which to divide the continuum of Mesoamerican culture history into manageable segments, but the Preclassic period is still an arbitrary construct. New discoveries will soon reveal earlier pottery, calling for a revision of its chronological boundaries.

Preclassic Maya societies, like those of Mesoamerica at large, were never uniform. The first known Preclassic occupation in the Maya world evidently represents a settled society with a mixed farming and foraging economy and a technology that included pottery making. Contemporary groups elsewhere in Mesoamerica had very different ways of life. In the Tehuacán valley, the earliest Preclassic societies had mixed economies in which seminomadic seasonal rounds marked continued heavy reliance on animals foods and wild plants in addition to domesticated plants.[15] Fully sedentary life developed only after 1000 B.C. At least one group along the Pacific coast of western Mesoamerica had settled in a permanent village by the beginning of the Preclassic period, but there is no evidence that its inhabitants cultivated plants.[16] Farther east, the late Archaic coastal foraging adaptation persisted, with no indication of farming or pottery, until 2000 B.C.

Most Preclassic communities do represent settled, pottery-making farming societies. It does not follow that sedentism, agriculture, and ceramic technology are linked in a fixed process of cultural development. These patterns certainly did not appear everywhere in Mesoamerica at once. By the late Preclassic period, though, a village farming way of life was established throughout the Maya world, setting the stage for the emergence of Maya civilization.

First Village Farmers (Early Preclassic Period: 2500–1400 B.C.)[17]

Cuello, on the eastern edge of the Maya lowlands, is the earliest known settled community in the Maya world.[18] A village may have existed there by 2500 B.C. Its oldest structure is a small, low, plaster-surfaced platform. Post holes in the plaster indicate that a timber-frame building stood on the round platform. This building, remodeled several times, was eventually leveled to make way for another, similar structure. A series of fire pits lined with pottery vessels stood before the new building. They were not ordinary domestic hearths, but their actual function is unknown. Later, a group of buildings neatly arranged around a small plaza superseded the single structure. The curved front of the platform along the patio's western edge has a plaster facing continuous with the court floor, indicating that the complex was built as a unit. The platform itself, of earth construction reinforced with stones along the upper edge, was surfaced with plaster and supported a rounded timber-frame building. Both floor and superstructure were renewed at least once.

The pottery made by the first Cuello villagers is the earliest found in Mesoamerica. Jars, bowls, and low-sided dishes are plain or simply decorated. The vessels are not particularly elaborate, but neither are they "experimental." As Cuello's early potters were in full control of basic ceramic technology, we may infer a long undocumented ancestry for Mesoamerican pottery making. The more ancient pottery tradition of lower Central America and northwestern South America is probably one ultimate source of the Mesoamerican craft. Early vessels from Cuello and elsewhere in Mesoamerica do resemble southern pottery in general ways. Very close links existed, at least sporadically, between certain regions of Mesoamerica and South America during the Early Preclassic period.

The early Cuello village had a mixed subsistence economy, combining cultivation and foraging. Manos and metates indicate the importance of plant processing. Maize and manioc, definitely part of the diet, were probably cultivated, and many other locally available plants, notably ramón, were potential basic foods. Hunting, trapping, fishing, and collecting provided a variety of animal foods. Brockets and other deer, turtles, and armadillos were most important, followed by rabbits, agoutis, peccaries, fish, and snails. Dogs, probably domesticated, also contributed to the diet. Cuello villagers manufactured most goods from local raw materials: points, knives, scrapers, and other sharp tools from chert; beads from marine shell; pigment from hematite. For heavy grinding tools, they imported sandstone, probably from the Maya Mountains, some 150 kilometers to the south. Jade for luxury jewelry came from even farther south—the Motagua Valley, 350 kilometers and more away. Burials provide the only indication of ritual activity. Pottery vessels, plain or decorated, simple jade and shell jewelry, and red hematite pigment were interred with the dead in graves sealed with plaster. Funerary offerings are more or less comparable in every grave (except that of a child), suggesting a basically homogeneous community with no great differences in wealth or social status.

Pottery like that of Cuello found at several other localities may indicate contemporary villages elsewhere in the Maya lowlands. Since the early Cuello pottery tradition persists with little change for more than a thousand years, though, these communities need not have been settled as early as Cuello.

Not long after 2000 B.C., another pottery tradition developed in southeastern Mesoamerica.[19] Barra pottery appeared first at a few small villages, hamlets, and campsites in the lagoon-estuary zone along the Pacific coast. Within a few centuries the Barra pottery tradition gave rise to the Ocós style, which spread to communities throughout the Intermediate Zone. The Ocós tradition extended east as far as Sakajut and El Portón, well within the Maya highlands. The basic distribution of pottery in the Ocós tradition corresponds to the probable homeland of the Proto-Zoquean language group, and these highland Ocós villages may represent an early eastern extension of its territory. Traditions of pottery manufacture can easily transcend language differences, though. Zoquean and Maya peoples may have shared the Ocós pottery tradition. There are no solid grounds for assigning Sakajut and El Portón to any specific linguistic group.

Though it represents a single basic tradition of manufacture, Ocós pottery varies considerably from region to region. Ocós communities were not uniform. Most were small villages with mixed farming and foraging economies, but local subsistence systems were quite variable. Some coastal villages depended heavily on fish, shellfish, and other marine resources in addition to plant foods.

Others eschewed these foods, perhaps because they relied more heavily on plants, wild or cultivated. Clusters of obsidian chips, apparently the teeth of decayed grating boards, suggest that such root crops as manioc may have been important contributors to the diet.[20] Inland communities developed other blends of farming and foraging. Local groups in every region did not undergo simultaneous shifts in their ways of life. In the dry highlands of central Mexico, people still followed seasonal rounds to some extent until 1000 B.C. or later. Many of their lowland contemporaries presumably did the same. One set of Barra pottery from the Chantuto region was made by coastal foragers with a shifting lifestyle much like that of the Archaic people who had camped on the same site.

Eventually some Ocós communities grew into large villages. A few even began to organize public construction projects, building temples on tall platforms. The people of San Lorenzo, in the Gulf Coast lowlands, undertook the greatest public works project.[21] They moved enormous quantities of earth to modify and enlarge the natural plateau on which the settlement was located. Pottery and figurines already embodied a few features of the later Olmec art style, and by 1500 B.C. San Lorenzo villagers had also begun to produce basalt sculpture. Their descendants completed the development of the Olmec style and the transformation of the plateau into a giant building platform.

At a few villages along the Pacific Coast, Ocós pottery includes vessels with an unusual iridescent pinkish coloring.[22] They are identical to a type common in contemporary communities in coastal Ecuador, but unknown elsewhere. Figurines, distinctive ear ornaments, and several other shared features of pottery manufacture and decoration confirm the relationship. For a short period, at least, intense interaction, probably involving direct communication by sea, linked these two regions. This South American connection reflects a late stage of a long-standing process. Barra and Ocós pottery, like that of Cuello, seems to reflect some South American norms of manufacture and decoration. Pottery making began in northwestern South America before 3000 B.C.[23] Ceramic technology probably spread gradually north and west, through lower Central America to Mesoamerica. Especially in coastal zones, the overall way of life was much the same throughout this area. In each region comparable village societies combined dependence on wild and cultivated plants with a strong orientation toward coastal and marine resources. No great differences in lifestyle presented barriers to communication. New ways of doing things probably spread freely and widely from community to community along both the Pacific and Caribbean littorals. Before the end of the Early Preclassic period sea-borne contacts linked some distant regions more directly, marking the beginning of a pattern of interaction that continued, at least intermittently, until the Spanish conquest.

The Rise of Civilization in the Intermediate Zone (Middle Preclassic Period: 1400–400 B.C.)

By the beginning of the Middle Preclassic period, precocious village societies in the Gulf Coast lowlands had developed into Mesoamerica's first truly complex culture: Olmec civilization.[24] San Lorenzo (Map 6) had grown into an important civic center, producing large public constructions and monumental stone sculpture.[25] The modification of the San Lorenzo plateau was completed. Thousands of tons of earth fill formed an artificial construction platform that may also be a giant effigy. Atop the plateau were many earth and clay mounds arranged around plazas. Larger structures were platforms for perishable public buildings, probably temples. Smaller mounds supported houses. Monumental basalt sculptures depicting dynastic as well as ritual and mythical themes were arrayed among the buildings. Twenty or more artificial ponds, each lined with bentonite (consolidated volcanic ash) and connected to an elaborate stone drainage system, dot the plateau.

To judge by the two hundred or so residential platforms, fewer than

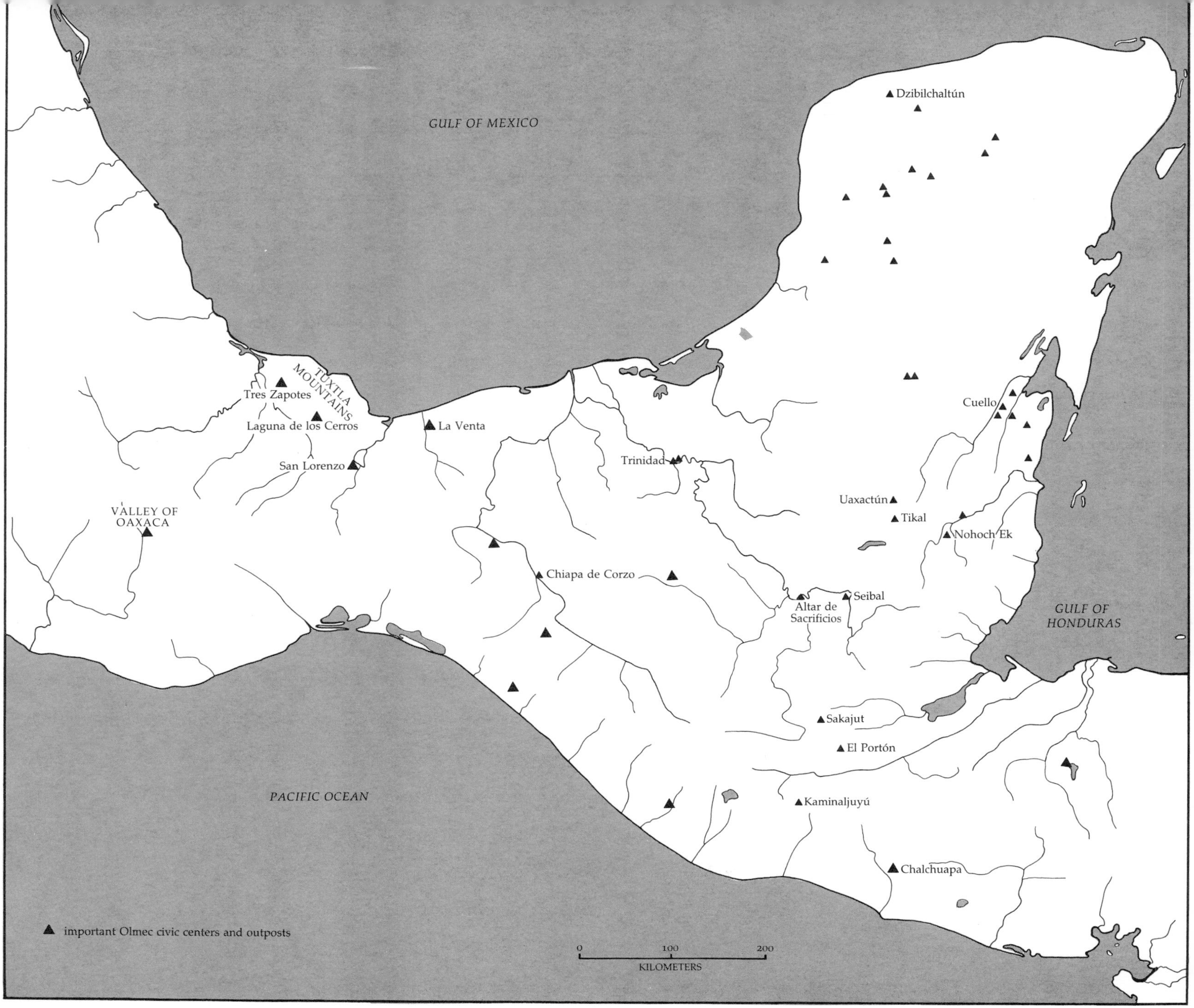

GULF OF MEXICO

GULF OF
HONDURAS

PACIFIC OCEAN

▲ Dzibilchaltún

Cuello ▲

▲ Nohoch'Ek

▲ Uaxactún

▲ Tikal

Seibal
▲ Altar de
Sacrificios

▲ Sakajut

▲ El Portón

▲ Kaminaljuyú

▲ Chalchuapa

Trinidad ▲

Chiapa de Corzo ▲

La Venta ▲

TUXTLA
MOUNTAINS

Tres Zapotes ▲

Laguna de los Cerros ▲

San Lorenzo ▲

VALLEY OF
OAXACA ▲

0   100   200

KILOMETERS

▲ important Olmec civic centers and outposts

Map 6. Middle Preclassic communities

a thousand souls lived on the plateau itself. A few hundred more probably lived in nearby residential communities, but San Lorenzo was never a great population center. It was nonetheless an important place, a center of religious, economic, and political power. Though San Lorenzo may not have been the capital of a single state that embraced the entire Olmec world, the people who lived there were the leaders of Olmec society. They exercised considerable power over the human and natural resources of a huge sustaining area. La Venta, Laguna de los Cerros, and other contemporary Olmec centers in the Gulf Coast heartland could not match San Lorenzo in wealth, religious importance, or political power. San Lorenzo's public works projects testify to the power and managerial expertise of its leaders. They planned and directed massive construction projects that involved the quarrying and placement of millions of cubic meters of earth fill. They also organized the importation of vast quantities of raw materials. The basalt used for the drainage system and for monumental sculpture—many thousands of tons of it—was brought from the Tuxtla Mountains, some 75 kilometers to the northwest. From distant areas, far beyond the Gulf Coast, came obsidian for tools and iron ores, mica, shell, and other materials for jewelry and ritual paraphernalia, as well as finished products. A variety of perishable goods, not preserved in the archaeological record, must have been imported as well.

The details of the mechanisms that transmitted these products to the Gulf Coast are unknown. In some instances, Olmec merchants doubtless traded with foreign groups, but there are no indications of what products may have been exported from the Gulf Coast. In a few areas, where especially valuable commodities were available, Olmecs established outposts in order to secure access to them.[26] Olmec enclaves in the Valley of Oaxaca procured iron ores and products manufactured from them for Gulf Coast centers. Olmec culture had a strong impact on peoples beyond the Gulf Coast. Olmec-style pottery and figurines appeared throughout the Intermediate Zone and in many parts of Central Mexico, most often in the houses and burials of wealthy, high-status people. The distribution of the Olmec style defines a sphere of economic and social interaction embracing much of Mesoamerica. Its most obvious economic function was to funnel valuable commodities to the Olmec centers on the Gulf Coast.

About 1000 B.C. San Lorenzo lost its preeminent position in the Olmec world, and La Venta emerged as its greatest center.[27] La Venta was another vital civic center without a huge resident population. It, too, boasted a wealth of monumental basalt sculpture (Figs. 26, 27), and its public architecture and massive construction projects surpassed those of San Lorenzo in size, in the formality of their layout, and in their organizational requirements. La Venta imported basalt from the Tuxtla Mountains on a truly massive scale. A new Olmec style of pottery and figurines defined the Olmec world dominated by La Venta.[28] Olmec exploitation of valuable raw materials outside the Gulf Coast heartland intensified. Highland Mexican products included special pottery clays, obsidian, iron ores, mica, and other valuable minerals. Jade, the most precious substance of all, came from the Balsas Valley of

26. Colossal basalt head from La Venta

27. Basalt "altar" from La Venta

Guerrero. Southern and eastern areas provided serpentine, obsidian, and possibly another variety of jade. The Pacific slope and piedmont sector of the Intermediate Zone was a major cacao-producing region in later prehispanic times. Chocolate, later a medium of exchange as well as the source of an aristocratic beverage, may already have become an important luxury item. Monumental relief carvings and cave paintings in the purest Olmec style, along with public architecture typical of the Gulf Coast, marked Olmec enclaves in other areas where particularly valuable commodities were to be had. La Venta continued to control a huge sphere until its collapse, about 500 B.C. In the following centuries, with no integrating force providing for continued interaction among its regions, the Olmec world dissolved.

Aside from the lower Usumacinta region, bordering on the Olmec heartland, few sections of the Maya area were part of the Olmec world.[29] There is an isolated Olmec relief carving in inland Chiapas, but Maya speech may not have extended so far west in the Middle Preclassic period. Olmec-style pottery and figurines occur in the highlands of Guatemala, though they are not common. They probably reflect Olmec interest in local obsidian sources. The Sula plain and the Lake Yojoa region, along the eastern fringe of the Maya world, had a definite Olmec presence. Here, too, the Olmecs probably sought cacao, a major product of the region in later periods. Local pottery-making traditions elsewhere in Maya country show faint echoes of Olmec styles, and some communities imported a few Olmec pots and jade objects. Most of the peoples of the Maya world evidently were not directly involved in the Olmec economic sphere.

In another sense, Olmec civilization did have an enormous impact on Maya cultural development, for the foundations of Classic Maya civilization rest on an Olmec heritage.[30] Maya culture reached its developmental peak in lowland tropical forests with an ecology similar to that of the Olmec heartland. Basic organizational patterns of Maya civilization had been established centuries earlier by the Olmec. Classic Maya society revolved around impressive civic centers that were foci of public activity, of social prestige, of religious authority, and of economic and political power. Here were temples, palaces, ball courts, and monumental art. Temples are the largest structures. They are also funerary monuments to important political figures whose deeds are recorded and celebrated in associated art and inscriptions. Few Maya centers had densely populated residential zones. Most people lived dispersed in the surrounding territory. Procurement of jade and other luxury goods, as well as utilitarian items, was an important function of Classic Maya political and economic organization. Enclaves of Mayas living far beyond their home territories reflect a basic pattern of Maya territoriality, representing a strategy of ecological diversification. Such enclaves expanded access to valuable raw materials and to varied environments for crop cultivation. They also facilitated communication and interaction. All of these patterns are found, at least in embryonic form, in Olmec civilization.

Classic Maya civilization's Olmec ancestry is traceable through the Izapan culture, which spread throughout the Intermediate Zone and much of the Maya highlands in the Late Preclassic period. Olmec art foreshadows Izapan art in subject matter, in style, and even in specific iconographic elements and glyphlike symbols.[31] The continuities from Izapan art to Classic Maya art are even more striking. Olmec, Izapan, and Maya stelae all portray historical themes. The hieroglyphic inscriptions that accompany Izapan art resemble later Maya writing in the overall structure and layout of texts, in the forms of certain glyphs, and even in the use of the complex and distinctive Long Count system of recording dates. In a very real sense, Maya symbol systems began with Izapan culture, which in turn has an obvious Olmec ancestry. Olmec-Maya continuities extend to religious institutions and symbols as well: the ball game, the supreme importance of jade, the use of red pigments with jade, ceremonial bloodletting, and many items of ritual paraphernalia.

The importance of these continuities has led some Mesoamericanists to the conclusion that Olmec civilization was really the first flowering of Maya civilization; that is, that the creators of Olmec civilization were ethnically and linguistically Maya.[32] If the early people of the Olmec heartland spoke a Maya language, the Gulf Coast would have been part of a continuous zone of Maya speech extending from the Huastec region to what is now the Maya lowlands. The corollary—that by the Classic period Maya speakers had moved entirely out of the heartland and subsequently lived almost exclusively outside what had been the Olmec world—is difficult to accept.

A more satisfactory hypothesis is that the early population of the Gulf Coast and the Isthmus of Tehuantepec, the creators of Olmec civilization, spoke Proto-Zoquean, the language ancestral to that of the Mixe and Zoque, who occupied much of the Intermediate Zone in late times.[33] The reconstructed vocabulary of Proto-Zoquean for the period around 1500 B.C. includes terms for many distinctively Mesoamerican items that were part of the Olmec cultural inventory: important plants, including basic crops; important domestic and wild animals; food-preparation terms; ritual and calendar terms; words relating to trade and commerce. Proto-Zoquean loan words are common in other Mesoamerican languages, some quite distant from the historic area of Mixe and Zoque speech. Proto-Zoquean must have been spoken by a group with wide-ranging connections. Probable Maya borrowings from Proto-Zoquean include words for cacao, gourd, tomato, papaya, tortilla, tamal, corn dough, incense, twenty years, dog, ax, sacrifice(?), turkey, lizard, bee, child, elder brother. The cultural importance of these items implies that Proto-Zoquean speakers were once extremely prestigious and influential. The people of the core of the Olmec world, in the Gulf Coast heartland and adjacent sectors of the Intermediate Zone, were probably Proto-Zoquean speakers, as were many Olmecs residing in enclaves outside this zone. Olmec Mesamerica was not linguistically uniform, though. In highland Mexico, eastern sectors of the Intermediate Zone, and parts of the Maya highlands, the Olmec world consisted of scattered enclaves of ethnic Olmecs living among and interacting with peoples who spoke different languages and who bore different cultural traditions. The wide adoption of Olmec pottery and figurine styles and of Proto-Zoquean words reflects the profound impact Olmec culture had on these local groups. In the lowlands, along the eastern edge of the Olmec heartland, in the Maya highlands, and in the piedmont zone to the south, Proto-Zoquean speakers mingled with their Maya-speaking eastern neighbors. Many Maya communities in these regions adopted significant facets of Olmec culture. Some linguists have postulated a close relationship between the two language families. If this hypothesis is correct, linguistic differences between speakers of Zoquean and Maya would not have been as extreme in the Middle Preclassic period as they were in later times. In any case, Olmec civilization was a multiethnic, polyglot phenomenon in its own time and in its heritage. Interaction of Maya and Zoquean peoples continued as a historical process along a linguistic frontier that extended from the Gulf Coast through the highlands and piedmont to the Pacific Coast.[34] In the Late Preclassic period Olmec-influenced Maya groups contributed to the rise of Izapan civilization, another multiethnic, polyglot culture. Izapan civilization in turn made a major contribution to the development of Maya civilization.

CHAPTER SIX

FOUNDATIONS OF MAYA CIVILIZATION

THE EVOLUTION OF VILLAGE SOCIETIES
(MIDDLE PRECLASSIC PERIOD: 1400–400 B.C.)

The Middle Preclassic period was an era of slow growth in the Maya world. At first, typical communities were small but prosperous villages with mixed subsistence economies. Simple farming and gardening, combined with exploitation of tree crops and other wild plants, provided a variety of plant foods. Hunting and trapping contributed animal protein. Specific crop plants and wild food sources varied from region to region, as did supplementary food-getting activities. Along the rivers and coasts, fishing and shellfish collecting were extremely important. Trade linked communities into local and regional economic networks. Many villages were able to import such commodities as obsidian, hard stone for grinding tools, and salt. Larger and wealthier communities could boast small-scale public works projects and a few small temples.

As communities grew, differences in wealth and social status within them became greater. Distinct local aristocratic groups began to emerge. By the end of the Middle Preclassic period, a few villages had grown to the size of small towns. The largest had perhaps a few thousand residents, definite elite groups, and several public structures. They probably dominated their local areas economically, if not politically, and they might be classed as minor regional civic centers. No Maya community, however, matched the great Olmec centers. None undertook such massive public construction or controlled such extensive procurement networks. Maya societies were simpler politically and economically, if not socially. Maya elite groups were less distinct from ordinary folk. They had not concentrated power and wealth in their own hands to the same degree as had Olmec leaders. Temples testify to the public aspects of Maya religion, and it was probably inseparable from politics, but the Maya produced nothing comparable to Olmec dynastic monumental art. The Maya world was largely outside the Olmec orbit. Some communities along the margins of the Maya area did participate in the Olmec economic sphere. Some, especially in highland Guatemala and northern Honduras, were probably Olmec enclaves in regions of Maya speech. Others, particularly in the west, represent the fringes of the main Zoquean distribution, for in this early period Maya-speaking peoples had not yet expanded to their eventual western limits. Zoquean and Maya peoples doubtless mingled in a variety of patterns along their common frontier.

Except in the eastern lowlands, Middle Preclassic communities are the earliest known in the Maya world. They were not necessarily initial, pioneering settlements in their respective regions, for increases in the number and size of villages brought a corresponding improvement in the archaeological record. Early Middle Preclassic pottery-making traditions in several regions share very general features of form and decoration.[1] Red slips and low-sided dishes or bowls were widely popular, but each community and region manufactured pottery according to its own distinctive norms. Maya communities did not wholeheartedly adopt the widely distributed pottery styles of the Olmec world, and the internal spheres of communication that later led to widely shared ideas about pottery making evidently had not yet emerged.

The people of Cuello, in the eastern lowlands, continued the long-established local cultural tradition.[2] They remodeled and enlarged their structures, but there is no indication of change in basic building types, architectural styles, or patterns of community layout. The old plaza complex, slightly enlarged and modified, remained in place. A new oblong plaster-coated platform along the west side of the complex had rounded ends and a straight front with a step leading down into the patio. The new thatched, timber-frame building atop the platform was probably also a bit larger than its predecessor, but its form and function are unknown. There are slight indications that later versions of this patio complex had public, ritual functions.

The community economy of mixed farming and foraging remained essentially the same. Maize and manioc were still probably the main crops, supplemented by hunting, fishing, and plant collecting. The people of Cuello still used mainly local raw materials—chert, marine shells, mineral pigments—but they continued to procure sandstone for grinding tools in the Maya Mountains, to the south. They also began to import obsidian from the Maya highlands, probably via the Motagua Valley, which was the source of jade. Burials still provide the only indication of ritual activity. Funerary offerings, including decorated pottery vessels, powdered hematite pigment, and shell beads, do not yet suggest sharp social distinctions.

Pottery like that of Cuello indicates contemporary villages at several nearby locations in the eastern lowlands, but nothing is known of the nature of these communities. To the south, in the Belize Valley, the earliest known occupations are contemporary with the later Cuello community.[3] They reflect a generally comparable lifestyle, but with its own regional flavor. Their pottery represents a distinctive local tradition. Many vessels share very general features with contemporary pottery to the north, but there is no indication of particularly intense contacts. Groups of a few small wattle-and-daub[4] dwellings on low platforms, roughly 50 meters apart, typically occupied riverbanks. These early houses may have had plaster floors laid on gravel foundations like their later counterparts, but none is sufficiently well preserved to provide details of construction or floor plan. Here, too, the economy was presumably based on mixed cultivation and foraging, but no direct evidence of farming has been found. Local raw materials—chert for cutting tools, marine shell for ornaments—were most important, but hard stone for grinding tools probably came from the Maya Mountains.

To the west, in the Pasión Valley, the earliest known communities are generally comparable to their eastern contemporaries, but they represent yet another distinct local cultural tradition. Altar de Sacrificios, at the confluence of the Pasión and Salinas rivers, was the site of a small village by about 1000 B.C.[5] At least four buildings clustered around a small plaza, with other houses scattered nearby. These dwellings, small timber-frame houses with wattle-and-daub walls, packed-earth floors, and thatched roofs, were built directly on the land surface. The economy was based on mixed farming and foraging and depended heavily on river resources. The surviving remains of jack beans, deer, and freshwater mussels represent only a small part of the diet. Most tools were fashioned from local stone, but igneous stone and obsidian were imported from the highlands. There is no indication that the community was other than homogeneous; the single known burial contained no funerary offerings at all. If we leave aside enigmatic objects, too often assumed to be ritual paraphernalia, and a little red sandstone table that may have served as an altar, small, hand-modeled pottery figurines represent the only possible evidence of ritual activity. The putative role of these female effigies in household fertility cults is far from certain. Early pottery from Altar de Sacrificios reflects a third regional manufacturing tradition that is also typical of Seibal, 50 kilometers upstream on the Río Pasión.[6] Seibal was presumably a comparable village, though the actual archaeological evidence is limited to small concentrations of pottery and household refuse in two areas of high ground. The people of Seibal also had access to highland sources of obsidian and igneous stone. Altar de Sacrificios and Seibal were more involved in the Olmec sphere than most other villages in the Maya lowlands. Though neither community adopted the Olmec style fully, their pottery reflects several Olmec norms of decoration. At Seibal, a jade bloodletter and a cache of jade celts laid out in a cross reflect Olmec ritual patterns. The Río Usumacinta would be the natural route of communication with the Olmec world. Contemporary villagers at Trinidad, on the lower Usumacinta, manufactured pottery resembling that of the early Pasión tradition as well as the Olmec-style pottery more typical of the region.[7]

Contemporary pottery from Sakajut and El Portón, near the headwaters of the Río Salinas, in the northern highlands, also resembles that of the Pasión tradition.[8] Both villages, situated on natural routes connecting the highlands and southern lowlands, may have been part of the exchange system that provided early Pasión communities with highland raw materials. This connection may also account for Olmec traits there. Pottery and public architecture (probably temple platforms) indicate that Sakajut and El Portón were more involved with the Olmec sphere than with the rest of the Maya world. Whether they were Zoquean outposts, Maya communities, or some hybrid of the two, Sakajut and El Portón were part of the Olmec world.

Contemporary communities in the central highlands were more like lowland Maya settlements.[9] Kaminaljuyú and its immediate neighbors were small villages with mixed farming and foraging economies. They show no signs of centralized economic and political organization or of sharp distinctions between socioeconomic groups. Their pottery represents another essentially independent local tradition, with few obvious connections with the Olmec style.

To the east, Chalchuapa was a major civic center with Olmec relief carving, monumental public architecture, and Olmec-style pottery.[10] Other types of pottery indicate connections with Kaminaljuyú, with the northern highland communities, and, less strongly, with Pasión and eastern lowland communities. These very general resemblances mark the beginning of a process of intensifying communication that eventually linked Chalchuapa closely to the central Maya highlands and to the Maya lowlands beyond.

The earliest known community at Tikal was evidently another small village.[11] Scanty data reveal no details of community organization. Like their contemporaries to the east and west, early Tikal villagers imported obsidian and hard stone from the highlands. Their pottery represents a fourth local tradition of manufacture. It shares only the most general features with pottery from other regions. Nearby Uaxactún was probably a comparable small village in this early period, but it is represented only by small pottery collections similar to those of Tikal.

There is no good evidence of settlements in central and northern Yucatan in this early period, though the region was not necessarily unpopulated. Pottery found at Becán and Maní resembles that of early villages in the eastern lowlands, suggesting that the first northern communities remain to be found.[12]

Except on the margins, most early communities in the Maya world were small villages. Societies were homogeneous, with no signs of sharp differences in wealth or social status. These communities did not have centralized political leadership and they did not undertake large public construction projects. They were essentially self-sufficient, relying on a combination of farming and foraging for subsistence and on local raw materials for most tools. Some villages did import such raw materials as obsidian, hard stones, and jade from distant regions, but there were no giant spheres of intensive economic interaction like those of the Olmec world.

After 800 B.C. the regionalism of the Maya area began to break down. Scattered regions formed larger and larger spheres of interaction. A Maya world emerged as a recognizable entity. This process is precisely the reverse of the one that was under way at the same time in the Intermediate Zone. The unity of the Olmec world had begun to dissolve even before the final collapse of La Venta. Perhaps increased communication and exchange within the Maya world disrupted Olmec procurement patterns, contributing to the breakup of Olmec economic hegemony and to the demise of La Venta's dominance. Such processes seldom have simple, one-way cause-and-effect relations, though. The decline of a monolithic Olmec economic sphere might easily have contributed to intensified trade with the Maya area by removing such obstacles as monopoly control of certain commodities and markets.

The emergence of a recognizable Maya world is the first stage of a remarkable process of coordinate evolution. The regions of the Maya world never lost their own distinctive cultural traditions, but they were never again entirely independent. Ideas and institutions developed in one region could spread to many distant communities. This interaction was the key process in the emergence of Maya civilization.

The clearest sign of increasing communication throughout the Maya world is a definite trend toward greater homogeneity in pottery production in widely scattered communities. The first widespread Maya pottery style, called Mamom, does not reflect cultural uniformity.[13] Many kinds of interaction linked many diverse communities. Pottery making did not suddenly become uniform throughout the Maya world. The eastern lowland version of Mamom, for example, developed from local antecedents long before other communities began to produce similar vessels.

Even in pottery production, local differences were not entirely submerged. Regional diversity is still apparent beneath the new veneer of features common to the Mamom style. This pattern of regional variations on common themes continued to characterize the Maya world throughout its preconquest history. In the eastern lowlands, the Pasión zone, the Tikal zone, and the highlands, pottery embodies elements of earlier local traditions as well as features of the common Mamom style. The Mamom style does not reflect external influence. It developed in several regions from a series of localized but generally similar ancestors. These regional traditions came to share certain features and to follow convergent developmental paths as the result of increasing communication. Greater differences distinguish the northern and southern lowlands, though communities in both areas produced pottery in the Mamom style. Highland pottery reflects a somewhat different tradition. Ties between highlands and lowlands were weaker than those linking lowland regions. Communication extended, at least indirectly, to the limits of the Maya world, though, for pottery made at Chalchuapa, in the eastern highlands, and at Chiapa de Corzo, in the Intermediate Zone, echoes the Mamom style.

The basic way of life of the peoples of the Maya world in the late Middle Preclassic period was much like that of their ancestors. The typical community was still a small, homogeneous, self-sufficient village of farmers and foragers. Communities grew and multiplied as the population of the Maya world increased. Connections between regions, particularly trade, intensified, though not uniformly.[14] Dzibilchaltún, in the north, relied on local raw materials, importing no obsidian, but most communities did participate in expanded economic spheres. Extensive exchange networks distributed raw materials more widely than ever. Cuello and other villages in the east had certainly begun to import obsidian by this time. Altar de Sacrificios and Seibal continued to acquire obsidian and igneous stone from the highlands. Mamom pottery became more uniform throughout the Maya world.

By the end of the Middle Preclassic period, a few of the largest and most prosperous communities had begun to show signs of emerging aristocratic groups and centralized political leadership. At Dzibilchaltún, in northern Yucatan, some large platforms probably represent public structures, and one building appears to be a community sweat bath.[15] Nohoch Ek, in the eastern lowlands, boasted a dressed-stone platform faced with stucco.[16] The largest public building complex of the time was a formal plaza group at Altar de Sacrificios.[17] It was probably a ceremonial precinct. The platforms flanking the plaza, one of which was 5 meters tall, were faced with shell and plaster and had stone masonry stairs. The timber-frame buildings atop the platforms have not survived, but their size and special construction features indicate that they were not ordinary dwellings. At Kaminaljuyú construction of large earth platforms flanking plazas probably began late in the Middle Preclassic period.[18] These were not ordinary dwellings, but public, probably ceremonial, structures. Altar de Sacrificios, Kaminaljuyú, and a few other settlements had achieved the status of minor civic centers. They probably dominated villages in their surrounding regions, but patterns of social, economic, and political organization did not change radically. These changes would come in the following period, as processes of population increase, community growth, and intensified interaction among regions throughout the Maya area continued. These trends, combined with the emergence of sharp social and economic differences within Maya societies, produced a new kind of social order.

THE RISE OF ARISTOCRACIES AND REGIONAL CIVIC CENTERS (LATE PRECLASSIC PERIOD: 400 B.C.–A.D. 250)[19]

The first sign of intensified interaction among the regions of the Maya area is the appearance of a new shared style of pottery manufacture.[20] This Chicanel pottery tradition did not appear suddenly throughout the Maya world. It grew out of variants of the Mamom tradition in the several regions, with slightly different timing in each instance, much as

Mamom had developed from antecedent regional traditions. Within a century or two, though, every community in the Maya lowlands (Map 7) manufactured pottery in the same basic Chicanel style.

Regional differences continued, reflecting the survival of distinctive local traditions. Northern and southern lowland communities remained distinct, but they shared many more patterns than before. Lowland peoples continued to import highland raw materials, and highland pottery reflects some features of the Chicanel style. Chalchuapa was now squarely within the highland Maya world, and many highland communities developed closer ties with those of the upper piedmont zone. To the west, the people of Chiapa de Corzo manufactured luxury pottery in the Chicanel style, and their public buildings also suggest ties with the Maya lowlands. Villages in the far western Maya highlands shared a basic tradition of pottery making with Chiapa de Corzo, but they adopted fewer distinctively Chicanel features. Maya-speaking peoples may have occupied both regions but there is no reason that Zoquean groups could not have shared elements of architectural style and norms of pottery production with their Maya neighbors.

Part of the explanation for the intensified interaction among regions may lie in accelerating population growth. Communities grew and multiplied throughout the Maya world. Expanded exchange is a related development: more communities were importing more goods.[21] Obsidian from highland Guatemala was widely distributed. Jade traveled as far north as Dzibilchaltún. Tikal and its neighbors in interior sectors of the southern lowlands began to import shell and stingray spines for jewelry and ritual paraphernalia.

This upsurge in luxury imports reflects the beginning of another continuing process within Maya societies: the widening of social and economic gaps between emerging aristocratic groups and ordinary farmers. Massive public architecture—temples certainly, and possibly palaces and administrative buildings—reflects the new specialist roles of these leaders. Religion, in the process of transformation, moved more and more into the realm of public activity and began to require specialized priest-managers. Public buildings imply political leaders with the authority and power to command the human and economic resources of large areas. Richly stocked masonry tombs in civic building complexes contrast sharply with plain burials beneath the floors of ordinary houses, illustrating the social and economic differences that had developed within Maya societies.

While these generalizations hold for the Maya area as a whole, developments were not uniform. Specific patterns of growth and development differ markedly from region to region.

The Izapan World

The Maya highlands, though linked to the lowlands, were also an integral part of the Izapan world.[22] The heart of this cultural sphere lay in the southern coast and piedmont zone. Izapa-style relief carving

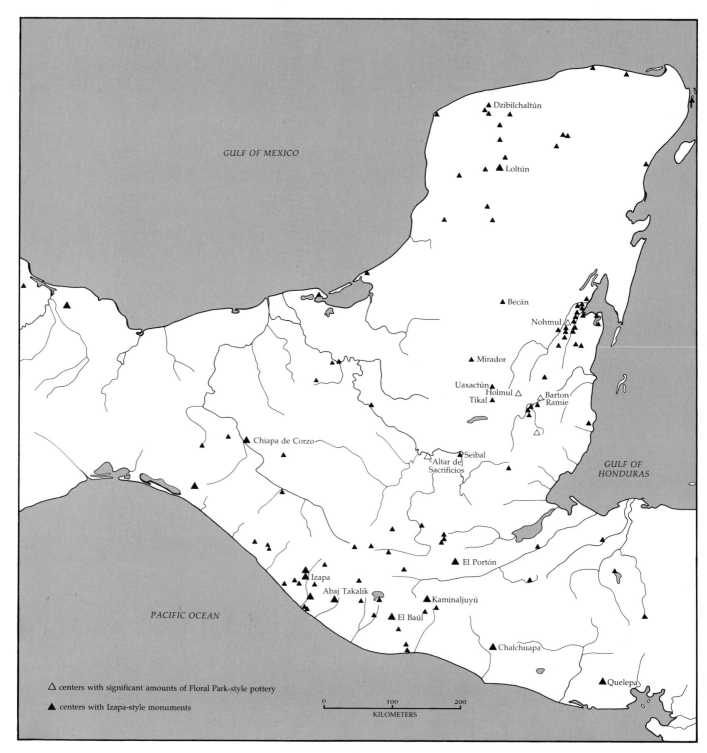

GULF OF MEXICO

Dzibilchaltún

Loltún

Becán

Nohmul

Mirador

Uaxactún
Holmul
Tikal

Barton
Ramie

Chiapa de Corzo

Seibal
Altar de
Sacrificios

GULF OF
HONDURAS

El Portón

Izapa

Abaj Takalik

Kaminaljuyú

PACIFIC OCEAN

El Baúl

Chalchuapa

Quelepa

△ centers with significant amounts of Floral Park-style pottery

▲ centers with Izapa-style monuments

0   100   200
KILOMETERS

Map 7. Late Preclassic communities

extends north and west through the Intermediate Zone to the Gulf Coast. This distribution recalls the old southeastern sphere of the Olmec world, and the style and iconography of Izapan art reflects a definite Olmec ancestry. Archaeological data are insufficient for a real understanding of Izapan "civilization." Izapa itself has the greatest concentration of relief carving, but it was not necessarily the place where the style originated or the "capital" of an Izapan state. There is no real evidence that there was a single Izapan cultural system comparable to Olmec civilization. Izapan relief sculpture actually shows a good deal of regional variation, as does associated architecture, pottery, and other items of material culture. This variety probably reflects both regional cultural differences and developmental change within the several centuries spanned by Izapan art. The distribution of Izapan art reflects a multiethnic sphere of interaction, embracing both Zoquean peoples in the Intermediate Zone and Maya societies in the highlands.

In style, Izapan art provides a historical bridge between Olmec art and Early Classic Maya art (Fig. 28).[23] Many elements of Classic Maya iconography and writing, intimately related to politics and religion, first appear on Izapan monuments. Izapan centers erected stelae—vertical stone shafts, commonly carved with elaborate scenes in relief and often accompanied by low cylindrical stone "altars." Many of these stelae depict richly dressed figures as well as cosmological themes. They foreshadow the Classic Maya stela complex, which glorified community leaders.

Glyphs and numbers are extremely rare at Izapa itself, but several Izapan monuments, including stelae at Kaminaljuyú, Chalchuapa, and El Portón, in the Maya highlands, bear hieroglyphic inscriptions.[24] A few texts include calendar dates in a system identical to the Classic Maya Long Count (Figs. 29, 30). The earliest, from Chiapa de Corzo, corresponds to 36 B.C. The latest, from El Baul and Abaj Takalik, in the southern piedmont, fall in the first and second centuries of the Christian era. The conceptual system is that of the Long Count: elapsed time is tabulated from the same fixed starting point, is divided into the same set of units, and is recorded in the same way. Even the format and several auxiliary features are those of the earliest Classic Maya lowland dates. At a few highland and piedmont centers, stelae and altars placed before large public buildings not only have reliefs and dates remarkably like those of Early Classic lowland Maya stelae, but also bear hieroglyphic texts in an ancestral version of the Classic script. The stela complex, embodying the essence of Classic Maya art and iconography, developed in the highland-piedmont zone during the Late Preclassic period. As in later lowland centers, the early southern monuments reflect a complex, hierarchical social and political order. They must celebrate the exploits of local leaders, who oversaw the construction of the elaborate public buildings, and who were often buried within them.

Kaminaljuyú consisted of several densely occupied neighborhoods.[25] Each had its own civic precinct, with earth and clay platforms supporting timber-frame thatched buildings. The largest public struc-

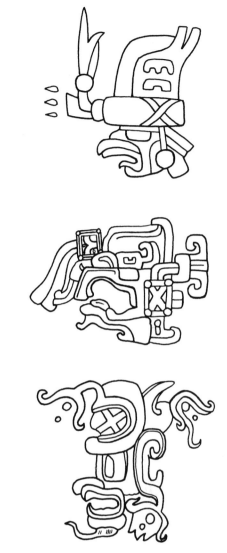

28. Continuities in Olmec, Izapa, and Maya art. Note that each mask has toothless jaws, an *X* or crossed-bands symbol, and flowers or other plant motifs in the headdress. *Above:* detail of relief carving II at Chalcatzingo, Morelos (reversed); *center:* detail of Izapan Stela 11 at Kaminaljuyú; *below:* detail of Maya mural from Bonampak (upper panel, Room 1, Structure 1). (Not to same scale.) (Adapted from Piña Chan 1955:69, Miles 1965a:Fig. 15a, and Carnegie Institution 1955.)

29. Stela C, Tres Zapotes. *Left:* front, with Long Count date 7.16.6.16.18, corresponding to the year 31 B.C. The text follows the single-column format of early Maya calendrical inscriptions, with a large introductory glyph including a jaguar head, representing the patron of the month, bar-and-dot numbers without period glyphs, and the corresponding ritual almanac position (6 Etz'nab). (Compare Figs. 15, 30, and 43.) *Right:* reverse with Izapan-style relief. (Adapted from M. Coe 1976:Fig. 4 and Marcus 1976b:Fig. 7.)

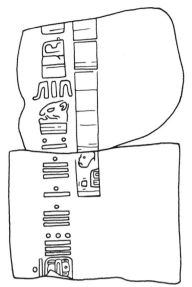
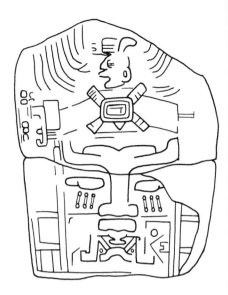

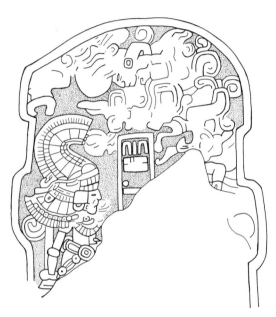

30. Stela 2, Abaj Takalik. This monument, accompanied by a plain stone altar, was erected on a sloping stone pavement before a building platform. A richly dressed figure faces a vertical hieroglyphic text with a face peering down from among swirling clouds above. The placement of the stela, as well as the format of its scene, the costume of the principal figure, and the hieroglyphic text with its Long Count date, typifies the early Maya stela complex. The text opens with an introductory glyph consisting of the typical three-part upper element and the earliest known use of the *tun* element; the month patron is missing. The numbers are largely destroyed, but the first was certainly 7; the second was probably 6, 11, or 16, so that the date would fall between 235 and 18 B.C. Charcoal from beneath the pavement on which Stela 2 was erected produced a date of 2100 B.P. ± 170. (Adapted from J. Graham et al. 1978:Pl. 2 and M. Coe 1976: Fig. 6.)

ture in each group was a tall, terraced temple platform, often containing a richly stocked tomb (Fig. 31). Nearby smaller structures include lower platforms that supported noble residences (Fig. 32). This community pattern, along with the stela complex, indicates a social order much like that of Maya centers of the Classic period. Emergent aristocratic groups, combining many varied political, religious, and economic roles, dominated social life.

Early Maya iconography was only one aspect of the art of the southern region in this period. Some monuments represent a related but distinct complex featuring the more mythical or cosmological themes so common in the art of Izapa. Others fall into an intermediate category. A few represent different stylistic traditions altogether. Abaj Takalik has stelae and altars in the Izapan and early Maya styles, some with hieroglyphic texts; plain stelae and altars; potbellied boulder sculptures; and a variety of miscellaneous carvings.[26] Kaminaljuyú and other important civic centers of the region have a comparable variety of monuments, suggesting a series of regionally distinct cultural traditions. The complex relations among them cannot be analyzed properly without a better historical perspective on chronological change during the Late Preclassic period. It is certain, though, that one component of the cultural potpourri of the Maya highlands and the adjacent piedmont zone during these centuries represents the foundation of Maya iconography, and of Classic Maya political-religious symbolism in particular.

The Maya Lowlands

Monumental public art, so typical of lowland Maya civilization in its florescent period, was less vigorous in the lowlands in this early developmental stage. At Tikal and Uaxactún, tomb paintings and painted

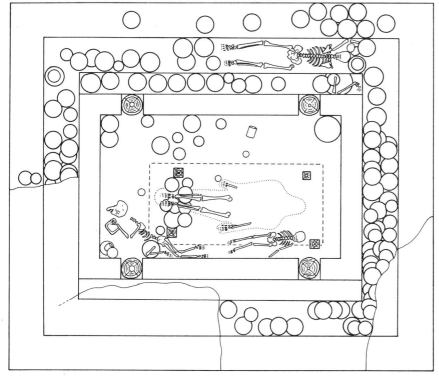

31. Tomb II, Mound E-III-3, Kaminaljuyú: plan of the tomb of one of Kaminaljuyú's great early leaders, dug into the floor of a temple platform. Five benches (uppermost not shown) step down to the burial chamber proper. The main occupant was laid out on a wooden litter (dashed line) supported by four wooden blocks and covered with mats. The body (dotted line), painted bright red, was wrapped in a burial cloth with a mosaic mask of green stone over the face. The bodies of two children aged 6 to 8, probably sacrificed to accompany the lord, were laid along the west edge of the chamber. Offerings were arrayed around the corpse. In addition to the illustrated pottery vessels, some of which contained the residue of burned incense, they include jade beads, stone ear ornaments, plaques encrusted with pyrite, gourds coated with stucco, obsidian and andesite blades, pebbles and chunks of minerals (iron oxide, hematite, mica, quartz), animal bones, fish teeth, stingray spines, several miscellaneous stone and bone objects, and probably a variety of perishable materials. The list of offerings, especially jade, is surely incomplete, for the tomb was partially plundered in antiquity. The burial chamber was roofed with wooden beams supported by four large wooden posts, and a third sacrificial victim, a young adult, was laid face down along an upper bench amid additional offerings, including 100 or more pottery vessels and a few stone beads. The entire tomb was filled with earth and capped by a new clay floor across the top of the platform, which continued to be used for ceremonial activities. The clay floor was renewed several times as the tomb fill slumped, and finally the old structure was entirely encased within a new clay-floored platform ascended by a broad stairway. The burial of an important person was often the occasion for such remodeling projects; an earlier (and even richer) tomb lay deep within Mound E-III-3. (Adapted from Shook and Kidder 1952:Fig. 15.)

and modeled stucco decoration on temple platforms and building facades (Fig. 33) echo the early Maya style of the southern highland-piedmont area.[27] A few broken monument fragments found at Tikal indicate the beginnings of stone relief sculpture, but neither center has produced evidence of Preclassic hieroglyphic writing. Development was not continuous in this region. Social changes, marked by large-scale public architecture and richly stocked tombs, proceeded quite rapidly until about the time of Christ (Figs. 33–36). The next few centuries represent a period of stabilization, with slackened population growth. New evidence from Mirador, to the north, indicates comparable stucco relief decoration on truly massive temple platforms.

By contrast, most centers in the Río Pasión and eastern lowland regions enjoyed steady growth and development through the beginning of the Classic period.[28] Processes of change were not uniform, though. Seibal experienced an early population expansion and building boom, followed by a period of decline that culminated in near

32. Structure 4a, Mound B-II-1, Kaminaljuyú: reconstruction drawing of a noble family's dwelling in one of Kaminaljuyú's civic areas. A platform with three low terraces, rising not quite 3 m. above the adjacent plaza, supported the dwelling itself, which had two rooms slightly sunken below the platform surface. Details of the timber frame and thatched roof are hypothetical. This building represents the sixth in a series of seven remodelings. (Adapted from Austin and Lothson 1969:Fig. 64.)

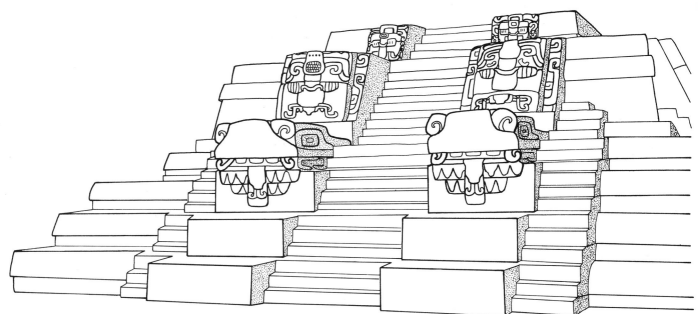

33. Pyramid E-VII sub, Uaxactún: reconstruction drawing of the front of a temple platform consisting of an earth-and-rubble core roughly faced with stone plastered with an outer coating of stucco. The modeled stucco masks, which adorn all four sides of the pyramid, represent the early Maya art style expressed in stone relief carving in the southern highland–piedmont region. The platform surface, slight more than 8 m. above the adjacent plaza, once supported a small timber-frame structure with a thatched roof. (Adapted from Proskouriakoff 1963a:5 and Ricketson and Ricketson 1937:Figs. 33, 39, 42, 43, 49, 50, Pl. 30.)

34. Temple platforms, North Acropolis, Tikal: plan of a temple group built about the time of Christ in Tikal's main ceremonial precinct. The northern (*top*) and eastern (*right*) platforms, rising about 4 m. above the acropolis floor, supported imposing temple buildings with modeled and painted stucco decoration. These two structures were nearly identical (see. Fig. 35). A temple of different design, also with modeled stucco ornamentation, stood on a lower platform at the head of the access stairs along the south edge of the acropolis. Two much smaller buildings occupied the southwest corner of the group. Tikal's early nobles, sometimes accompanied by their sacrificed retainers, were interred in vaulted tomb chambers within the acropolis itself (see Fig. 36). The tombs, painted inside with elaborate figures, were richly stocked with burial offerings. (Adapted from W. Coe 1967:42.)

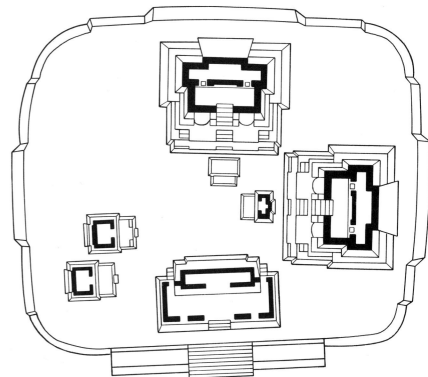

abandonment by A.D. 300. Here early monumental art consists mainly of occasional modeled and painted stucco decoration on civic buildings. There are no monuments with Long Count dates and no hieroglyphic texts.

Unlike Tikal and Uaxactún, many centers in an arc stretching across the eastern and southern flank of the lowlands added new features to the standard Chicanel pottery style just before the time of Christ.[29] Vessels with swollen legs and true polychrome painting (red and black paint over an orange ground) (Fig. 37) are the most striking elements of the new Floral Park style. Many Floral Park features have antecedents in earlier pottery-making traditions of the Maya highlands and adjacent piedmont regions.[30] This connection is especially obvious at Chalchuapa, in the east. The appearance of the new style in southern lowland centers marks another, very intensive episode in the continuing relationship between highlands and lowlands. At few, if any, centers did Floral Park replace the Chicanel style entirely. The two traditions coexisted within each region, marking a clear differentiation between ordinary and luxury pottery. Aristocrats at certain prosperous centers adopted Floral Park pottery, using it for tomb offerings and in ritual activities. Ordinary people at these centers continued to manufacture pottery according to the old Chicanel norms, as did the residents of smaller, less prominent communities. The great popularity of Floral Park pottery at a few centers (Altar de Sacrificios, Barton Ramie, Nohmul, Holmul) might even indicate enclaves of people from the highland-piedmont zone.[31] If highlanders did live in these communities, they were probably involved in the ongoing trade in obsidian, jade, and other raw materials.

Other communities in this arc did not adopt the southern luxury pottery tradition so wholeheartedly, nor did centers farther north and west.[32] Tikal, Uaxactún, and centers along the middle Río Usumacinta occasionally imported Floral Park vessels. Some features of the style were added to local pottery-making traditions, but there was no real shift away from the Chicanel style. Trade networks distributed Floral Park pottery as far west as Chiapa de Corzo. Here Floral Park imports contrast sharply with new local styles that marked a decided withdrawal from the Chicanel sphere.

Though it was a regional phenomenon, mainly restricted to the eastern and southern fringe of the lowlands, the Floral Park style and its southern relations represent the advent of luxury polychrome pottery, an important feature of Classic Maya civilization. Like the early distribution of Maya sculpture and writing, it is another indication of intense highland–lowland contacts, suggesting that many of the foundations of Classic Maya civilization were laid in the Maya highlands. During the Late Preclassic period many southern innovations spread gradually northward into the lowlands, where they were elaborated in later centuries.

In central Yucatan, patterns of growth and development followed yet another course.[33] Becán began to produce Chicanel-style pottery at about the same time as centers farther south, but few other changes

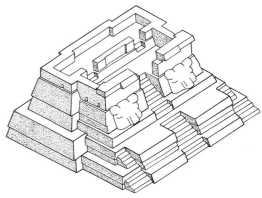

35. Structure 5D-Sub 1-1st, North Acropolis, Tikal: reconstruction drawing of a temple built in Tikal's civic-ceremonial center about the time of Christ. The floor of the rear room stood about 4.5 m. above the acropolis surface. This building is the northern (top) structure in the plan of the North Acropolis in Fig. 34; the eastern (right) building was nearly identical. The stucco masks flanking the stairway of the stucco-faced earth-and-rubble platform probably depicted jaguars. The projecting upper facade of the masonry building itself was ornamented with modeled stucco brightly painted in red, pink, black, and cream. The platform is very much like contemporary temple platforms at nearby Uaxactún, and the moldings along the sides and rear foreshadow the platform architecture of the Classic period (compare Figs. 33 and 52). (Adapted from W. Coe 1965:Fig. 4.)

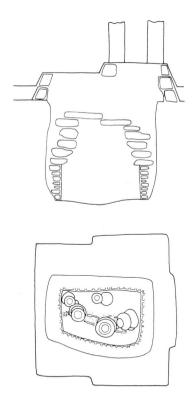

36. Burial (167) chamber, North Acropolis, Tikal. *Above:* east–west section through the center of the small building just in front of the eastern temple (see Fig. 34). The burial chamber was built at the bottom of a pit that cut away all but the edges of a preexisting platform. The chamber itself had stone walls roughly plastered with mud and a vaulted roof; the corbeling technique (stones projecting progressively toward the center, eventually bridged by a single slab) does not show clearly because the section parallels the room's long axis. After the burial ceremonies, the chamber was covered with earth and rubble and a low red-painted platform was built over the pit. The small one-room masonry shrine atop the platform was decorated with polychrome frescoes; it may also have been vaulted. *Below:* plan of the burial on the chamber floor, with outlines of the excavation and the platform indicated. The shaded area indicates the body of the tomb's principal personage, one of Tikal's early nobles. A pair of large bowls on the chest contained the disarticulated skeleton of a second adult—perhaps a kinsman, since both suffered from some disease that produced unusually thickened skull bones. A second pair of bowls containing an infant, possibly stillborn, was placed over the noble's hips. A shell necklace and bracelets had adorned the body. Other offerings left in the tomb included a green stone figurine, nine pottery vessels, and two red-painted gourds. (Adapted from W. Coe 1965:Figs 6, 10.)

took place until the beginning of the Christian era. During the last centuries of the Late Preclassic period Becán enjoyed a surge in population growth and engaged in the first really large-scale public construction. The greatest public works project was a massive ditch and embankment, probably a fortification. It is nearly 2 kilometers in circumference and encircles the entire center. There is no evidence here of early Maya monumental art or Floral Park ceramics.

In the northern lowlands, population growth and social change were relatively steady throughout the Late Preclassic period, though again developments were not uniform.[34] Dzibilchaltún, in the northwest, quickly grew into the region's largest civic center, with several large public buildings (Fig. 38) and a substantial population. In the first century B.C. it experienced a drastic decline. Dzibilchaltún imported jade and other raw materials from highland Guatemala, but did not adopt the early Maya tradition of monumental art. A relief carving near the mouth of Loltún cave (Fig. 39) and several portable pieces indicate that early Maya art and writing had already been adopted elsewhere in the north.[35] Northern lowland pottery represents a regional version of the Chicanel style, with no significant Floral Park features.

Coordinate Evolution

By A.D. 250 complex processes of growth and development had forever transformed homogeneous Maya societies. The old pattern of comparable villages had given way to elaborate settlement hierarchies. Civic centers (Fig. 40) provided social and economic focal points for surrounding villages, hamlets, and isolated farmsteads. In every part of the Maya world at least one center outstripped its fellows and rose to a position of regional dominance before the end of the Late Preclassic period. Smaller outlying communities may not have changed radically, but evidence of widening social and economic gaps abounds at larger civic centers. The contrast between simple burials under house floors and elaborate vaulted masonry tombs stocked with luxury goods in public architectural complexes testifies to the emergence of distinct aristocracies. Most of these public buildings were temples, and the practice of burying high-ranking individuals in sacred public places suggests the aristocratic ancestor cults typical of later Maya societies. Early stelae and altars also mark the inception of the Classic-period pattern of intertwined political, economic, and religious organization. Monuments to political leaders had strong sacred overtones in their iconography and in their association with temples.

Civic architecture and other massive public construction projects represent one obvious facet of the political and administrative roles that fell to the new leadership. They were able to command and mobilize human and economic resources on a regional scale, and they organized them to carry through well-planned public works projects. Aristocratic groups played key economic roles as well, for the imported luxury goods that adorn their tombs indicate far-flung procurement networks. Nobles must also have been involved in organizing the acquisition and distribution of obsidian, hard stones, and other widely used utilitarian goods. The emergent leadership may already have taken on managerial roles in subsistence economics as well, for the conversion of swamps and low river margins to new agricultural land had already begun, at least in the eastern lowlands.[36] The excavation and maintenance of canal systems and the concurrent creation of raised fields by landfill operations does not actually require administrative oversight, but specialists were certainly available and probably eager to expand their spheres of control.

Though all Maya societies experienced the same basic evolutionary transition between 400 B.C. and A.D. 250, the process was not uniform, and the Maya area did not become homogeneous. Developmental profiles vary from region to region, and even within regions. Styles of pottery and architectural decoration indicate the survival of vigorous local cultural traditions most clearly. Centers in the Maya highlands featured earth and clay public building platforms. Associated monumental stone sculpture was quite varied, including a stela-altar complex memorializing leaders in relief carving and hieroglyphic texts. Southern lowland public buildings often had stone construction and stucco decoration. Architectural decoration reflects the same emergent Maya monumental art style, but stone sculpture is rare and there is no evidence of writing. Some lowland centers also adopted a new highland luxury pottery style. In the northern lowlands stone and stucco public buildings were large but quite plain. Pottery complexes there did not reflect southern innovations.

The stela complex of the highland-piedmont zone was ancestral to that of later Maya civilization. Early southern pottery also foreshadows many of the features of Classic Maya luxury pottery. The foundations of important aspects of Classic Maya civilization were laid in the south, but Maya civilization was not a highland invention transferred to the lowlands. Early public buildings in southern lowland centers, with stone facings and stucco decoration, set the pattern for monumental architecture of the Classic period. The origins of polychrome pottery do not lie in either region. The development of Maya monumental art and luxury pottery were regional events, while similar social changes occurred throughout the Maya world during these centuries. Individual features of Classic Maya civilization can be traced to developments in particular regions. The emergence of Maya civilization itself was an areawide process.

The regions of the Maya area participated in parallel, linked evolutionary processes. Many factors were important in stimulating and fueling these developments.[37] There was no single cause. A huge fortification at Becán suggests that conflict and the need for defense may have contributed to the rise of powerful political leaders in central Yucatan, but defense was not an areawide preoccupation. The need to import exotic raw materials surely played a similar role in other regions. Population growth occurred in every region, but demographic trends were far from uniform. Population pressure presumably contributed to the growth of new institutions in many regions, but it was

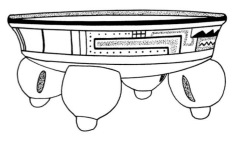

37. Floral Park–style bowl, Holmul. The four swollen legs are hollow and contain loose pottery pellets so that they serve as rattles. The polychrome geometric design is done in red and black paint over an orange ground. This bowl was one of several vessels interred with one of Holmul's nobles in a burial chamber excavated into a platform mound just after the time of Christ. (Adapted from Merwin and Vaillant 1932:Pl. 18d.)

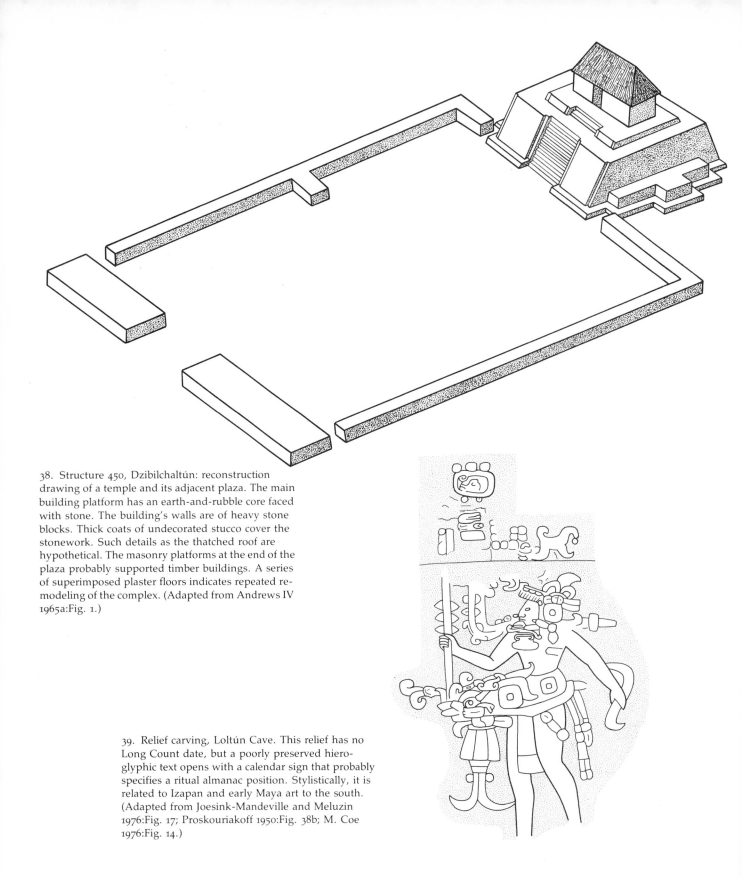

38. Structure 450, Dzibilchaltún: reconstruction
drawing of a temple and its adjacent plaza. The main
building platform has an earth-and-rubble core faced
with stone. The building's walls are of heavy stone
blocks. Thick coats of undecorated stucco cover the
stonework. Such details as the thatched roof are
hypothetical. The masonry platforms at the end of the
plaza probably supported timber buildings. A series
of superimposed plaster floors indicates repeated remodeling of the complex. (Adapted from Andrews IV
1965a:Fig. 1.)

39. Relief carving, Loltún Cave. This relief has no
Long Count date, but a poorly preserved hieroglyphic text opens with a calendar sign that probably
specifies a ritual almanac position. Stylistically, it is
related to Izapan and early Maya art to the south.
(Adapted from Joesink-Mandeville and Meluzin
1976:Fig. 17; Proskouriakoff 1950:Fig. 38b; M. Coe
1976:Fig. 14.)

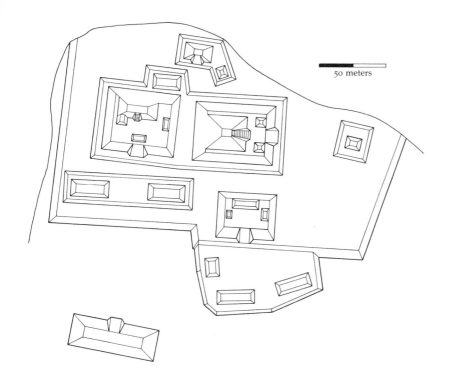

40. Plan of Cerros: the central public precinct of a regional civic center. Clusters of smaller structures, mostly oridinary residences, were scattered throughout the surrounding area. (Adapted from Freidel 1979:Fig. 3.)

50 meters

not the one driving force. The connections among the regions of the Maya world created an environment in which a variety of localized causal factors contributed to the emergence of Classic Maya civilization. New political institutions developed in one region under the pressure of conflict or population pressure might spread because they also facilitated commercial activities. Networks of communication stretched across the Maya world. They brought its several regions to the threshold of civilization together.

CHAPTER SEVEN

CLASSIC MAYA CIVILIZATION

Growth processes that began during the Preclassic period culminated in Classic Maya civilization—one of the most splendid achievements of native America. Populations continued to expand. Civic centers grew larger and more powerful. The gap between aristocrats and common people widened. Nobles acquired greater political and religious authority, and wielded more power. Specialists multiplied in every field. Architecture, arts, and crafts all reached new aesthetic peaks. In writing and the intellectual sphere generally, Classic Maya sophistication was unrivaled in the Americas. The Classic period was a time of cultural florescence throughout the Maya world.

The original definition of the Classic period, based on events in the southern lowlands, must be broadened to embrace related developments elsewhere in the Maya world. Most of the traits traditionally associated with the beginning of the Classic period—large public buildings, corbeled vaults, polychrome pottery, the Long Count calendar, writing, and the Maya style of monumental art—actually appeared rather earlier in one or another part of the Maya area.

The Classic period does embrace the first great florescence of Maya civilization, but it also includes two centuries of cultural decline in parts of the southern lowlands. The end of the Classic period still coincides roughly with the demise of the great civic centers in the southern lowlands, but this "collapse" was really a process of decline that began early in the ninth century and lasted well into the tenth. Related developments produced great changes in societies throughout the Maya world, but they did not bring about the end of Maya civilization. In the north and in the highlands, new civic centers came to power after A.D. 1000. A few of them controlled regions larger than any Classic Maya realm.

The most striking development marking the onset of the Classic period is the appearance of the stela cult in the southern lowlands. A few centers in the heart of the southern lowlands began to erect stelae with portraits of their richly dressed rulers and dated hieroglyphic texts recording the main events of their lives. At the same time there were changes in pottery and other craft styles. Several regions experienced intensified population growth. Many centers enjoyed building booms, especially in civic architecture. Each of these developments has obvious roots in processes under way throughout the Maya area in the Late Preclassic period. The stela complex was directly descended from the much earlier tradition developed in southern highland and piedmont centers. Late Preclassic public buildings at several southern lowland centers embodied the basic stylistic and construction features of Classic Maya civic architecture. The new widely shared pottery style had evolved from the Floral Park style. In every way, Classic Maya civilization is an outgrowth of Late Preclassic Maya culture—an intensification and expansion of Late Preclassic cultural patterns.

Like earlier Maya societies, those of the Classic period were diverse. Expanding economic and political systems intensified communication among communities throughout the Maya world. Many patterns were widely shared, but Classic Maya civilization was never a single homogenous cultural system. It comprised several interacting cultures, each with its own regional flavor, its own variations on the same basic themes. Each regional culture represented a distinctive blend of its unique local heritage and patterns developed in other parts of the Maya world. The Classic civilization of the southern lowlands was a synthesis of styles and institutions with diverse historical origins. Public architecture had mainly local antecedents, while luxury pottery and monumental art owed much to earlier developments in the Maya highlands and adjacent piedmont zone. Other regions achieved different syntheses of local developments and borrowed patterns.

THE EARLY CLASSIC PERIOD (A.D. 250–600)

Processes of growth and development that had begun in the Late Preclassic period continued during the Early Classic period as the new patterns of Maya civilization took hold. As in earlier centuries, these trends were not uniform throughout the Maya world, nor were they smoothly continuous in any one region. Traditional connections among regions persisted and even intensified. Long-distance commerce continued to flourish. The stela complex spread rapidly outward from the heart of the southern lowlands.

At the same time, regional differences, particularly in craft styles,

41. Corbeled vault, Copán. Higher courses project farther and farther toward the center until they can be spanned by a single block; there is no true keystone.

became more pronounced. This increasing regionalism probably reflects closer ties among centers within regions, rather than diminished communication among regions. The sharpest contrasts developed between highland and lowland areas, though commerce continued. Styles and institutions were more widely shared within the lowlands, but differences between northern and southern sectors became more pronounced.

The Lowlands

The cultural synthesis that established the basic form of Classic Maya civilization took shape first in the central sector of the southern lowlands, in the Tikal-Uaxactún region.[1] There is no evidence of substantial population increase at Tikal or Uaxactún at first, but the construction of public buildings accelerated. As in the Late Preclassic period, a few of these buildings may be palaces or elite residences, but most are temples. Architectural style, decoration, and construction techniques all follow patterns established in the preceding period. Corbeled vaulting (Fig. 41) was now certainly in use in above-ground buildings as well as in subterranean tombs. A new tradition of pottery making featuring elaborate polychrome painting (Fig. 42) replaced Chicanel. This Tzakol style essentially represents the spread of an evolved version of the Floral Park tradition (see Fig. 37) throughout the southern lowlands and beyond.

The most striking innovation is the stela complex.[2] Tikal's Stela 29 (Fig. 43), carved with the Long Count position 8.12.14.8.15, corresponding to A.D. 292, is the earliest dated monument to turn up so far in the Maya lowlands. Thirty-six years later, Uaxactún erected its first dated stela. For the next fifty years they were the only centers to do so. By the early fifth century, four or five smaller centers in the surrounding region were erecting monuments. During the second half of Cycle 8 of the Maya calendar (which ended in A.D. 434) the stela complex was restricted to a very small area in the heart of the southern lowlands (Map 8). Uaxactún has by far the largest number of early dated monuments. Together, Uaxactún and nearby Tikal produced half of all Cycle 8 stelae.

In style as well as content these early lowland stelae are squarely within the tradition of the Cycle 7–early Cycle 8 stela complex established in the highland-piedmont zone (Fig. 30). The disappearance of the stela complex from its original homeland in the Early Classic period evidently marks a change in highland sociopolitical systems, or at least in the mechanisms that reinforced the positions of highland aristocracies. There is no question that early lowland stelae (Figs. 43–45), like their highland ancestors, were memorials to powerful local political leaders and their families. These stelae reflect a social order in which aristocrats held the highest social ranks and dominated political, economic, and religious life. They filled specialized political roles that had economic and religious overtones. Ancestor motifs and other themes on the monuments appear to refer to noble family lines. Monuments

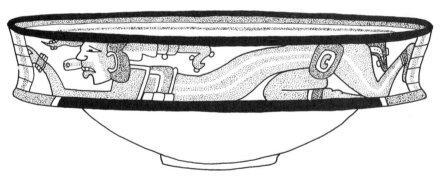

42. Tzakol-style bowl, Uaxactún. The projecting flange is a typical Early Classic trait. The designs on this polychrome bowl, featuring human figures along with geometric elements, were executed in red and black paint over an orange ground. This bowl was one of nine vessels placed as funerary offerings in an Early Classic burial at Uaxactún. (Adapted from R. E. Smith 1955:2, Figs. 3e, 76b5.)

are almost always associated with public buildings, and the practice of burying important people in well-built tombs within temple complexes continued. These patterns suggest aristocratic ancestor cults.

Tikal was the only center to carve an emblem glyph (Figs. 43, 45), formally designating it as a political unit, on its monuments during Cycle 8. The same emblem glyph appears at least once in the early inscriptions of Uaxactún, implying alliance or perhaps political domination. Tikal and Uaxactún evidently had something of a head start

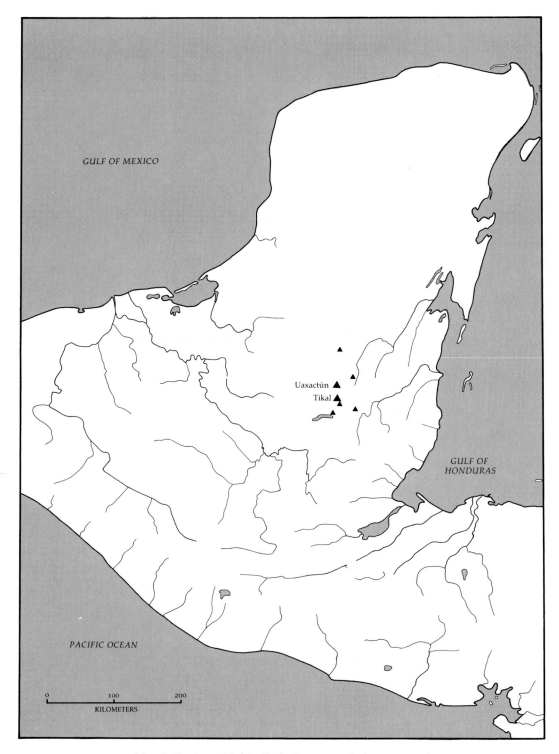

GULF OF MEXICO

PACIFIC OCEAN

GULF OF
HONDURAS

Uaxactún ▲

Tikal ▲

0   100   200
KILOMETERS

Map 8. Centers with late Cycle 8 monuments (A.D. 292–434)

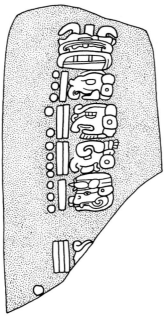

43. Stela 29, Tikal. The Long Count position, 8.12.14.8.15, is the earliest known from the Maya lowlands, corresponding to A.D. 292. The date is arranged in a single column, like the earlier Cycle 7 inscriptions, but the numbers are now written vertically as coefficients of glyphs representing the periods of the Long Count, as in later typical Initial Series dates (see Figs. 15, 29, 30). The introducing glyph includes the patron of the month (Zip). The dot just above the break is all that remains of the ritual almanac notation. The other side of the monument bears the portrait of a richly dressed noble with a scepter tucked under his right arm. As on many Izapan and early Maya monuments, the head of a deity or deified ancestor peers down from above. The headdress element on the head just in front of the noble's right hand is identical to Tikal's emblem glyph (see Figs. 30, 45); this is the first known use of this symbol. The monument, found broken in an ancient rubbish heap, must originally have been erected before an Early Classic public building, as were later Tikal stelae. (Adapted from M. Coe 1976:Fig. 15; W. Coe 1967:95; Marcus 1976b:Fig. 10.)

along the road to political power in the opening centuries of the Classic period.

This precocious political development may be related to the external connections of the two centers, for the ruling aristocracies of Tikal and Uaxactún developed close ties with foreign nobles toward the end of Cycle 8.[3] At Uaxactún, a stela erected in A.D. 377 portrays a foreign figure in non-Maya dress, carrying an *atlatl* (spear thrower), a Mexican weapon hitherto unknown in the Maya world. Less than two years later, the Tikal ruler known to Mayanists as Curl Snout came to power. Curl Snout had himself depicted on his inaugural monument (Fig. 44) in a pose and costume typical of the nobles of Teotihuacán, the great urban capital of highland central Mexico. His tomb contained, in addition to the usual ritual paraphernalia, imported vessels and other objects indicating a Teotihuacán connection. At about this time three other burials at Tikal involved Mexican-style cremation rites.

The relationship continued, though perhaps less intensely, during the reign of Stormy Sky, who succeeded Curl Snout about A.D. 425. Stela 31, erected to celebrate the first katun (twenty years) of his reign, depicts Stormy Sky in typical Maya regalia, but with Mexican emblems among his accoutrements (Fig. 45). Two subordinate figures in highland Mexican dress flank Stormy Sky; they carry atlatls and shields adorned with be face of Tlaloc, the central Mexican rain god. Stela 31 emphasizes Stormy Sky's genealogical links with his Mexican-influenced predecessor, for Curl Snout is the "ancestor figure" gazing down on him. The text mentions the accession of both rulers. By the time Stormy Sky died, about A.D. 455, Tikal's Mexican connection was definitely on the wane. His tomb, like his monuments, was more traditional than Curl Snout's, with fewer Mexican imports.

44. Stela 4, Tikal. This monument is the first erected in honor of the early Tikal ruler nicknamed Curl Snout, after the curlicue protruding from the face of the portrait glyph that records his name. The stela records the date of his accession to rule in A.D. 378 (8. 17.2.16.7). Elements of Curl Snout's regalia and his frontal seated pose are typical of portraits of nobles at Teotihuacán, the great central Mexican city. Stela 4 was moved in the Postclassic period and reerected upside down alongside an inverted altar. Its correct orientation has been restored, but its original location is unknown.

For a very brief period, Mexican cultural elements became very popular among the rulers of Tikal and Uaxactún. It is even possible, though far from certain, that Curl Snout himself was a foreigner. He certainly established a ruling line with a strong Mexican affiliation at Tikal. Stormy Sky's monuments emphasize his ties to Curl Snout, but they incorporate Mexican symbols only as minor elements. The quick decline of Mexican emblems does not square with the notion that foreign rulers took over Tikal. It suggests instead an episode of especially intense alliance, perhaps including marriage ties, between local Maya rulers and foreign aristocrats. These foreign connections may have influenced the course of political development at Tikal and Uaxactún, but they do not represent the implantation of a foreign civilization in the Maya lowlands. Lowland Maya societies had already developed the essential features of civilization. The stela cult, reflecting the basic patterns of Classic Maya political organization, had been present in the heart of the southern lowlands for at least a century by the time Curl Snout came to power.

Though Maya tomb offerings include green obsidian from central Mexico and Maya pottery has been found at Teotihuacán, the ties between lowland Maya centers and Teotihuacán were probably not direct. Teotihuacán maintained an active presence in the Maya highlands, most notably at Kaminaljuyú (Map 9).[4] Stylistic nuances of Mexican material found there point to an enclave of Mexicans, but more likely from some part of Teotihuacán's southeastern dominions than from the central Mexican metropolis itself. Teotihuacán's sphere of influence embraced most of the Intermediate Zone, from the Gulf Coast to the Pacific Coast and piedmont. Curl Snout's burial at Tikal is very much like Mexican tombs at Kaminaljuyú. The Mexicans who came to Tikal, and who may have maintained a resident enclave there, were almost certainly "colonial" Teotihuacanos from Kaminaljuyú. Commerce was surely an important component of this interaction, as lowland aristocracies added central Mexican obsidian and Teotihuacán-style pottery to the traditional imports from the Maya highlands. After Curl Snout's reign, Mexican imports fell off rapidly, though economic ties with the highlands continued. Local potters still manufactured a few Teotihuacán-inspired vessels and Mexican emblems did not disappear entirely from monumental art, but these are plainly minor elements in overwhelmingly Maya contexts.

The heart of the southern lowlands experienced renewed growth during the late fifth and early sixth centuries.[5] Tikal enjoyed a burst of monumental construction activity and a population surge. Inscriptions at centers as distant as Yaxchilán mention Tikal, already emerging as a powerful political center with influence extending far beyond its local area. Tikal had begun to take on the features of a regional capital, a status it certainly achieved in the Late Classic period.

This growth was interrupted in the sixth century. Between 9.5.0.0.0 and 9.8.0.0.0 (A.D. 534–593), Tikal, Uaxactún, and many dependent centers ceased to erect new stelae and sharply cut back their public building activity.[6] In part, this slackened growth may be related to

45. Stela 31, Tikal. This monument was erected about A.D. 445 to mark the end of the first katun of Stormy Sky's rule. His costume is essentially Maya, but such elements as the skull in his headdress are Teotihuacán-inspired. The figures on the sides of the stela are dressed as Teotihuacán warriors; they carry atlatls, and the shield at the right is decorated with the face of Tlaloc, the central Mexican rain god. The head gazing down from above is that of Stormy Sky's predecessor, Curl Snout. The Tikal emblem glyph appears in the headdress of the head in the crook of Stormy Sky's arm. His name glyph appears as part of his headdress. The deity head emerging from this glyph, along with elements of the headdresses on the heads at his belt, may be other lineage emblems. The hieroglyphic text mentions Curl Snout's accession as well as that of Stormy Sky, emphasizing the genealogical link between them. Stela 31 originally stood before one of the Early Classic temples of the North Acropolis. In the eighth century it was moved up into the rear room of the temple itself. Here it was burned and incense burners were broken around it. Then the upper part of the temple was destroyed and the whole building was encased in a new construction. Two nobles were buried in the heart of the structure before the remodeling, and the ceremonial "sacrifice" of the ancient monument may have marked some momentous event in the affairs of Stormy Sky's descendants, who had returned to power at Tikal late in the seventh century, after a long lapse. (Adapted from Robertson et al. 1972:Pls. 133-35.)

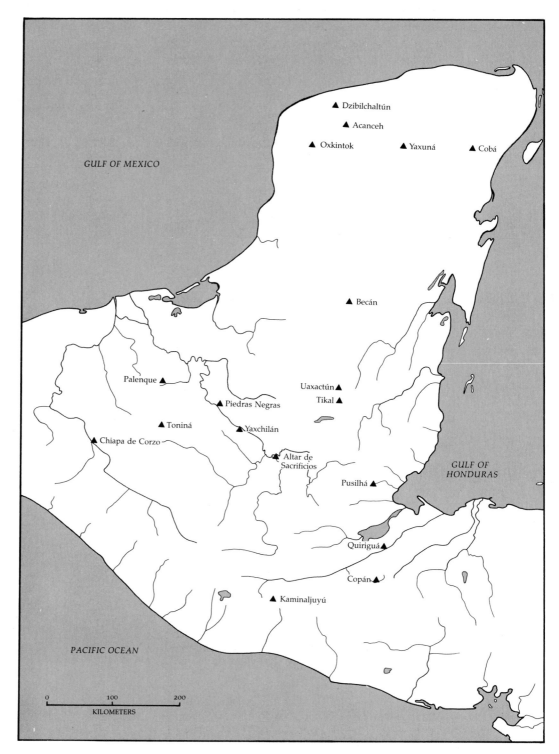

Map 9. Early Classic centers

political and economic reorientations following the withdrawal of Teotihuacán's presence. A corresponding period of slackened growth marks a brief but pronounced episode of decline throughout the southern lowlands.

Elsewhere in the southern lowlands, the development of the regional patterns of Classic Maya civilization was even more gradual. Mexican ties were much less intense.[7] Tomb offerings and special caches sometimes include imported central Mexican obsidian and Teotihuacán-style pottery (Fig. 46). Local potters adopted some features of the Teotihuacán style. Mexican symbols sometimes appear in monumental art. There is nothing comparable to the Mexican interlude at Tikal, though.

In the eastern lowlands, where Floral Park pottery was so popular, the new Tzakol ceramic style was in widespread use from the beginning of the Classic period.[8] Otherwise, the basic way of life was much the same as it had been in the closing centuries of the Late Preclassic period. Population growth continued. Some older civic centers faded into obscurity, but new, larger ones replaced them. Monumental public architecture and richly stocked burials testify to the expanding political and economic power of local aristocracies, but eastern centers did not adopt the stela cult until early Cycle 9 (mid-fifth century). Development was evidently steady in the east. In the sixth century the stela complex, in temporary eclipse to the west, spread to Pusilhá and other eastern centers.

The same general pattern holds for the southeastern region, where Copán was erecting monuments in association with temples and palaces very early in Cycle 9.[9] Copán's early pottery reflects a regional adaptation of the basic Tzakol style. The stela complex continued through the sixth century without interruption, though Copán dedicated many fewer monuments during the interval from 9.5.0.0.0 to 9.8.0.0.0. Quiriguá, 50 kilometers to the north on the Río Motagua, erected two stelae late in the fifth century, but there is no evidence that an important civic center had emerged there before the very end of the Early Classic period.

To the west, along the Río Pasión, the first two centuries of the Early Classic period saw no appreciable change in the traditional way of life.[10] At Altar de Sacrificios the Late Preclassic building boom continued in the Early Classic period, but the Tzakol pottery style and the stela complex did not appear until the mid-fifth century. Public building activity declined during the late fifth and early sixth centuries, but Altar continued to erect sculptured monuments. Altar de Sacrificios was the first civic center in the west to take on the full Classic pattern of Maya civilization. In the sixth century, the rise of Yaxchilán and Piedras Negras, down the Río Usumacinta, ended Altar's preeminence. The style of early monuments at all three centers closely resembles that of Tikal and Uaxactún. The westward and northward spread of the stela complex may reflect an expanding sphere of political influence centered in the Tikal region. Tikal's emblem glyph appears in a Yaxchilán text just before that center acquired its own emblem glyph in

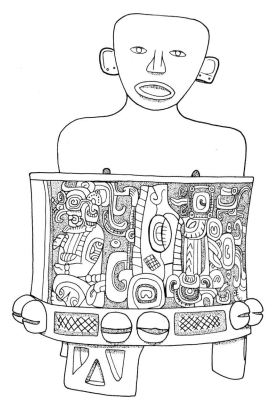

46. Tripod vase and figurine, Becán. These objects were part of a cache placed in the rubble of an Early Classic building on the occasion of a major remodeling operation. The vase is Maya. Its carved design, filled in with red pigment, represents Chac, the Maya rain god, seated before the open mouth of a monstrous reptilian creature. The ceramic statuette, found seated within the vase, is almost identical to Teotihuacán figurines. It is hollow and the front and back are separate pieces. Within it were ten smaller, solid pottery figurines, including an effigy of Tlaloc, the central Mexican rain god, three Teotihuacán warriors, and what seem to be emblems of Mexican military orders, along with four non-Teotihuacán warrior figures. The new structure erected over the ruins containing the cache seems to have been built in the distinctive *talud-tablero* style, typical of Teotihuacán platforms (see Fig. 47). (Adapted from Ball 1974b:cover ill.)

9.4.0.0.0 (A.D. 514). Shortly thereafter, Piedras Negras began to use its own emblem glyph, and contemporaneous Yaxchilán texts mention lords from all three centers. During the sixth century, a marked interruption in the stela complex reflects an unsettled period of reduced growth comparable to that farther east.

Farther north, middle Usumacinta communities had not yet adopted the patterns of Classic Maya civilization.[11] No important Early Classic civic center has been identified in this region. Local pottery complexes are quite varied, with only occasional echoes of the Tzakol style. Regionalization also affected the Palenque area, away from the river. Typical Chicanel complexes gave way to an essentially localized pottery tradition at the beginning of the Early Classic period. Not until the fifth and sixth centuries do imported southern polychromes and local versions of the Tzakol style indicate a significant renewal of ties with the rest of the southern lowlands. Monumental public construction also began at this time, but on a modest scale. Palenque did not become a major civic center with massive public architecture and monuments until the Late Classic period.

At Becán, too, few real changes marked the beginning of the Early Classic period.[12] Pottery making reflects a regional variant of the Tzakol style as well as strong influence from northern traditions. Public works activity continued. The ditch-and-bank fortification was kept in repair and some new civic architectural complexes appeared. The basic form of the older center was hardly altered, though. Many Late Preclassic buildings evidently remained in use until they were replaced in the Late Classic period. Fifth- and sixth-century pottery indicates intensified contacts with southern lowland centers and a corresponding weakening of northern ties. At the same time, Becán's potters adopted a few elements of the Teotihuacán style, and the center imported small quantities of central Mexican obsidian. A cache of Teotihuacán-style figurines in a structure that may have had Teotihuacán architectural features (Fig. 46) might even indicate a foreign enclave. If so, it must have involved Mexicanized Mayas from the south rather than central Mexicans or colonial Teotihuacanos. Tikal's intense Teotihuacán ties were already waning by this time, and Becán's Mexican connection must have been even more indirect. There is no clear evidence of reduced growth at the end of the Early Classic period in central Yucatan.

Early Classic developments in northern Yucatan were varied.[13] Pottery-making traditions, even more diverse than their Preclassic ancestors, shared few features with the southern Tzakol stylistic sphere. Yaxuná, Acanceh, and a few other minor civic centers undertook public works projects during the first two centuries of the period, but Dzibilchaltún, already in decline in the Late Preclassic period, was abandoned. Renewed public construction at Dzibilchaltún in the fifth century heralds a general period of revival and renewed external ties in the north. After 9.2.0.0.0 (A.D. 475) Oxkintok and other northern centers were erecting stelae and carving hieroglyphic inscriptions, and the spread of the stela complex continued during the rest of the Early Classic period. Pottery complexes echo Tzakol stylistic features and some centers imported luxury pottery from the southern lowlands; salt, extracted along the coast, was probably the principal export. Scattered Mexican pottery shapes and design features indicate sporadic and very indirect interaction with the Teotihuacán world. There is no indication of an episode of slackened growth like that in the south. Cobá and other centers in the northeast dedicated their first monuments during the sixth century.

The Highlands

A disastrous eruption of the volcano Ilopango about A.D. 250 produced widespread disruption in the highlands and piedmont.[14] Settlement patterns and trade networks underwent radical shifts, particularly in the east (though Quelepa, far to the east, was apparently beyond the zone of direct impact). Chalchuapa and many smaller centers were abandoned, and many surviving communities suffered drastic population declines. Kaminaljuyú, still the major highland Maya center, survived with reduced influence. Civic constructions were much more modest than those of the Late Preclassic period. Kaminaljuyú produced no new monumental art. Pottery represents a development of the local Late Preclassic stylistic tradition. Features shared with the lowland Tzakol style reflect continuing trade relations.

Beginning in the fifth century, Kaminaljuyú enjoyed a period of renewed growth as it became closely involved with the Teotihuacán world. At the same time, lowland-style polychromes mark intensified contacts with the rest of the Maya world to the north. The southern fringe of the Maya world contracted in this period as the piedmont and coastal zone became part of the Teotihuacán interaction sphere, stretching from Veracruz south and east through the Intermediate Zone. Disruption in the aftermath of the Ilopango disaster may have paved the way for this Teotihuacán expansion. Eastern communities, nearer the volcano, rebounded more slowly. Traditional ties with other highland regions to the west were broken, and new trade networks linked the eastern highlands with the southeastern fringe of the Maya lowlands.

Kaminaljuyú's connection with Teotihuacán began as an exchange relationship, probably indirect, marked by the appearance of central Mexican obsidian and a few other Mexican imports in aristocratic burials. Late in the fifth century, Teotihuacán-style tomb offerings became more popular and public buildings began to incorporate elements of Teotihuacán's distinctive architectural style. Teotihuacán's influence on Kaminaljuyú peaked early in the sixth century. A series of new public building complexes in a thoroughly Teotihuacán style transformed the center. Even construction techniques and materials followed Teotihuacán norms foreign to the local architectural tradition (Fig. 47). Tombs in these buildings were richly stocked with Teotihuacán-style pottery and central Mexican imports (Fig. 48). The Teotihuacán presence was quite localized in these building complexes at Kaminaljuyú. They must have housed enclaves of foreigners, probably noble merchants from one of Teotihuacán's eastern provinces.

47. Structure B-4, Kaminaljuyú. The main temple building, of which no trace remains, undoubtedly once stood on the platform summit, about 8 m. above the adjacent plaza. The wall stubs on the jutting lower platform represent a smaller shrine. Each terrace consists of a sloping lower section (*talud*) surmounted by a vertical inset panel framed by a projecting molding (*tablero*). This platform design is typical of the architecture of Teotihuacán. A tomb chamber beneath the stair contained the body of an Early Classic noble along with three adolescent retainers or relatives, a dog, and several parrots and quails, all sacrificed to accompany him. Mortuary offerings included pottery vessels decorated in the style of Teotihuacán (see Fig. 48) as well as local wares, pyrite-encrusted plaques, grinding stones, obsidian tools, bone awls, mica, shells and shell ornaments, stingray spines, a gourd containing liquid mercury, and a wealth of jade jewelry and ornaments. This burial provided the occasion for the construction of this building over the remains of earlier platforms; it later underwent several additional remodelings. (Adapted from Kidder et al. 1946:Fig. 113.)

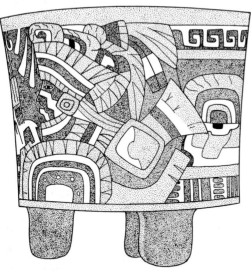

48. Tripod vase, Kaminaljuyú. This vessel was one of a pair included among the funerary offerings placed with the body of the noble in a tomb chamber (B-I) beneath the stairway of a temple platform (B-4, Fig. 47). The design, representing a Teotihuacán warrior, is executed in red, green, and black paint on a thin stucco coating over the black fabric of the pottery. This vase may be an import from central Mexico rather than a local copy in the Teotihuacán style. (Adapted from Kidder et al. 1946:Fig. 174d.)

Other parts of the center reflect the local Maya tradition. Outside of Kaminaljuyú, Teotihuacán architectural elements are quite rare. Kaminaljuyú, the economic center of the Maya highlands, was an ideal staging point for foreigners seeking obsidian, jade, and other highland products. From here they could also establish contact with Kaminaljuyú's traditional lowland trading partners. The lords of Teotihuacán reinforced the relationship by fostering a small Maya enclave within their own city.

By the late sixth century the Teotihuacán presence at Kaminaljuyú was on the wane. Teotihuacán architectural and pottery styles had a lasting impact on the tastes of the Maya aristocracy and on local craft production, but Teotihuacán elements played progressively reduced roles within the local highland Maya tradition. By the mid-seventh century, local styles were universal again.

The fluid Maya–Zoque frontier in the western highlands stabilized in the Early Classic period, as the distribution of Maya peoples took on the basic contours that persisted until the conquest.[15] Chiapa de Corzo and other far western centers in the central depression of Chiapas drifted away from the Maya world before the end of the Late Preclassic period. In the western highlands, Early Classic pottery reflects fully Maya styles for the first time. The Tzakol style did not penetrate this far west. Local traditions of pottery production and decoration represent another regional style that evolved independently from a variant of the Chicanel tradition. Populations grew and new hilltop settlements replaced valley communities. Sharp changes in craft styles may mark an influx of new peoples. If so, the Tzeltal and Tzotzil, inhabitants of the region at the time of the conquest, would be the leading candidates. The Tzeltalan branch of the Mayan language family separated from the proto-Cholan stock not long after the time of Christ. A westward expansion of Tzeltalan peoples from the southern lowlands or an adjacent foothill region of the northern highland slopes could account for the advent of Maya pottery styles in the west. The stela complex appeared at Toniná and a few nearby centers in the sixth century.

1. Ball court, Copán (Late Classic period).

2. Temple of the Sun, Palenque (Late Classic period).

3. Main temple complex (North Acropolis), Tikal (Late Classic period).

4. Temple of the Magician, Uxmal (Late Classic period).

5. Temple of the Warriors, Chichén Itzá (Early Postclassic period).

6. Small temple at Tulum, on the east coast of Yucatan (Late Postclassic period).

7. Temple, Iximché (Late Postclassic period).

8. Market at Sololá, near Lake Atitlán, in the Maya highlands.

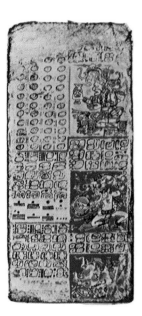

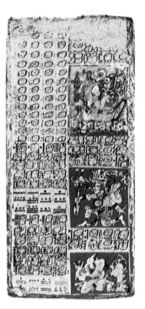

9. Astronomical table, Dresden Codex. These pages tabulate the appearances and disappearances of the planet Venus as morning and evening star and set out the associated supernatural influences on human activity. The codex was painted in Yucatan, probably in the thirteenth century.

10. Palace scene painted on a polychrome vase from the Maya lowlands. The seated ruler at the right gazes into a mirror of polished obsidian held by a retainer. One of the glyphs may be Yaxchilán's emblem glyph. Dumbarton Oaks, Washington, D.C.

By the sixth century the basic patterns of Classic Maya civilization were firmly established. Civic centers with elaborate public architecture reflected powerful aristocracies with well-defined leadership roles. Stelae provided public confirmation of their power and prestige. A few lowland centers, concentrating authority and power to an unusual degree, moved toward positions of regional dominance. In the lowlands, only the west lagged behind in adopting the full pattern of Classic Maya civilization. Regional differences, sharper than before, marked distinct northern and southern lowland areas. Sharper contrasts set the Maya highlands apart. After their early lead in the development of Maya monumental art and writing, central and eastern highland centers ceased to memorialize their leaders with stelae and hieroglyphic texts. Like Teotihuacán's expansion, this retreat may have to do with massive disruptions caused by the eruption of Ilopango. Highland Maya communities did not revert to homogeneous village societies. Civic centers and aristocracies survived, but they no longer relied on the stela complex to celebrate the lives and works of their leaders.

THE LATE CLASSIC PERIOD (A.D. 600–1000)

Remarkable, almost uniform, growth and development took place throughout the Maya lowlands during the first two centuries of the Late Classic period. Settlement systems were transformed into complex hierarchies as more communities grew into civic centers, smaller centers became larger, and the largest centers amassed greater power. Civic centers were hubs of social, religious, economic, and political activity for extensive surrounding regions. A few of the most powerful were able to translate prestige and influence into real political power, fashioning states of regional scope. Northern centers, building on smaller, simpler Early Classic foundations, progressively came to rival their great southern lowland counterparts. Ubiquitous stelae and hieroglyphic texts testify to comparable social and political institutions throughout the lowlands. Aristocrats took on new managerial roles. Occupations became increasingly specialized, particularly in the realm of craft production and building trades. Subsistence, more varied than ever, involved intensive agricultural techniques. Trade networks expanded, embracing wider areas and handling a greater volume and diversity of materials. Populations grew, becoming particularly dense in the immediate environs of powerful civic centers.

Processes leading to intensified regional differences and to increased homogeneity were at work simultaneously in the Late Classic Maya world. Shared patterns went beyond the very basic similarity in the overall way of life that had always existed throughout the Maya world. Settlement systems, civic centers, and the social order they imply had always been generally comparable. Now monumental art, the stela complex, and writing had spread throughout the lowlands. A common basic belief system sustained social and political institutions everywhere. The symbol systems used to express these concepts were so similar from region to region that they almost imply a single Maya religion. Specific shared elements were confined to aristocratic segments of lowland Maya societies. They were mainly products of interaction among the ruling groups of the several regions of the Maya world. Monumental art and hieroglyphic texts document some of the social and political ties that linked the aristocracies of various centers. Similar interchanges took place in the intellectual sphere among priest-scientists devoted to astronomical, astrological, and other esoteric investigations. Between A.D. 687 and 756, for example, inscriptions at all lowland centers reflect the adoption of a new uniform system of tabulating lunar periods.[16] Long-distance exchange, increasingly centralized in the hands of noble merchants and administrators, also promoted communication. The emergence of regional states with expanding spheres of influence was a powerful stimulus intensifying these connections.

On closer inspection, the apparent homogeneity of the Maya world dissolves into a kaleidoscopic picture of regional variations on the same set of basic themes. Late Classic Maya monumental art has stylistic coherence and stands apart from the art of other Mesoamerican peoples. At the same time, regional styles of sculpture and painting are readily apparent. No one could mistake modeled stucco decoration from Palenque for the work of a Copán artist, or confuse the stelae of Quiriguá and Tikal. Styles of public architecture and architectural decoration show the same pattern of diversity within a single basic tradition. The elaborate mosaic facades of Uxmal's temples and palaces do not obscure their relationships to homologous buildings in the south (Color Plate 4). Regional differences in crafts are still more pronounced. Pottery manufacture involved a tremendous array of regional styles, though symbolic scenes and designs on luxury vessels were comparable everywhere.

In the ninth century, a new process intervened. The progressive decline that began at this time utterly transformed the Maya world. Its most devastating effects were felt in the southern lowlands, where every great center of the Classic period presently ceased to function. Related processes were at work in the north, but here an intense episode of foreign influence produced different results. Highland Maya societies participated less directly in these processes, but they, too, felt the effects of external pressures. These pressures, along with disruption of communication and exchange networks resulting from the collapse of lowland centers, produced radically reoriented economic and social systems in the highlands as well.

Demography and Settlement

Maya populations reached their greatest size and widest distribution during the seventh and eighth centuries. The distribution of swampy land, variable farming conditions and communication facilities, the clustering of people around major centers, and other

THE WORLD OF THE ANCIENT MAYA

factors produced considerable variation in population density. All of the best areas for settlement had been occupied for hundreds of years.

The basic unit of settlement everywhere was the domestic plaza complex with three or four or more small thatched wattle-and-daub buildings (Fig. 7) grouped around open courtyards.[17] These one-room dwellings, each on its own low platform, correspond to the single-family dwellings of today's Maya. Each housed a couple with their unmarried children. Plaza complexes grew as sons married and established new households in adjacent buildings around the courtyard. Clusters of several domestic plazas form hamlets in rural areas and neighborhoods within larger centers. Kinship and marriage ties must have been especially strong within these communities of a hundred or a few hundred souls, and they must sometimes have corresponded roughly to lineages and other formal kin groups, though there are no solid grounds for assuming that they always did so. Houses and domestic plazas larger and more elegant than the norm must be the dwellings of family and lineage heads with local political, economic, and religious leadership roles. Minor civic structures—small temples and aristocratic residences—were focal points for several basic communities. They reflect the more formal minor offices of administrative systems. Even in outlying areas, these minor civic centers were usually subordinate to larger ones. At the apexes of these hierarchies were such great regional capitals as Tikal.

Calculating actual population sizes and densities is very inexact at best. Even gross estimates, though, help us to understand Maya society and economies. Estimating ancient Maya populations requires an accurate count of houses in the area under study; precise dating to determine how many were occupied simultaneously during the period of interest; and a reliable indication of the number of people who lived in each house. The third factor is the most difficult, for even the most intense archaeological investigations seldom produce evidence for such precise reconstruction. The usual solution is to resort to census information gathered in Maya communities early in the colonial period. Estimating the first two factors accurately presupposes very extensive archaeological investigation. Domestic buildings are the least conspicuous Maya structures, and only an intensive search will produce a reliable count. Only excavation can distinguish with certainty between residences and small structures with other functions. Determining contemporaneity is even more difficult, requiring a very fine-scale chronological framework and good samples of datable objects (usually pottery) from each house. Only specially designed investigations will provide these data. In the Maya world, where impressive public buildings consume so much attention, such projects are rare.

The best data for population estimates come from Tikal, one of the largest and most thoroughly investigated Maya centers.[18] Here only a sample of the many thousands of structures could be excavated. Unlike most lowland centers, where settlement thins out gradually away from the civic nucleus, house density at Tikal drops off sharply beyond the bank-and-ditch constructions that define the basic residential community on the north and south. Excavation of more than 200 small buildings showed that 80 percent were houses dating to the eighth and early ninth centuries, the period of Tikal's greatest florescence. As most houses had been remodeled, they appear to have been occupied continuously during most of this time span. Some were surely occupied for shorter spans, but inconspicuous and destroyed houses missed by the survey should compensate in part for this error. When these figures are extrapolated to the center as a whole and multiplied by 5 (the average number of people per family in the early colonial period), the result indicates about 10,000 people in central Tikal alone. This figure makes no allowance for the occupants of palaces and other large buildings. Estimates of the population of the community within the bank and ditch run as high as 50,000. "Greater Tikal," including the surrounding region under the center's direct influence, must have embraced many thousands more who came often to the civic center for markets, social events, and ceremonies. However imprecise these estimates may be, they eliminate the possibility that Tikal was a sparsely populated "ceremonial" center.

Tikal, if not the largest of all Maya centers, was certainly among the most populous. Even at its peak it remained relatively open, without the extreme density of structures and people usually associated with such urban centers as Teotihuacán. Still, at Tikal and the other great Maya centers, daily life and social relations must have had something of an urban flavor. Certainly Maya centers performed all the civic functions of central places.

Subsistence

The concentration of even 10,000 people at a single civic center indicates that subsistence was diverse and involved intensive agriculture.[19] Basic milpa farming was the cornerstone of Classic Maya subsistence and maize was a mainstay of the diet, but this could not have been the only farming system. Estimations of the productivity of prehistoric maize farming are far less reliable even than those of populations. Changes in climate, soils, and the plants themselves make estimates of prehistoric yields of maize per hectare sheer guesswork. It is also difficult to determine the amount of land each community used for maize farming. Today Maya farmers often cultivate milpas 50 kilometers or more from their homes. It is impossible to know how far Classic Maya farmers were willing to travel to reach their fields. Allowing for the length of fallow cycles and the percentage of farmland given over to other crops is equally difficult. Even with maximum estimates for every factor, potential maize production would still be too low to support the populations of the great centers.

Scanty direct evidence in the form of occasionally preserved plant remains and indirect indications provided by historical documents and ethnographic studies do suggest some of the subsistence strategies that complemented milpa farming. In the first place, maize was never the sole crop. Milpas typically include beans, squashes, chiles, and other plants. Garden plots and wild plants added a tremendous variety of fruits, vegetables, and spices as well as medicinal herbs. Most of these plant products are not potential staples, but a few are. Manioc, sweet potatoes, and other root crops known to later Maya peoples produce higher yields than maize, though they are low in protein. Animal food was a relatively minor component of the Maya diet, but along the rivers and coasts fish and shellfish were quite important. In some areas the Maya may even have dug special canals to serve as fisheries. Where marine foods provided a ready source of protein, root crops could have been major foods. Manioc is mainly a lowland crop, but it can be grown as high as 2,000 meters. In the eastern lowlands manioc was certainly eaten, and probably cultivated, early in the Preclassic period.

The ramón or breadnut tree, growing wild today in many parts of the Maya lowlands, is another potential prehistoric staple. Recent Maya peoples have used ramón trees as a source of emergency food in times of famine. Ramón nuts, high in vegetable protein and fat, can be processed, like maize, into a nutritious flour. Ramón nuts store quite well. Experiments conducted in prehistoric *chultunes,* bell-shaped underground chambers found in many Maya centers, show that ramón nuts stored in them will last up to eighteen months, while maize rots in a few weeks. Ramón trees can produce much more food than maize (more than 1,100 kilograms per hectare), and with much less effort. The trees require little or no cultivation. They are more reliable than maize, and will produce some nuts even in very dry years. Ramón trees continue to produce nuts for decades, so that an orchard might provide a continuous source of food for a century or more without a single fallow period. Ramón trees need not even have been planted. Allowed to proliferate in fields, around houses, or in open areas within centers, they could provide a significant dietary supplement. Ramón trees are particularly common in the heart of the southern lowlands, where they are densest near the ruins of ancient Maya centers. *Chicosapote* fruit trees show the same distribution. In both instances, these stands of wild trees may reflect prehistoric orchards. These trees, along with the *balché* (whose bark is the source of a fermented ceremonial beverage), the *pom* (whose resin is used for incense), and several other important fruit- and fiber-producing trees, cluster densely around the ruins of Cobá, in northeastern Yucatan. Here they are associated specifically with high-status residential areas, suggesting that aristocrats owned, or at least controlled, most trees of economic value and almost all of those with ceremonial importance.

Agricultural techniques were by no means limited to the simplest form of milpa farming. Low-lying swampy areas too wet for ordinary rainy-season cultivation can be planted for an extra dry-season crop. In the lowlands as well as the highlands there are extensive remains of prehistoric terrace systems that converted otherwise useless slopes into a patchwork of level farm plots. In many lowland regions prehistoric land reclamation projects transformed swamps to full-time productive land. These raised-field systems involved the piling up of earth or muck to raise portions of the swamp near or above the water table. The

49. Pottery "mask," La Sierra. The sensitively modeled face with closed eyes, perhaps part of the decoration on an incense burner, represents the portrait of a dead person or possibly a deity of death.

elevated areas, rich in rotting vegetation, formed giant soggy compost heaps that could be farmed almost continuously with enormous productivity. Canals within the raised-field systems must have promoted fish cultivation, facilitated transport and communication, and provided a ready source of drinking water for the dry season.

Some large centers may have imported food from less densely populated regions. Coastal groups probably exported their nearly inexhaustible supply of fish and shellfish. The widespread exchange networks that crisscrossed the Maya world might have distributed food as routinely as imperishable commodities. Certainly they must have functioned sporadically to transfer local surpluses to areas where crop failure or population growth produced food shortages.

It is very unlikely that the population of the Maya world at large ever approached the limits of its carrying capacity. It is possible, though, that subsistence systems were near their limits in the most densely populated zones. Faced with endemic strain on normal subsistence strategies and increasingly frequent food shortages, some aristocracies may have chosen counterproductive responses. Shortened fallow cycles would provide immediate relief at the expense of long-term environmental degradation as soil nutrients were exhausted. Increased labor input could have raised productivity, but only at the cost of greater strain between peasants and rulers. Even if they avoided these traps, the Late Classic leaders of some lowland centers must have presided over societies with very fragile subsistence economies. The largest centers were quite vulnerable to the vagaries of weather and a host of other disruptive elements. Food shortages probably contributed to the widespread decline that swept across the Maya world at the end of the Late Classic period.

Economy, Society, Politics

The economies of the great civic centers and of the regions they dominated must have been as intricate as the subsistence systems.[20] The quality and standardization of craft products, especially pottery, suggest a well-developed pattern of economic specialization. (Fig. 49, Color Plate 10). Though the evidence is less conclusive, larger centers could probably also boast specialists in stone flaking and grinding, lapidaries, jewelers, weavers, tailors, tanners, feather workers, wood carvers, painters, sculptors in stone and plaster, carpenters, masons, and other building-trade specialists. Some neighborhoods within centers or outlying satellite communities probably housed concentrations of specialists in the same activity, resulting in a form of community specialization. Most people in every region were full-time farmers, and many craft specialists must have maintained some involvement in farming. Makers of luxury goods and other craftsmen most closely involved in the activities of the aristocracy sometimes maintained large dwellings in or near the public sectors of the great civic centers, though, suggesting an elevated socioeconomic status.

If craft specialization typified an emergent "middle class," other specialist roles were the province of the upper levels of Maya society.[21]

Aristocrats monopolized positions of great authority and power and those requiring extensive mastery of esoteric knowledge. Political, religious, and economic organization were inextricably intertwined, with aristocracies providing the key personnel. The highest-ranking members of the most noble families filled the top positions in the rulership and priesthood. Cadet lines and lesser aristocratic families produced lower-ranking priests and religious functionaries, scribes, long-distance merchants, architect-engineers, minor military officers, and a variety of political and economic administrators. The lower echelons of the aristocracy probably included many part-time farmers and craftsmen as well.

It is unlikely that these social groups were rigidly bounded classes. Relative status and power within the aristocracy fluctuated as old noble families lost influence and new ruling dynasties emerged. Mechanisms of social mobility probably permitted advancement from group to group as well. Though social gaps widened throughout the Classic period, with greater differences between ordinary farmers and high-ranking nobles, there is no reason to suppose that the system was ever closed or inflexible. Institutions like the modern *cargo* system could have been important in social integration.[22]

Cargo systems consist of sets of ranked religious and civil offices (cargos) held by adult males. Today national governments dominate the political life of most Maya communities, so religious cargos are more prominent. In Zinacantan, a Tzotzil community in the western highlands, the cargo system is a central feature of social and religious life. A cargo holder must leave his home in the countryside to live in the ceremonial center of the community for his period of service. He must pay for his own subsistence, for hospitality, and for ceremonial materials. Full participation in the system—a year at each of the four levels of the hierarchy—is very expensive indeed in lost income and direct expenses. Not every Zinacanteco can afford (or wishes) to conform to the ideal. For those who do, the rewards in personal fulfillment and social prestige are great. A cargo holder enjoys great prestige and much attention during his term of office, and a man who completes all four cargos becomes an honored community elder. In Zinacantan the cargo system provides a successful organizational framework for the religious life of a community of more than 8,000 dispersed throughout an area of more than 100 square kilometers. The cargo system of neighboring Chamula successfully serves more than 40,000 people. These systems are not simply remnants of ancient institutions. They are also, in part, responses to contemporary social conditions. Zinacantan's cargo system is much more elaborate today than it was a century ago and modern Zinacantecos are much more eager to participate than were their great-grandfathers. Today's cargo systems owe something to Spanish religious institutions, but they do have roots in precolumbian Mesoamerica as well.

Comparable prehispanic institutions could have functioned to distribute minor offices far down the social scale and to allow people who normally lived in outlying areas to participate directly in the political and religious affairs of civic centers. Families whose members performed these offices exceptionally well, or who used periodic sojourns close to centers of status and power to forge lasting alliances, might in the course of a few generations rise into the lower echelons of the aristocracy.

Success in commerce and exceptional military achievement were other potential routes to permanently elevated status. Both mechanisms operated among the Quiché at the time of the conquest. The Aztecs had institutionalized such mechanisms of social advancement. Several important political offices were reserved for commoners elevated to noble rank because of notable performance on the field of battle.

At the apex of the social order, all public activities merged in the person of the ruler. Stelae and other monuments at the great civic centers depict rulers in religious, political, and military roles. There is no question of their economic ascendancy. The distribution of minor palaces and temples defines administrative subdivisions within the great centers, reflecting an internal hierarchy of political and religious offices. To judge by the settlement patterns of surrounding territories, regional bureaucracies were equally complex. Several levels of subordinate centers with public buildings served as hubs of civic affairs for outlying villages, hamlets, and farmsteads. Whatever the extent of nonaristocratic participation at lower levels, the direction of political and religious activity was firmly in the hands of the aristocracy. Long-distance commerce, largely concerned with procuring luxury goods, was another essential facet of public activity. Nobles organized and controlled this trade.

Ultimately the aristocracy dominated the entire economy. Merchants may have delivered imported food and utilitarian goods, along with luxury imports, to the ruler, who then saw to their distribution. Much craft production was directly geared to consumption by the aristocracy and many other specialists were concerned with public activity. Nobles and craft specialists alike depended on farmers, and rulers must have collected and distributed food surpluses. On occasion, political leaders must have extended their influence into the sphere of agricultural and craft production, particularly in the Late Classic period. With increased specialization, administrative intervention was probably sometimes necessary to avoid the collapse of fragile economic systems in the face of crop failure or problems with the supply of raw materials. There is no reason to suppose that economic transactions among social groups were like those of a monetary economy. It is quite conceivable that officials routinely collected the bulk of all production—food, utilitarian craft goods, and luxury items alike—for redistribution. Undoubtedly farmers and craftsmen exchanged some of their surplus products directly at local and regional markets, but here, too, the aristocracy had a supervisory role, at least in maintaining order. Perhaps, as in Aztec markets, there were also officials to regulate weights and measures and standardize exchange rates. Classic Maya economies involved a balance of market and redistributive features.

Religion, too, was intimately bound up with politics. Rulers of the great civic centers were political officials, but they were also religious figures. Monumental art, above all the stela complex, provided public statements of the divine sanction that was the basis of political sovereignty. Elite ancestor cults were a part of the same belief system. Divine ancestors might replace more abstract deities as the "protector" figures depicted with current rulers (Figs. 43, 45). Along with high priestly roles, rulers had godlike personal qualities stemming from divine ancestry.

Religion influenced political activity in other ways, as well. Maya belief systems universally feature a unitary conception of time and the universe in which supernatural elements have direct roles in current events. Because time determines these influences, they are cyclical and predictable. Astrology was the chief science, embracing religion, astronomy, history, and prophecy. The calendar system lent meaning and order to every facet of life.

At the local level, Maya societies were highly integrated, with the key personnel of political, religious, and economic systems recruited from the upper echelons of the social hierarchy. Connections among aristocracies also produced the most important links among communities and regions. Tikal and a few other very powerful civic centers dominated political systems of regional scope, but there was never a single state that embraced all of the Maya world. Economic networks that distributed luxury goods and exotic raw materials are only the most obvious linkages that connected the regions of the Maya world in a larger cultural system. The single system of hieroglyphic writing and coordinated calendar in use at all civic centers indicates continuing communication throughout the lowlands during the Classic period.

Farmers and craftsmen must occasionally have undertaken to procure special foods or raw materials from distant regions on an ad hoc basis. In general, though, most ties between communities, especially over long distances, involved nobles. Communication among aristocracies, essential to the continued functioning of many aspects of Maya civilization, was in many ways institutionalized. Enclaves of Mayas living away from their home communities in other parts of the Maya world, and even beyond, must have been as common in the Classic period as in later times. Some were probably established quite purposefully by ruling groups; others were not. These enclaves—whether of nobles forging alliances, merchants procuring exotic goods, craftsmen tapping distant markets, or farmers taking advantage of differing environmental conditions—contributed to communication at every level, from local to interregional. Kinship ties and political alliances between noble families of different civic centers played key roles in the emergence of regional political systems, and they often linked the great centers of distant regions. These ties were especially intense within the southern lowlands, where monuments and burial offerings frequently record intermarriage, formal or ceremonial visits, and other sorts of interchange among aristocracies.

A polychrome vessel found in the richly stocked eighth century

tomb of a noblewoman at Altar de Sacrificios (Fig. 50) provides vivid documentation.[23] The painted scene shows a ceremony, part of the lady's funeral rites. The hieroglyphic text identifies among the participants a noble from Tikal and another who is either the great Bird Jaguar, ruler of Yaxchilán, or a personal emissary. Other offerings in the tomb included pottery imported from the Yaxchilán–Piedras Negras zone, from the Tikal area, and from the Chamá region of the highlands.

The cultural decline that swept across the Maya world in the ninth and tenth centuries also reflects the close connections among Maya centers and the degree to which aristocracies depended on them.[24] In

THE WORLD OF THE ANCIENT MAYA

50. Design on a polychrome vase, Altar de Sacrificios. This scene, painted in black and several shades of red over a creamy brown slip, records the funeral ceremonies of a middle-aged noblewoman. The cylindrical vase was found with the body of a younger woman, evidently a relative, buried with her. The younger woman appears in the scene seated at the lower left in the act of committing suicide with a large flint knife like one actually buried with her. The glyphs identify the man seated above her as a noble from Tikal and the man dancing before them in jaguar-skin trousers, mittens, and headdress as Bird Jaguar, the great eighth-century ruler of Yaxchilán. The three male figures to their right are other relatives or supernatural celebrants. Fifteen imported vessels were found in the tomb: those from the middle Usumacinta area were presumably Bird Jaguar's offerings; those from the central lowlands must have been brought by the noble from Tikal; and those from the Chamá region may have been the gifts of the lower seated figure in the fanged mask (whose glyphic text includes an unknown emblem glyph). The participation of these nobles in the funeral rites testifies to the importance of networks of kinship ties linking aristocrats from widely separated centers. A date in the text places the funeral in the year A.D. 754. Many Late Classic polychrome vessels were made expressly as mortuary offerings, and they often depict funerary rites and underworld deities. (Adapted from R. E. W. Adams 1971:frontis. and 1977a:Figs. 1–3; G. Stuart 1975:774–76.)

the southern lowlands, foreign interference in communication networks touched off a process of decline that eventually brought about the collapse of every major civic center. To the north and south, where contacts among aristocracies were less intense and less crucial to the maintenance of the social order, processes of decline were less drastic.

Regionalism

Comparable civic centers, widespread styles of monumental art and craft production, the stela complex, hieroglyphic writing, and the Long Count calendar give Classic Maya civilization an air of overall uniformity. Beneath this veneer is a wealth of regional diversity. The traditional tripartite subdivision of the Maya world into northern lowlands, southern lowlands, and highlands reflects real spheres of interaction. Similarities are certainly greatest within each of these areas, but none is uniform. Many lines of communication crossed areal "boundaries" to link distant civic centers.

THE SOUTHERN LOWLANDS Continuous intense contacts among southern lowland centers never obscured the fundamental differences that continued to characterize each region.

The central zone Early investigations in the heart of the southern lowlands laid the foundations of Maya archaeology. Styles, institutions, and organizational features of Tikal and Uaxactún have often been treated as the basic cultural patterns of the southern lowlands, and even of "true" Classic Maya civilization in general.

Late Classic Tepeu pottery (Fig. 49, Color Plate 10), first defined at Uaxactún, represents a widespread regional style shared throughout the southern lowlands and beyond.[25] Its spread may reflect Tikal's enormous social, political, and economic influence. Tepeu pottery is by no means uniform, though. There is no "standard" Late Classic Maya pottery style.

Tikal (Map 10, Fig. 51), by far the largest center in the southern lowlands, was among the most powerful of all Late Classic Maya civic centers.[26] Civic activity at Tikal in the Late Classic period, and for a millennium before that, revolved around the Great Plaza (Figs. 52–57, Color Plate 3), flanked by the center's mightiest temples and most elegant palaces.

To the east, Temple I, also called the Temple of the Giant Jaguar, soars to a height of more than 45 meters (Fig. 52). Nine superimposed terraces form the steep pyramid that supports the temple, reached by a single majestic stair. The intricate insets and moldings of the terraces form a field for the play of light and shadow. The temple building has three high, narrow, vaulted rooms with carved wooden lintels spanning the inner doorways. The innermost lintel depicts a huge jaguar, perhaps a divine protector of the royal family, towering over the figure of a Maya noble. The hollow roof comb atop the temple had an ornamental function, leading the eye upward from the line of the stair and providing an additional field for decoration. The face of the roof comb, now badly eroded, once portrayed a huge seated lord flanked by scrolls, brightly painted in cream, red, and perhaps blue and green. The temple itself, like others at Tikal, may also have been painted red. A small open-ended ball court, without markers, stands at the foot of the temple (Fig. 53).

Temple II (the Temple of the Masks), lower but equally well proportioned, faces the Temple of the Giant Jaguar across the Great Plaza (Fig. 54). Grotesque masks, now mostly destroyed, once flanked the central stairway. The temple building, like its opposite number, has three vaulted rooms, with a carved wooden lintel over the middle door. It, too, carries a decorative roof comb, this time depicting a huge

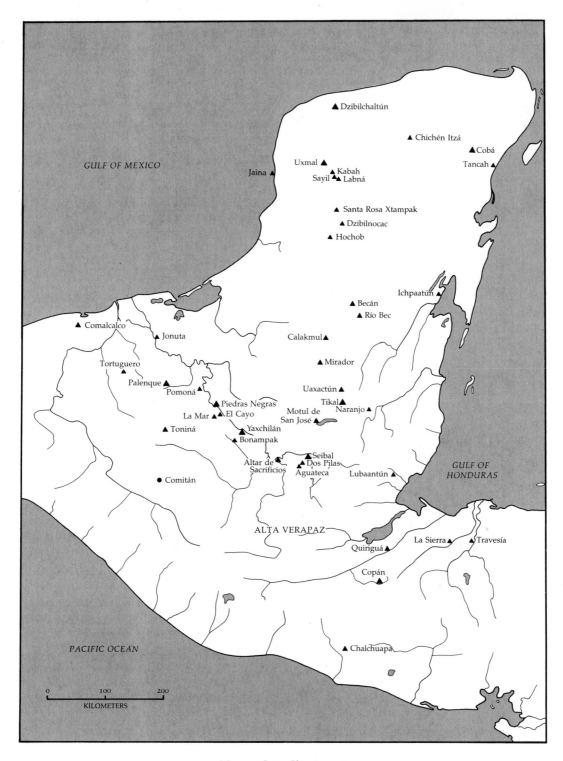

Map 10. Late Classic centers

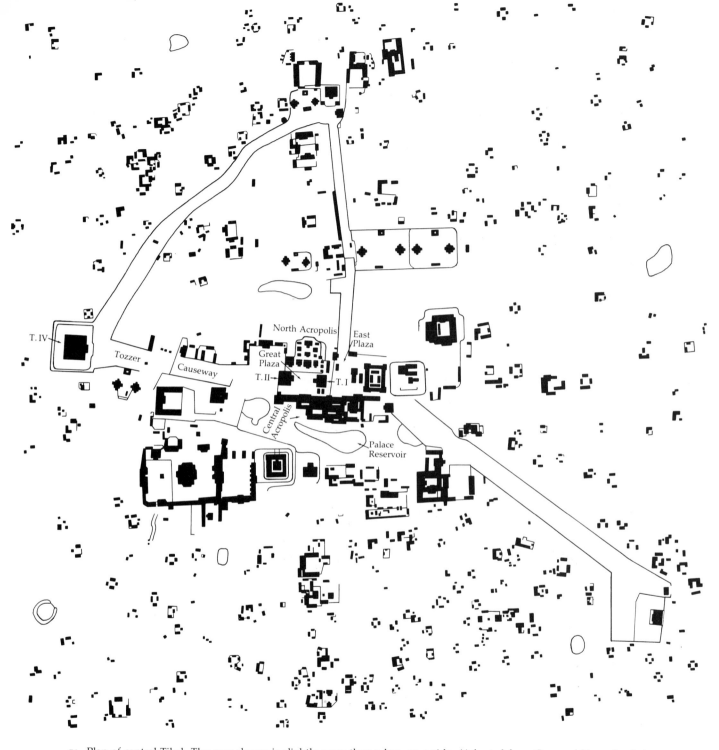

51. Plan of central Tikal. The area shown is slightly more than 2 km. on a side. (Adapted from Carr and Hazard 1961.)

face. On special occasions priests must have come out of the temple onto the great stone platform before it to review activities in the plaza below or to perform ceremonies in full view of the crowd.

The North Acropolis, a massive complex of temple buildings, closes off the north side of the Great Plaza (Fig. 55, Color Plate 3). Stelae and altars set before the temples and along the north edge of the plaza record the exploits of Tikal's great rulers. Many of them were entombed within the temple buildings.

The Central Acropolis (Fig. 56), an immense building group south of the Great Plaza, is Tikal's greatest palace complex. At its peak it consisted of a series of long, multiroomed buildings up to three stories

53. Ball court, Great Plaza, Tikal. The foot of Temple I appears in the background, just beyond the open end of the ball court.

high, grouped around six courts connected by stairways and passages (Fig. 57). The buildings had elaborate carved decoration and room interiors were fitted out with domestic features: dowels from which to hang curtains across doorways, benches, niches, and even thronelike seats with stone armrests. Tikal's aristocrats certainly used these buildings, though probably not for domestic purposes alone. The palaces were also suitable for a variety of administrative activities: royal audiences, meetings among nobles, and many everyday bureaucratic functions. In fact, they have no obvious kitchen areas, so food was probably prepared elsewhere and brought in by retainers. A small thatched kitchen building stands just outside the palace complex.

More temples, another ball court, and several other public buildings occupy the adjacent East Plaza (Fig. 58). A large quadrangle defined by a series of long, low buildings may have been Tikal's marketplace, for here the rooms have none of the benches or other domestic fixtures found in the palaces. Nearby is a small building fitted inside with a

water channel and a fire pit. Here Maya nobles reclined on wide benches as they enjoyed the steam baths prescribed in connection with curing and other ritual activity. Additional public building complexes cluster around the Great Plaza area on every side. Nearby are four of Tikal's ten reservoirs, natural ravines or quarries sealed and converted to water storage to ensure a steady supply of water through the dry season.

The Great Plaza, the hub of public life, embodied Tikal's greatness. The aristocrats who lived and worked in the palaces were at the center of political, economic, religious, and social life. Ceremonies in the

55. North Acropolis, Tikal. Stelae and altars are set along the northern edge of the Great Plaza, before the temples of the North Acropolis and before Temple I (*right foreground*).

nearby temples confirmed their fitness to reign. Reliefs and hieroglyphic texts on stelae, altars, lintels, and elsewhere recorded their great achievements, and those of their ancestors (Fig. 59).

Past rulers died, but they did not depart. Entombed in the temple complexes, they remained to protect and guide their descendants. The Late Classic buildings were but the latest in a long series of superimposed remodelings. Most of the temples were not just scenes of ceremonies: they were funerary memorials to the illustrious dead. The Great Plaza complex as a whole was a monument to Tikal's aristocracy and its ancestor cult.

Public activity was not entirely centralized in the Great Plaza. Broad raised causeways, paved with plaster and flanked by parapets, connected this civic core with other complexes of public buildings—temples, palaces, ball courts. To the west, the Tozzer causeway leads to Temple IV (Fig. 60). With its roof comb reaching a height of 65 meters, Temple IV is among the tallest standing precolumbian struc-

THE WORLD OF THE ANCIENT MAYA

56. Central Acropolis, Tikal.

tures in the Americas. More than 190,000 cubic meters of building
material went into its construction. Farther from the Great Plaza, temples and palaces become smaller and less elaborate and stelae and
altars less frequent. Many outlying building clusters represent lower
levels of the administrative hierarchy: subordinate civic units that
served the immediate needs of the people who lived in the dwellings
clustered around them. Ordinary farmers occupied most of the houses,
but some residential groups contained workshops of potters, stone
knappers, woodworkers, masons, sculptors, and other craft specialists. One compound evidently housed dental workers—cosmeticians
patronized by nobles who wished to improve their front teeth with
inlays of jade. As one moves farther from central Tikal, the density of public and domestic buildings alike thins out gradually. Beyond the ditch-and-bank constructions that define the primary settlement to the north and south, building density drops off sharply. The
basic Tikal community covers an area of about 123 square kilometers.

57. Interior court and multistory palace, Central Acropolis, Tikal.

At its Late Classic peak, Tikal housed a population in the tens of thousands.

Tikal dominated a political and economic sphere that embraced a large territory, and its indirect influence was enormously widespread.[27] Uaxactún, a smaller civic center less than 20 kilometers to the north, is well within what would otherwise be reconstructed as Tikal's immediate sustaining area.[28] The two centers may have been peers in the Late Preclassic period, but Tikal gradually gained the upper hand. Uaxactún's nobles began to mention Tikal in their monumental texts in the early Classic period. In the Late Classic period, Uaxactún occupied a distinctly subordinate status. It was one of many dependent centers dominated by Tikal. Tikal evidently chose to control part of its immediate sustaining area as it did outlying areas—through a separate but subsidiary administrative center.

Tikal controlled the region to the east through Naranjo, which in turn dominated subsidiary communities in its region. Hieroglyphic

THE WORLD OF THE ANCIENT MAYA

texts at Naranjo indicate that several local rulers married noblewomen from Tikal. Such marriage alliances between dominant and subordinate centers, probably quite common, enhanced the status of local ruling lines and cemented the positions of minor centers within the orbits of regional capitals. Comparable ties presumably connected Tikal with communities to the north. Mirador and neighboring centers may not have been formal dependencies, but styles of architecture, monumental art, and pottery do indicate influence radiating from Tikal.

Calakmul, though, with more than one hundred stelae, probably dominated its own political sphere. The eastern fringe of the lowlands was certainly beyond Tikal's immediate political and economic control. Lubaantún and other independent civic centers controlled modest territories. Here again, though, architecture, sculpture, and pottery do suggest links with Tikal and its dominions.

Tikal's contacts, often involving political marriage alliances, extended well beyond the heart of the southern lowlands. Stylistic and textual evidence indicates especially close relationships with Rio Pasión centers, to the south and west. Tikal may even have brought part of this region within its political orbit for a short time early in the Late

58. Mexican-style building, East Plaza, Tikal. The talud-tablero design of the platform recalls the architecture of Xochicalco and other Mexican civic centers (see Fig. 97). This structure suggests that Tikal's ties with central Mexico did not end with the decline of Teotihuacán.

59. Stela 9, Tikal. This monument, carved in A.D. 475 to honor the early ruler whose portrait it bears, still stood along the north edge of the Great Plaza during the Late Classic period.

Classic period. Yet farther afield, hieroglyphic texts at Yaxchilán suggest that Tikal nobles played important roles in local political affairs on at least one occasion. Again, they probably forged marriage alliances with the local aristocracy. Tikal's fame extended northwest to Palenque and southeast to Copán. These regional capitals all mentioned one another in hieroglyphic texts. The eighth-century rulers of Copán even shared names and titles with a Tikal dynasty.

Río Pasión Late Classic styles of architecture, monumental art, and luxury pottery indicate a continuation of traditionally close relationships between Pasión centers and the Tikal region.[29] Seventh-century texts at Dos Pilas refer again and again to the deeds of a Tikal noble, including what seems to be the real or symbolic capture of a local lord. Dos Pilas, if not the entire region, was surely subject to Tikal at this point. Tikal's influence on the Pasión region evidently waned thereafter. In the eighth century Dos Pilas, along with Seibal, Aguateca, and other western centers, recorded mainly local events, with only occasional references to Tikal.

The new independence of Pasión centers may reflect a general decline of large political spheres. During this time many modest civic centers grew larger and more powerful, and many smaller communities took on the civic functions of minor centers and began to erect their own monuments. Altar de Sacrificios, never a major center, maintained alliances with Yaxchilán, down the Usumacinta, as well as with other Pasión centers and Tikal. Bird Jaguar, the great eighth-century ruler of Yaxchilán, evidently participated in person in the funeral rites of a noble Altar lady along with nobles from Tikal and from the Alta Verapaz region of the highlands (Fig. 49). Seibal enjoyed its greatest growth and influence in the ninth century, under heavy foreign influence. Monumental art and architecture of this period point to strong northern connections. As processes of decline were setting in at other centers, Seibal in effect became a regional capital. Texts of this late period at Seibal, Tikal, and Calakmul mention for the first time Motul de San José. Motul was another formerly minor center that rose briefly to a position of regional importance late in the Classic period.

The southeastern frontier The southeastern region of the Maya lowlands had its own very distinctive styles of architecture, sculpture, and polychrome pottery painting. Copán, on the banks of a small river flowing through hilly forested uplands on the fringe of the Maya highlands, was the greatest civic center in the southeast.[30] It was the nucleus of a sphere of influence comparable to Tikal's.

Copán was not isolated from the great centers to the north and west. The Sky dynasty, which ruled the southeast in the eighth century, evidently shared one component of its ancestry with a leading family at Tikal. The Copán emblem glyph appears occasionally in Tikal texts, and one Copán stela mentions Tikal along with Calakmul and Palenque. These alliances notwithstanding, Copán was not subordinate to Tikal or any other center.

Public activity at Copán revolved around a compact central zone of

THE WORLD OF THE ANCIENT MAYA

60. Temple IV, Tikal. The roof comb stands 65 m. above the adjacent plaza, making Temple IV one of the tallest standing precolumbian buildings in the Americas. The terraced platform is unrestored.

temples and palaces, thick with monuments to local leaders. Copán's civic core is less extensive than Tikal's and individual buildings are smaller, but the two precincts were functionally equivalent—each the heart of a powerful regional capital. Copán's buildings are relatively simple in design, but most are elaborately decorated with reliefs in stone and stucco (Figs. 61–64). As at Tikal, sculpture and hieroglyphic texts associated with public buildings record the achievements of great rulers, but their style is quite distinctive. Architectural decoration and free-standing monuments alike feature very deep relief (Figs. 65–67). Some stelae almost have the character of sculpture in the round rather

61. Structure 11, Copán.

than relief. Costumes and other pictorial details are very elaborate. Even hieroglyphs are ornate, often integrated with the design of the monuments (Fig. 68). The overall effect is almost florid. The central ball court (Fig. 69, Color plate 1), unlike those at Tikal, has temples atop the playing walls, macaw-head markers along both sides, and sculptured plaques set flush in the floor along the center line.

The "suburbs" of Copán embrace most of the valley. Several imposing building complexes not far from central Copán appear to combine residential and civic functions. Smaller residences are the norm in outlying areas. A causeway runs from the main civic precinct into an area of dense building groups just upstream, branching to reach the most important complexes. This sector was evidently a principal aristocratic residential zone, for most of the buildings were large houses. One branch causeway leads to a cluster of five building complexes that must have housed one of Copán's most prominent families and its retainers. The largest platform facing the main plaza supported a masonry palace or temple with three vaulted rooms fitted with stone benches. A hieroglyphic text on the bench in the central room points to political functions, while the decoration suggests religious overtones. The room

THE WORLD OF THE ANCIENT MAYA

62. Architectural decoration, Structure 11, Copán. This figure, popularly called the Storm God, holds a torch or scepter featuring the day sign Ik ("wind").

63. Altar of Venus, Copán. The head of the deity appears between the halves of the glyph for Venus (see Fig. 19e, Color Plate 9).

64. Old Man of Copán. This tenoned head once adorned the corner of the Temple of the Inscriptions, atop Structure 11.

interiors were painted in conformity with color-direction symbolism: red for the east room, black for the west, and green for the central chamber, overlooking the plaza. High-ranking family members lived in the large residences that occupied other platforms flanking the plaza. The lineage's noble dead were buried with their luxury pottery and jade jewelry in stone tombs beneath the platforms or under the plaza floor. The four subsidiary building groups housed lower-ranking family members and retainers.

Below the great center, the Río Copán flows west and north into the Motagua. Quiriguá, 50 kilometers away on the Río Motagua, was

65. Stela A, Great Plaza, Copán. The small stone chamber below the monument was the repository for pottery and other offerings associated with its dedication in A.D. 731.

THE WORLD OF THE ANCIENT MAYA

ideally situated to control the distribution of obsidian and jade from the west.[31] Domination of Quiriguá and its subsidiary sphere extended Copán's effective control over a large zone to the north. Sculpture and architecture reflect close ties between the two centers from a very early period, and the Sky dynasty ruled Quiriguá early in the Late Classic period. Cauac Sky, who came to power at Quiriguá in A.D. 724, was probably from Copán, and his early construction projects included a copy of Copán's ball court. Not long after his accession a mysterious

66. Stela H, Great Plaza, Copán. This stela commemorates the exploits of a noblewoman of Copán.

67. Altar, Great Plaza, Copán. This grotesque beast stands before Stela D.

68. Stela B, Great Plaza, Copán. The ornate glyphs on the reverse of this monument are integrated with the overall design.

political event resulted in a rupture of relations with the old capital. Quiriguá enjoyed a building boom and general growth during the half century of Cauac Sky's rule. New monuments, notably the enormous stelae and zoomorphs (Fig. 70), mark the evolution of a distinctive Quiriguá style. The rupture of A.D. 737 may have taken Quiriguá out of Copán's economic sphere as well, for Late Classic pottery shows few links with the luxury styles of Copán. Even distinctive Copador vessels, with their glittering red hematite paint, so widely distributed south of Copán, are quite rare at Quiriguá.

East of the Copán valley, civic centers subordinate to the regional capital dot the upper Río Copán and cross the watershed into the Chamelecón drainage.[32] Copán's larger sphere of influence stretched as far as the Sula plain. This was a frontier zone in which Maya and Central American peoples mingled to produce an intricate mosaic of contrasting cultural patterns, and probably peoples of hybrid cultural identity as well.

La Sierra, on the western fringe of the frontier zone, dominated its valley and probably a good part of the surrounding region. La Sierra's most imposing public buildings feature dressed stone architecture in the Maya tradition (Fig. 71), but the center does not have a typical Maya community layout. Small domestic structures cluster around a civic core with temples, large residences (Fig. 72), and a ball court, but none of the buildings are grouped into formal plaza arrangements (Fig. 73). Irregular groupings of buildings have the appearance of having grown by accretion. The stela complex did not spread this far east. La Sierra's pottery, utilitarian and luxury vessels alike, places it firmly within Copán's orbit of influence, though Copador ware is rare. The variant Maya style of the Sula plain forms another important component of La Sierra's polychrome pottery tradition (Fig. 74). This Ulua polychrome style also appears at Copán, in smaller quantities. La Sierra imported vessels

THE WORLD OF THE ANCIENT MAYA

from lowland regions to the north and exported a few of its own polychromes, at least to one of Quiriguá's dependencies. La Sierra seems to combine rural aspects of Copán's southeastern regional patterns with some facets of the easternmost Sula Valley variants of Classic Maya styles. It may have been a multicultural cosmopolitan community, with enclaves of foreign Mayas or even non-Maya people.

East of La Sierra, in the Sula plain, the cultural situation was even more complex. Some centers, such as Travesía, have dressed-stone public architecture and pottery within the Maya tradition. Others, with quite different styles, evidently represent non-Maya groups. Still others represent multicultural or hybrid communities.

Luxury pottery styles indicate that Copán, and to a lesser extent Sula Valley centers, maintained connections with Chalchuapa and neighboring communities in the southeastern Maya highlands. The distinctive Copador type of luxury pottery is particularly common in the south. Here, too, the stela complex and hieroglyphic texts are absent.

Río Usumacinta Usumacinta centers reflect another set of variations on the themes of Classic Maya civilization.[33] Late Classic pottery at Piedras Negras, Yaxchilán, and nearby centers reflects a distinctive regional variant of the Tepeu style. Mexican elements and military themes, particularly popular in monumental art, probably reflect proximity to the western frontier and its expansion-minded Mexican and Maya-Mexican peoples. Architectural features also point to downstream connections.

Yaxchilán, an enormous center on the Río Usumacinta, was the capital of the region's most powerful state during the Late Classic period. Despite its importance, no extensive archaeological investigations have been undertaken at Yaxchilán, so almost all available data

71. Stairway, La Sierra. This stair, constructed of carefully dressed and fitted blocks, ascends the largest temple platform in the civic core. It appears here in the process of excavation.

72. House, La Sierra: interior of one of the two rooms of a substantial residence with thick walls built of cobbles set in clay mortar and a paved floor. Dense deposits of pottery found with this building suggest that it may have been the residence and workshop of a family of potters.

come from studies of its hieroglyphic inscriptions. Bonampak, 25 kilometers to the southwest, on a tributary stream, is the most famous of Yaxchilán's dependencies, though it was of minor political and economic importance. Bonampak's architecture and low relief sculpture reflect the impact of Yaxchilán styles. Hieroglyphic texts confirm the relationship, again suggesting marriage alliances between local lords and aristocratic women from the regional capital. One of these noble wives appears in the famous murals recording a successful raid on a nearby center (Fig. 75).

Piedras Negras, farther down the Usumacinta, was a large center, with many stelae set before its temples and palaces. Eight sweat baths

73. Central zone, La Sierra. These mounds, here un-cleared and unrestored, were faced with stone, and each supported a masonry building. They are laid out with respect to local topography, not organized into neat plaza units.

THE WORLD OF THE ANCIENT MAYA

suggest an unusual regional emphasis on this ceremonial activity. In the earlier part of the Classic period, Piedras Negras probably rivaled Yaxchilán in importance, for two early Yaxchilán texts mention Piedras Negras and its lords. In the Late Classic period Yaxchilán emerged as the dominant center, as its rulers were important enough in the affairs of Piedras Negras to be mentioned in several texts. Piedras Negras maintained other foreign ties as well, for its texts also refer to Tikal lords. The jaguar-protector theme on monuments in Piedras Negras probably indicates genealogical ties with Tikal's aristocracy. Piedras Negras' relations with distant centers were not always so positive. One lord of Aguateca designated himself "captor of Turtle Carapace," a common title at Piedras Negras.

In the eighth century, Yaxchilán asserted its dominance in the Usumacinta region. Bird Jaguar (Figs. 24, 25) or a close kinsman took a major role in the succession at Piedras Negras. Through Piedras Negras, Yaxchilán could control El Cayo and the other subsidiary centers of its sphere. Yaxchilán's external links stretched southeast to Altar de Sacrificios, where Bird Jaguar or his representative also participated in local affairs (Fig. 49). Northwestern connections were even stronger. The mansard roofs, roof combs, and facades of Yaxchilán's buildings strongly recall those of Palenque, where texts occasionally refer to Yaxchilán. A variant method of recording dates at Yaxchilán, like the Mexican elements in its art, points to northern connections, in this instance with western Yucatan.

The western frontier The western regional variant of Classic Maya civilization, most fully represented at Palenque, is as distinctive as that of Copán's sphere in the southeast.[34] Beyond Palenque to the north lies

74. Ulua-style polychrome vase, La Sierra. Glyphlike heads at the rim and base and the richly dressed standing figure plainly reflect Maya canons of pottery decoration, but the frontal face that bulges out at the right does not.

75. Judgment of captives, Bonampak. This small section of a narrative mural sequence recording a raid on another center shows a nude prisoner pleading his case before the victorious lords. Other captives, whose hands are bleeding, sit on the lower terrace alongside a sprawling corpse whose foot rests against the severed head of a sacrificed prisoner.

the frontier zone in which Maya groups mingled with Mexican peoples of the Gulf Coast. Signs of contact with the culturally diverse peoples of the frontier are prominent at Palenque and other centers in its region.

Pottery in the west reflects this frontier status. Some luxury vessels reflect the Tepeu style, dominant in the south, but most western pottery represents a distinctive regional tradition. From the very beginning of the Late Classic period, a fine paste pottery tradition, typical of the frontier and the Gulf Coast, is prominent. This pottery often has a strongly Mexican flavor in style and iconography. With time, fine paste wares grew in importance as Tepeu-style polychromes declined, reflecting the increasing influence of frontier people and a progressive northward reorientation of lines of communication. These trends were intimately connected to the processes of decline that brought sweeping changes to the Maya world at the end of the Classic period.

Palenque, not a particularly prominent center in earlier centuries, dominated an extensive political sphere in the Late Classic period. By the end of the eighth century, though, processes of decline had set in, and Palenque was among the first southern centers to lose its power. Palenque's temples and palaces are striking architecturally, but few are

76. Stucco relief, Palace, Palenque.

THE WORLD OF THE ANCIENT MAYA

77. Palace, Palenque.

immense. Mansard roofs, roof combs, and trefoil arches are all quite distinctive. Stelae are rare. Most of Palenque's monumental art consists of architectural ornamentation—delicate painted stucco and stone relief panels (Fig. 76). The ball court, by contrast, is small and plain. Palenque's elevated situation, in the foothills overlooking the coastal plain, provided local planners with considerable scope to blend architecture with topography. The layout of the civic core manifests exceptional care in the placement of buildings in relation to one another and to the uneven terrain.

The Palace (Fig. 77), a maze of interior courts and subterranean rooms and passages, is Palenque's most unusual building. Sculptured plaques and texts suggest that it was the administrative heart of the center as well as an aristocratic residence complex. A unique four-level square tower (Fig. 78) dominating the Palace provides a stunning view of the surrounding countryside stretching north to the sea. A glyph for the planet Venus painted on the wall of one of the landings of the tower's interior stair (Fig. 79) may indicate that it was an astronomical

78. Palace tower, Palenque.

observatory as well. Behind the Palace, the small stream flowing through the center was chaneled into a vaulted aqueduct.

The temples of the Sun, Cross, and Foliated Cross form a compact group behind the Palace (Fig. 80, Color Plate 2). They and the nearby Temple of the Inscriptions (Fig. 81), Palenque's most imposing structure, are monuments to the dynasty of Palenque's greatest ruler. Pacal (Shield) came to power in 9.9.4.2.8 (A.D. 615) and presided over Palenque's swift rise to regional dominance until his death in 9.12.11.5.18 (A.D. 683). His son and successor, Chan Bahlum (Serpent Jaguar), began his reign in 9.12.11.12.10 (A.D. 684). The Temple of the Inscriptions was built above Pacal's crypt, which is reached by a vaulted stair

79. Venus glyph, Palace tower, Palenque.

80. Temple group, Palenque: Temple of the Cross (*far left*), Temple of the Foliated Cross (*background*), Temple of the Sun (*right*).

81. Temple of the Inscriptions, Palenque. This building is a monument to the dynasty of Pacal, Palenque's great seventh-century ruler. Pacal's crypt, almost directly beneath the small altar at the base of the stairway, is reached by a vaulted stair that descends into the pyramid from the upper temple building.

that descends from the floor of the temple building through the heart of the pyramid to a level below the ground. Pacal's body lies in an immense sculptured stone sarcophagus along with his jade mask, ear spools, necklaces, rings, and a treasure-trove of other jade and mother-of-pearl ornaments. Stucco reliefs adorned the walls of the crypt. Pottery vessels and beautifully sculptured stucco portrait heads littered its floor, sprinkled with red cinnabar pigment. The corpses of five or six sacrificial victims, slain in connection with Pacal's funeral rites, guarded the sepulcher and its antechamber. After the funeral ceremonies the crypt was closed with a huge stone block, the antechamber and stair were filled with rubble, and the temple floor was

THE WORLD OF THE ANCIENT MAYA

sealed with large flush slabs. Only a slender pottery tube leading upward from the crypt to near the temple floor provided for communication between Pacal and his descendants in the upper world.

Reliefs on Pacal's sarcophagus identify him in death with the sun god, as does a jade effigy of the sun god buried with him. Reliefs in the Temple of the Cross, the monument celebrating the succession of Chan Bahlum, reaffirm this association. The inner tablet of the sanctuary (Fig. 82) shows Pacal on the left, holding the sun god's head. A crosslike complex of supernatural elements resting on another sun-god head separates him from his simply dressed successor. The outer doorjambs represent a later stage in the narrative. Chan Bahlum, now dressed in royal regalia and holding the scepter symbolic of royal authority, stands on the left, in the place of the dead king. He faces an underworld god on the opposite jamb. The whole symbolic arrangement represents the transfer of royal authority and power from Pacal to Chan Bahlum, under the special auspices of the sun god. The accompanying hieroglyphic texts record the same events.

Palenque's architects designed these buildings with such sophistication that the sun itself appeared to confirm these symbolic associations. As the sun sets on the day of the winter solstice, when it is lowest and weakest, its last light shines through a notch in the ridge behind the Temple of the Inscriptions, spotlighting the succession scenes in the Temple of the Cross. At every other time of year they are in shadow. Observers in the Palace saw the sun, sinking below the ridge behind the Temple of the Inscriptions (Fig. 81), follow an oblique path along the line of the stair to Pacal's tomb. Symbolically, the dying sun confirmed the succession of Chan Bahlum, then entered the underworld through Pacal's tomb. No more dramatic statement of the supernatural foundations of the authority of Palenque's ruling line is imaginable. The design of Palenque's civic precinct blends architecture, natural topography, monumental art, and belief systems into a structured environment that symbolically confirms the social and political order.

Through a hierarchy of lesser centers, Palenque controlled a substantial region. Texts at Tortuguero mention noble Palenque women as well as men, suggesting that here, too, marriage alliances were among the ties that bound subsidiary centers to the regional capital. Pomoná, the most prominent of Palenque's dependencies, probably lay near the frontier with the Piedras Negras–Yaxchilán political sphere. Palenque's texts occasionally refer to the latter center. References to Tikal in Palenque texts, and to Palenque on carved bones in the tomb of a noble buried beneath Tikal's Temple of the Giant Jaguar, suggest a close alliance between the two capitals. Hieroglyphic texts indicate other ties stretching as far south and east as Copán. Hieroglyphic texts also link Palenque with Toniná, to the south at the edge of the western highlands, and a few monuments at Palenque and its dependencies reflect the Toniná style.

Tortuguero and Jonuta lay near the western and northern limits of Palenque's sphere, on the fringe of the frontier zone. Comalcalco, a

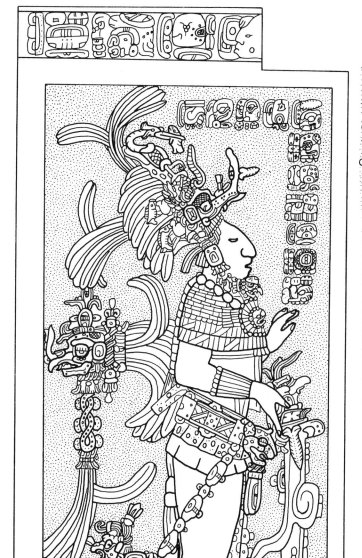

82. Relief panels, Temple of the Cross, Palenque. The central scene, showing Pacal on the left and his son, Chan Bahlum, on the right, is in the sanctuary within the temple. The panels at the left and right, from the outer doorjambs, show Chan Bahlum again, facing an underworld god. The entire sequence and the associated hieroglyphic texts represent the transfer of rule from Pacal to his son. (Adapted from Schele 1976:Fig. 6.)

major civic center near the coast, was well within the frontier zone. Its architecture and stucco reliefs include features of Palenque's style, but other elements indicate ties with Mexican groups and with western Yucatan. Its architectural techniques, featuring brick construction, are unique in the Maya world. Its pottery includes features of the fine paste tradition. Comalcalco was beyond the limits of the Tepeu polychrome style and the stela company. Like La Sierra and the Sula Valley centers, Comalcalco was on the fringe of the sphere of influence of a great Maya regional capital. At the same time it was part of a culturally complex frontier zone, in which peoples of Maya, non-Maya, and hybrid cultural identity mingled. Comalcalco's blend of styles reflects this diversity of cultural traditions.

THE NORTHERN LOWLANDS Late Classic Maya civilization in the northern lowlands consists of a series of regional societies only loosely linked with their southern contemporaries. Northern styles of architecture and monumental art are quite distinctive, though they are part of the Classic Maya tradition. The stela complex, the calendar, and the writing system also reflect basic Maya patterns, though evey hieroglyphic writing shows considerable regional distinctiveness. Few northern texts are so well understood as those of southern centers, and details of the political histories and foreign alliances of northern centers are correspondingly sparse. Southern styles of polychrome luxury pottery faded rapidly from northern pottery-making traditions in the Late Classic period, especially at western Yucatecan centers. Such imported goods as obsidian and jade reflect some continuing connections with the south, probably increasingly indirect. During the eighth and ninth centuries many northern regions interacted with southern centers only through the geographically and culturally intermediate communities of central Yucatan.

Western Yucatan Early Classic traditions persisted at the centers of western Yucatan during the first century or two of the Late Classic period.[35] Local styles of public architecture and pottery reflect continuing, though not intense, ties with the south. By the ninth century, southern features had faded as highly distinctive new regional styles emerged. The advent of the western Yucatecan style is roughly coeval with the beginning of the decline in the western lowlands. New Mexican elements accompanied both developments. Disruption of communication networks in the west may have severed a principal link between northern and southern lowlands at the same time that newly intensified contacts with Mexican and Mexican-influenced peoples of the frontier zone affected both areas.

Uxmal, in the Puuc hills of western Yucatan, was among the largest and most powerful of the northern civic centers, with a sphere of influence comparable to those of the south. This Puuc sphere is especially distinctive in its architectural tradition. Public buildings—temples, palaces, ball courts—correspond to the functional types of southern centers, but architectural style and construction techniques differ sharply. Rubble-cored walls faced with thin stone veneers, free-

83. Temple of the Magician, Uxmal. This view shows the rear of the building.

standing and engaged columns, and plain lower building facades topped by intricate stone mosaics combine to produce a sharp contrast with southern civic buildings.

Uxmal's civic core embodies the fullest expression of the Puuc architectural style. Wide plazas and other open areas lend Uxmal a feeling of spaciousness unknown in the more crowded southern centers. The layout is especially compatible with the surrounding open Yucatecan terrain. The Temple of the Magician (Fig. 83, Color Plate 4) is Uxmal's most massive structure. The unusual smoothly faced elliptical pyramid surmounted by an elaborately ornamented temple building was rebuilt five times. The adjacent Nunnery Quadrangle, four multiroomed buildings with mosaic facades arranged around a central court (Figs. 84-86), was probably a palace-administrative complex. A stela stands before the main building, opposite the arched entranceway. A small ball court lies between this complex and another broad platform supporting two of the most pleasingly proportioned Maya buildings ever

84. Nunnery Quadrangle, Uxmal. A stela stands before the main two-story palace, which is decorated with elaborate stone mosaic scenes and masks.

built: the Governor's Palace (Fig. 87) and the House of the Turtles (Fig. 88). The Great Pyramid, a large temple building ornamented with mosaic masks of a grotesque supernatural being, stands on an adjacent platform. Surrounding building complexes reflect the same simplicity of design combined with ornate decorated facades. Mexican elements are common in Uxmal's monumental art, and its pottery incorporates fine paste styles of the western frontier. Uxmal even had a tzompantli, or skull-rack platform, identical to those on which central Mexican peoples displayed the heads of sacrificial victims. Perhaps Uxmal housed an enclave of Mexicans.

The distribution of Puuc-style buildings in the surrounding region reflects Uxmal's sphere of direct political and economic control. A paved causeway runs 16 kilometers southeast from Uxmal to Kabah, a smaller dependency (Figs. 89–91). Sayil and Labná were two other prominent subordinate centers in the immediate region.

The island of Jaina, just off the west coast, was evidently especially sacred ground, for aristocrats from several western mainland centers chose it for their final resting place. The small island accommodated

THE WORLD OF THE ANCIENT MAYA

85. Nunnery Quadrangle, Uxmal: view of the arched entrance, with the Governor's Palace (*left*), House of the Turtles (*left center*), and Great Pyramid (*center*) in the background.

86. Mosaic decoration, Nunnery Quadrangle, Uxmal: detail of the upper facade of the building in Fig. 85; the mosaic decoration itself represents the facade of a building.

87. Governor's Palace, Uxmal.

many hundreds of tombs stocked with rich offerings, including the famous polychrome figurines.

The Puuc architectural style spread quite widely, extending at least as far east as Chichén Itzá, as did central Yucatecan styles (Figs. 92, 93). Chichén was at this time still a minor civic center, perhaps subordinate to Uxmal.

Dzibilchaltún, in the northwest, also has buildings in the Puuc style, but it was surely not a dependency of Uxmal. Dzibilchaltún grew into an enormous center in the Late Classic period. Clusters of houses and small public buildings surround the core of temples, palaces, and stelae. Raised causeways connect the major civic complexes. Nearly 8,400 buildings on platforms occupy central Dzibilchaltún, and many more perishable structures without platforms once stood among them. Outlying building groups extend well beyond the central zone of 20 square kilometers. Dzibilchaltún was a huge community with a population numbering in the tens of thousands. It was surely a regional capital with its own political and economic sphere. Here, too, potters adopted fine paste styles. Unusual inscriptions and a tzompantli again indicate Mexican connections. Dzibilchaltún and Uxmal may both have housed enclaves of Mexicans or Mexicanized Mayas from the western frontier region.

Eastern Yucatan   Cobá was the largest and most powerful center in eastern Yucatan.[36] A causeway more than 100 kilometers long connects Cobá with Yaxuná, just south of Chichén Itzá, pointing to close ties with western centers. Cobá has many complexes of temples and palaces connected by a network of internal causeways and surrounded by extensive residential areas (Fig. 94). Stelae and inscriptions here suggest very close connections with southern centers. One monument refers to a noble Tikal woman who married into Naranjo's aristocracy. Cobá has an unusually large number of stelae memorializing women. Some of their portraits incorporate motifs usually reserved for male rulers: ceremonial bars symbolic of authority and prisoners beneath their feet. Similar stelae at Tancah, Ichpaatún, and several other centers suggest that royal women from southern centers played exceptionally important roles in the north. Here they evidently assumed high political offices in addition to their roles as royal spouses.

Central Yucatan   Communities in Central Yucatan, geographically intermediate between northern and southern lowlands, maintained close ties with Uxmal and its Puuc sphere, and to a lesser degree with southern centers.[37] Central Yucatecan buildings have elaborate facades ornamented with stone mosaics, but unlike Puuc structures, they are

88. House of the Turtles, Uxmal: detail showing turtle effigies along the upper facade.

89. Arch, Kabah. This monument marks Kabah's end of a paved causeway that connects the center with Uxmal.

90. Codz Pop, Kabah. Some 250 mosaic masks decorate the facade.

91. Codz Pop, Kabah: detail of mosaic masks on the lower facade. The two square pierced objects at right center are ear ornaments of adjacent heads. The lighter projecting stone is the grotesque nose of the head on the left.

92. Puuc-style building, Chichén Itzá.

93. Iglesia ("church"), Chichén Itzá. This building reflects the architectural styles of central Yucatan.

94. Temple, Cobá.

usually faced with plaster. Masks of long-nosed demons are especially common on building corners. Doorways often take the form of mouths of grotesque monsters, particularly in the Chenes region, in the northwest (Fig. 95). One of the early versions of Uxmal's Temple of the Magician (Fig. 83, Color Plate 4) was built in this style. Farther south and east, in the Río Bec region, architecture echoes southern styles more strongly. Towers at the corners of low buildings imitate the form, but not the function, of tall southern temple pyramids. Stairs are too steep to climb and "temples" atop the towers are false, solid constructions.

Becán's potters incorporated variants of the Tepeu polychrome style and of the style of the Puuc sphere into their local tradition. In the eighth century Becán's increasingly regionalized pottery suggests that external relations, particularly with southern centers, weakened. Pottery from Santa Rosa Xtampak and Dzibilnocac, in the Chenes region, shares some stylistic features with the Río Bec tradition and has some southern elements, but it is most like the pottery of Puuc centers and Dzibilchaltún. There is, in effect, a cultural gradient from the Puuc area

through the Chenes zone to the Río Bec region, with increasing evidence of contacts with the southern lowlands.

THE HIGHLANDS   Toniná, on the northern flank of the highlands to the west, dominated a substantial political and economic sphere.[38] Monumental art and craft styles represent another distinctive regional variant of Late Classic civilization. Hieroglyphic texts indicate that the region's closest external links were with Palenque's sphere, to the north. Palenque and a few of its dependencies occasionally erected monuments in the Toniná style. Centers in the Comitán valley, farther south, erected dated stelae in another regional style. The stela complex and monumental art evidently did not extend farther west into the highlands, though some communities there imported pottery from the southern lowlands. Settlement systems indicate political regionalization, with no really dominant centers. Most communities were quite

95. Restored version of Structure 2, Hochob, in the Museo Nacional de Antropología, Mexico City. The elaborate facade, in which the doorway represents the open mouth of a reptilian monster, typifies central Yucatecan architecture, particularly in the Chenes region.

small, located in defensible positions on ridges and hilltops. Near the end of the Classic period, the influence of the western frontier reached the western highlands. Several communities imported fine paste luxury pots for funerary offerings.

Central and eastern highland regions were less closely linked with the rest of the Maya world during the Late Classic period.[39] The stela complex, Long Count calendar system, and hieroglyphic writing, first developed in highland and piedmont centers, went out of use at the beginning of the Classic period. Such architectural features as corbeled arches, universal to the north, did not extend to highland centers. The mechanisms of communication that spread these traits throughout the rest of the Maya world evidently did not embrace most of the highlands. After the decline of Teotihuacán's influence, the central highlands underwent a process of regionalization, marked by the resurgence of local Maya traditions. In some regions, particularly along the northern fringe of the central highlands, traditions of pottery making continued to reflect lowland styles. Lowland centers still imported jade, obsidian, and other highland commodities, but few, if any, central highland communities maintained close ties with lowland centers. In the east, lowland connections were stronger, especially between Chalchuapa and Copán's sphere.

No highland community could compare with the great lowland centers in size, architectural magnificence, or political and economic influence. None controlled a political and economic sphere comparable to those dominated by the great lowland regional capitals. Cotio, a small civic center in the Valley of Guatemala, is typical of many Late Classic highland centers. A compact cluster of a few low platform mounds faced with adobe plaster supported small thatched buildings. These structures, along with a single small ball court, comprised the entire civic precinct.

Decline

Beginning about A.D. 800 in the west, center after center across the southern lowlands stopped erecting stelae.[40] Public building activity slackened or ceased altogether, populations declined, and most centers quickly lost power and central administrative functions. Social, economic, and political systems were devastated, reduced to shadows of their climax forms.

Changes were not instantaneous. Some communities continued to function as civic centers for a brief period. Public construction continued at some centers, on a reduced scale, for a few decades after the last stelae and hieroglyphic texts were carved. Seibal even experienced a ninth-century boom in public building and a peak of monument dedication while other centers in the region were in decline. Before the end of the century it, too, declined. By 10.4.0.0.0 (A.D. 909) the last Long Count date had been carved and no southern lowland center retained its power. By the middle of the tenth century, the civic core of every southern center was an abandoned ruin, though surrounding areas retained at least remnants of their former populations. Squatters in the ruins of a few centers made pitiful attempts to recapture lost grandeur.

At Tikal survivors tried to maintain corrupt versions of the old institutions.[41] They reerected broken stelae, sometimes with the hieroglyphic inscriptions upside down. Ashes and fragments of crude incense burners in temples testify to ineffectual attempts to maintain the traditional ceremonial regime. The old sacred buildings, still holy places, were now refurbished only with graffiti scratched on the walls (Fig. 96). The whole of the aristocratic component of Maya civilization had been swept away, along with, in some regions, a good proportion of the peasant population that had sustained it.

At Palenque, public construction waned in the mid-eighth century.[42] The latest Long Count date (9.18.9.0.0), on a carved pottery vessel, corresponds to A.D. 799. Aristocratic activity ceased altogether shortly thereafter. Within a decade, Piedras Negras, La Mar, El Cayo, Bonampak, and all of the smaller centers in the Usumacinta region had erected their last dated monuments. Yaxchilán alone may have held out for another decade or two, until just after the beginning of the tenth cycle (10.0.10.0.0, A.D. 840). As at Palenque, the last monumental public architecture and the end of the aristocracy came shortly thereafter.

At all of these centers the decline is related to contacts with the north and west—the Gulf Coast frontier, where Maya and Mexican peoples intermingled. The distinctive "fine paste" pottery tradition is the most widespread indicator of this interaction. This pottery tradition developed first on the Gulf Coast among Mexican or Mexican-influenced Maya peoples marginal to the Classic Maya world. Its appearance at Maya centers, often accompanied by Mexican elements in architecture and sculpture, reflects a process of foreign influence on Maya societies by Mexicans, or frontier peoples with hybrid cultures, or both. On the western fringe of the lowlands, fine paste pottery appeared as early as the seventh century, along with southern-style polychrome pottery. These early fine paste wares are highly variable and probably represent indirect contacts with frontier peoples. Fine paste wares became progressively more dominant at western Maya centers during the eighth century as southern features waned. At Palenque this was also a time of declining public construction. By the end of the eighth century, as aristocratic activity ceased at Palenque, a

96. Graffito, Temple II, Tikal. The scene depicts an episode of human sacrifice. (Adapted from Maler 1911:Fig. 10.)

new fine paste style with strongly Mexican decoration had appeared.

Farther south, similar developments are associated with the slightly later decline of the centers of the Usumacinta region. Mexican elements appeared on the stelae of Piedras Negras and Yaxchilán as early as the eighth century. The people who occupied Piedras Negras in the early ninth century, after the decline of the aristocracy, manufactured fine paste pottery. The later fine paste style made an appearance toward the end of the century.

At Altar de Sacrificios the last dated monuments were erected late in the eighth century as public construction declined.[43] Fine paste pottery appeared at this time alongside remnants of the old polychrome tradition. Toward the middle of the ninth century the late fine paste style appeared at Altar, at first as an import, but with growing popularity. By the beginning of the tenth century major construction activity had ended, and the remaining population that occupied Altar until mid-century manufactured pottery exclusively in the late style.

Events associated with the decline of Seibal illustrate the complexity of the external pressures involved in the collapse.[44] Until the late eighth century, Seibal reflected typical southern lowland patterns. At the beginning of the ninth century, the center entered its greatest period of temple construction and stela dedication, but the monuments have a decidedly foreign, northern flavor. At first, new stelae depict leaders with unusual facial features in typical southern lowland aristocratic dress. Later monuments portray figures whose countenances and garb point north, to western Yucatan. Seibal's architecture also incorporated Yucatecan features in this period. Throughout the ninth century, the late fine paste pottery style progressively displaced the polychrome tradition. Seibal continued to dedicate stelae until 10.3.0.0.0 (A.D. 889), but after that the center quickly lost importance. It was abandoned early in the tenth century. Seibal evidently came under the domination of a foreign group in the ninth century, and the alien features are extensive enough to suggest the possibility of an actual influx of foreign Maya aristocrats. Western Yucatan was itself influenced by Mexicanized peoples of the frontier zone, and Seibal's foreign Maya nobles may have helped to transmit the late fine paste style and other Mexican features into the Pasión region.

There is no reason to associate the foreign elements everywhere with a single people. Mexicanized Maya peoples of the eastern Gulf Coast were probably involved in exchange networks stretching up the Usumacinta.[45] Their descendants, the Mexican-influenced Putún, who later occupied the Acalán region, certainly were. Peoples of hybrid Maya-Mexican culture, and even non-Maya Mexicans, were probably involved as well. Each Maya center was subjected to a unique concatenation of foreign influences. The common thread is the increasing impingement of people with cultural patterns foreign to southern Classic Maya civilization, emanating ultimately from the western frontier of the Maya world.

This interaction also carried elements of Maya culture from the Gulf Coast to the north and west in the ninth and tenth centuries.[46] Maya-

97. Temple platform, Xochicalco. The figure seated within the coils of the feathered serpent is executed in a Maya style.

98. Portrait of a noble, Cacaxtla. The figure and his costume are thoroughly Maya in style, but the hieroglyphs represent a Mexican writing system. The glyph above and behind the figure is probably his calendar (birth day) name: 3 Deer, equivalent to 3 Manik in the Yucatec calendar. (Adapted from Foncerrada 1979:Fig. 7; López and Molina 1976:5.)

style relief carvings and hieroglyphs on buildings at Xochicalco (Fig. 97), in the central Mexican highlands, may reflect an exchange of esoteric information among priests or aristocrats. Mural paintings in a palace at Cacaxtla depict battle scenes and even nobles in a thoroughly Maya style (Fig. 98), though Mexican glyphic texts accompany them. The fact that local leaders chose to have their portraits painted in the Maya manner suggests close economic and/or diplomatic relations, perhaps involving marriage ties, with distant Maya centers in the Gulf Coast frontier region or along the Usumacinta.

Pressures from the frontier were less intense east of the Usumacinta. At Tikal and Uaxactún, building activity and dedication of stelae slackened early in the ninth century.[47] The latest Long Count date at these centers is 10.3.0.0.0 (A.D. 889) but there was no major construction after 10.0.0.0.0 (A.D. 830). At Tikal, population dropped by as much as 90 percent from the eighth-century peak. This was a radical change but not a sudden disaster. Over the course of several generations, a reduced birth rate and increased death rates among key groups, especially women of child-bearing age, could easily account for the overall loss. Fine paste pottery appeared alongside remnants of the polychrome tradition, but after the decline had set in.

Civic centers in the Río Bec zone of central Yucatan were in eclipse by the early decades of the ninth century.[48] Outlying populations were declining but not decimated. Becán initiated no major construction after about A.D. 830. Squatter-type occupations appeared in the old public buildings. Pottery of the late ninth and early tenth centuries reflects the late fine paste style as well as ties with northern lowland styles.

Civic centers in the eastern and southeastern lowlands ceased to function before the middle of the ninth century, but here fine paste pottery is quite rare.[49] If peoples of the western frontier had an impact in the east, it was quite indirect. In the Belize valley, the decline of the aristocratic group was not immediately disastrous for the population as a whole. Away from major civic centers, domestic life went on. Vigorous village communities survived well into the tenth century, at least. Quiriguá, too, may have survived as a community for a considerable time after the demise of its aristocracy, but it certainly lost its status as a great civic center. This pattern may be widespread, especially in the east, though there is no doubt that at Tikal and Uaxactún outlying populations declined with the centers on which they depended.

While peoples of the western frontier played key roles in the decline of centers in the Usumacinta and Pasión regions, they were certainly not directly responsible for the collapse of centers farther east. Even in the west the collapse cannot simply be blamed on a foreign invasion, for there is little evidence of widespread population intrusions or of intense military activity. Rather, the decline involved complex processes in which external pressures exacerbated stresses inherent in the structure of Maya societies.[50] Different combinations of factors resulted in slightly different processes and timings in each region.

One serious internal stress resulted from the population expansion of the preceding millennium. By the eighth century populations throughout the lowlands had reached new peaks of size and density. Aristocratic segments of society, well fed and cared for, were probably expanding most rapidly. Subsistence systems were able to feed these larger numbers of people, but at considerable cost. An increased degree of management and greater labor requirements would have increased production but created new stresses. The temptation to intensify food production at the expense of environmental stability by shortening fallow cycles must have been nearly irresistible. The inevitable result would have been environmental degradation. Even without this misfortune, the newly intensified farming systems became increasingly fragile. With subsistence systems stretched to their limits, even slightly reduced production resulting from minor environmental fluctuations could assume the proportions of serious emergencies. In this situation, any further increase in population, agricultural intensification, or environmental damage could only increase the frequency and severity of food shortages. Attempts to compensate by importing food would distribute the strains to other communities, with the probable side effect of increased competition and friction among centers and regions. Serious food shortages, even very fleeting ones, could only widen social and economic gaps, already a source of tension between wealthy aristocrats and peasants eking out a bare existence. Increased pressure on all segments of society was inevitable as aristocrats faced greater and greater administrative burdens and as their demands for increased labor from the peasant sector escalated.

The continued success of Maya civilization demanded maintenance of an intricate pattern of articulation among many complex systems. Pressure at any key point could disrupt the fragile balance, setting off self-reinforcing cycles that magnified difficulties and spread them throughout the Maya world. The penetration of the western lowlands by foreigners carrying Mexican cultural patterns was one such trigger. Armed incursions were not necessary, though they probably occurred sporadically, on a small scale.

Any substantial intrusion of foreign elements into communication networks would result in serious disruption of the connections among Maya centers, sending shock waves throughout the southern lowlands. In the first place, any disruption of exchange and distribution networks would make communities extremely vulnerable to local crop failures. Second, the aristocratic segment of Maya civilization depended on intensive interaction among centers. Local aristocracies were cosmopolitan, with wide-ranging social, political, and economic ties. Efficient communication networks were as essential to the maintenance of local political and religious systems as was the uninterrupted flow of luxury goods. Anything that interfered with such practices as the ceremonial confirmation of local rulers' legitimacy at regional capitals or increased the difficulty of nobles' participation in special events (marriage rites, inaugural celebrations, funerals, and the like) at distant centers struck at the very foundations of southern lowland Maya society. International facets of aristocratic life were the first to go, with the disappearance of the stela complex, monumental art, the Long Count calendar, and the writing system, and the dissolution of luxury pottery styles. Presently, as the malaise deepened in each region, aristocracies lost control, centers ceased monumental construction activity, and all other signs of public activity faded.

Foreign elements spread, filling partial vacuums. External influences and the spread of Mexican cultural patterns are implicated in the decline of southern centers as both cause and effect. In the west they were a triggering mechanism, setting off a chain reaction that eventually weakened all of the interconnected southern centers, even on the eastern fringes of the lowlands. At Tikal foreign elements appeared only after the decline was under way. Farther east they are barely represented at all, and there are indications that the decline had a narrower effect on aristocratic segments of society there.

The processes of decline that brought Maya civilization to an end throughout the southern lowlands affected northern civic centers differently.[51] Here, too, aristocracies had close connections with peoples of the western frontier in the Last Classic period, perhaps even closer than their southern counterparts. Ninth- and tenth-century pottery at Uxmal, Sayil, Kabah, Dzibilchaltún, Chichén Itzá, and many other centers reflects fine paste styles as well as Yucatecan traditions. Other indications of Mexican influence are common, particularly at Uxmal and Dzibilchaltún, where non-Maya inscriptions, sculpture, and tzompantlis suggest the presence of enclaves of Mexican aristocrats.

These signs of foreign influence coexisted for a considerable time with the peak of cultural development at northern centers. If foreign intervention triggered the decline of southern centers, it evidently had a different, or at least delayed, effect in the north. Part of the reason lies in the long-standing tradition of regional distinctiveness in the north. Though trade continued, northern centers were marginally involved in the communication networks that linked the centers of the southern lowlands in the Late Classic period. Northern monumental art and architecture became very distinctive, and southern styles of luxury pottery were hardly represented at all in the northern complexes. Social and political ties between northern and southern aristocracies grew weak in relation to the intensity of contacts within each region. The northern lowlands were also more regionalized internally. Unlike the southern area, they did not constitute a single sphere of interaction. In the north, new alliances with Mexican or Mexican-influenced peoples of the western frontier may have partly replaced ties with southern centers. Northern aristocracies, less dependent on external communication and more receptive to foreign alliances, were less vulnerable, perhaps even receptive, to intensified pressures emanating from the western frontier.

In any case, northern civic centers continued to flourish during the tenth century, though a process of decline may have begun at some centers. Late in the century, external pressures intensified. Large numbers of Mexicans and Mexican-influenced Mayas moved into Yucatan from the west, bringing about a massive reorientation of Maya civilization in the north. This influx of foreign people and ideas may simply have accelerated a process of decline that had already set in. In any case, Uxmal, Dzibilchaltún, and the other civic centers, at least in the west, declined rapidly. Most were effectively abandoned, though regional populations were not decimated. The tradition of powerful civic centers did not end in the north, for a hybrid Maya-Mexican aristocracy established a new dynasty. Chichén Itzá soon emerged as the most powerful center in Yucatan, indeed in all the Maya world, bringing most of the northern area under its political and economic sway.

In the western highlands small communities, already located along ridges and on hilltops, show few signs of disruption at the end of the Late Classic period.[52] Elsewhere most highland societies underwent radical alterations late in the tenth century, as civic centers ceased to function and many communities were abandoned. New centers that emerged in the eleventh century were almost uniformly situated on hilltops and in other defensible locations. Some were actually fortified. The newly pressing need for defense may reflect increasing foreign penetrations, for the highland region was subject to external pressures from more than one quarter. Influences emanating ultimately from central Mexico continued to reach the Maya highlands by way of the southern coast and piedmont throughout the Classic period.

Connections between central Mexico and southeastern Mesoamerica did not end, and may even have intensified, with the collapse of Teotihuacán and the breakup of its sphere.[53] Widespread cultural instability and population shifts attended the collapse of the great central Mexican city and the chain reactions ultimately reached far to the east. Linguistic and ethnographic evidence suggests that the ancestors of the Pipil groups scattered along the coast and piedmont at the time of the conquest split from their parent central Mexican popula-

THE WORLD OF THE ANCIENT MAYA

tions in the Late Classic period. The increasing popularity of fine paste pottery in highland Maya communities toward the end of the period indicates closer contacts with the Gulf Coast frontier region. At first these links may have been quite indirect, reflecting the close ties that already existed between northern highlands and southern lowlands, but northern influences persisted long after the failure of southern lowland communication and exchange networks. After A.D. 1000 highland aristocracies maintained very close relations with the Maya-Mexican rulers of northern Yucatan.

Like the northern lowlands, the highlands did not comprise a single sphere of interaction. Highland aristocracies were even less dependent than their northern lowland counterparts on communication with distant centers. They were less vulnerable to foreign intervention. Still, faced with increasing external pressures and influxes of foreigners, they too succumbed.

CHAPTER EIGHT

NEW ORIENTATIONS: THE POSTCLASSIC MAYA

The Postclassic period was originally defined as a time of widespread new cultural orientations involving some degree of decline or decadence after the aesthetic achievements of the Classic period.[1] In the traditional view, Classic societies were peace-loving, theocratic, and introverted, preoccupied with farming, arts, crafts, religion, and other domestic concerns. They gave way, sometimes in violent episodes of destruction and conquest, to new societies with a thoroughly secular and militaristic cast. The advent of these new warlike, expansionist societies brought a general upsurge in international trade, warfare, and conquest. The Classic Maya decline, once thought to involve the sudden, spectacular collapse of all great civic centers in the face of foreign military intervention, seemed to epitomize the nature of the transition from Classic to Postclassic society.

The contrast traditionally drawn between Postclassic and earlier societies does contain a kernel of truth, but the differences have been seriously exaggerated. Postclassic societies, and the new cultural orientations they reflect, have definite roots in the Classic period.

Continuities between Classic and Postclassic Maya societies have been underemphasized. Widespread decline and cultural reorientation did mark the end of the Classic period, but there was no areawide collapse. Even in the southern lowlands the decline was a process in which foreign intrusion, not necessarily sweeping military conquest, was one of the many factors. In the northern lowlands and in the highlands, continuities from Classic to Postclassic are quite prominent.

Conquest-period Maya societies in the north were distinctly less impressive than their Classic-period counterparts in the scope of their political and economic organization and in the quality of their architecture, arts, and crafts. Early Postclassic northern societies, however, were much more like their predecessors. Chichén Itzá (Map 11) controlled a political and economic sphere at least as extensive as that of any Classic center. Only the most subjective aesthetic judgment could brand its art and architecture decadent.

Native Maya historical traditions describe events and conditions of the Postclassic period.[2] Their references to conflict and conquest exaggerate the scope of Postclassic reorientations. Postclassic Maya societies, on the threshold of history, seem more different from their predecessors than they really were. Warfare and sacrifice are indeed prominent themes in Early Postclassic Maya art, especially in the north. This emphasis reflects in part strong Mexican influence, in part traditional Maya activities. None of these themes was unprecedented in the Maya world. Warfare and conquest are well represented among the political events recorded in Classic Maya art and inscriptions (Figs. 20, 25, 75).[3] Human sacrifice was certainly not unknown to Classic Maya societies; it is a common theme on polychrome pots (Figs. 50, 75, 96). Tzompantlis, platforms supporting racks for the display of sacrificed victims' heads, appeared at Uxmal and Dzibilchaltún with other Mexican elements in the Late Classic period. Postclassic Maya societies were not identical to their Classic-period ancestors, but they were not so radically different as the traditional view suggests. Cultural orientations and emphases had shifted; basic Maya patterns had not.

THE EARLY POSTCLASSIC PERIOD (A.D. 1000–1200)

The Lowlands

Toward the close of the tenth century the long-standing involvement of Mexican and Mexican-influenced frontier peoples in the affairs of northern Yucatan intensified. European and traditional Maya histories refer again and again to the complex comings and goings of the Itzá, a Maya group foreign to northern Yucatan, and to Mexicans who often accompanied them. Diego de Landa, third bishop of Yucatan, recounting preconquest history, explained:

> It is believed among the Indians that with the Itzas who occupied Chichen Itza, there reigned a great lord, named Kukulcan. . . . They say that he arrived from the west; but they differ among themselves as to whether he arrived before or after the Itzas or with them. . . . [A]fter his return he was regarded in Mexico as one of their gods and called Quetzalcoatl; and they also considered him a god in Yucatan on account of his being a just statesman; and this is seen in the order which he imposed on Yucatan, after the death of the lords, in order to calm the dissensions which their deaths had caused in the country.[4]

Kukulcán is a Yucatec translation of Quetzalcoatl ("quetzal bird–

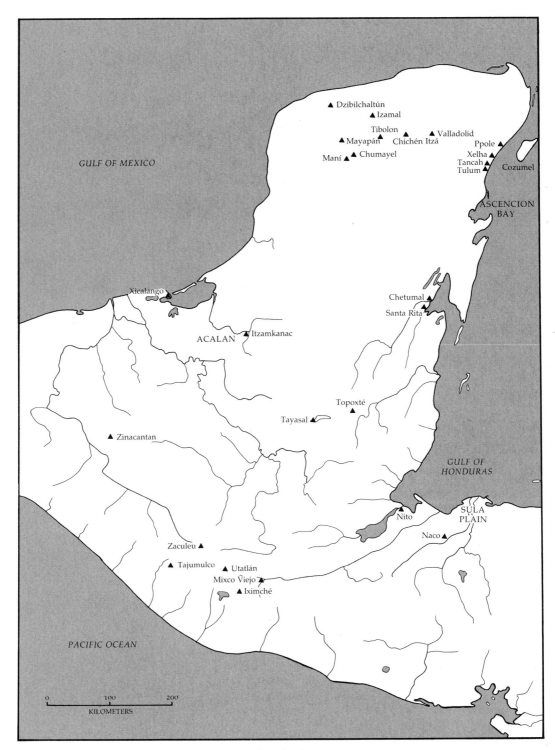

Map 11. Postclassic centers

snake"), the Nahuatl name for the "feathered serpent," the great central Mexican culture hero.[5] The Aztec Quetzalcoatl, patron of priests and priestly knowledge, inventor of agriculture, writing, and the calendar, was the conquest-period descendant of an ancient Mesoamerican god. A feathered-serpent diety was certainly known to the lords of Teotihuacán, and perhaps to the Olmecs. Largely overshadowed in Aztec belief by their warlike tutelary gods, Quetzalcoatl had been far more prominent among the Toltecs. He was closely identified with the ruling line at Tula, the Toltec capital. Quetzalcoatl—sometimes the god, sometimes an important man bearing his name—was the great protagonist of Toltec legendary history. Garbled Aztec versions of Toltec history describe the end of the great Toltec empire in terms of an epic metaphorical conflict. A priestly faction led by the devout Quetzalcoatl battled the warlike forces of Tezcatlipoca, devotees of human sacrifice. In the dénouement, Quetzalcoatl and a small band of loyal retainers left the Toltec capital to undertake an eastward journey attended by mythical events.

Aztec history is a blend of descriptions of events and interpretations of them, with a liberal dose of myth, all cast in strongly didactic and symbolic terms. The Aztecs rewrote central Mexican history as a great allegory to illustrate and reinforce their own understanding of the underlying meaning of the past. Aztec accounts of the deeds of Quetzalcoatl must not be understood as straightforward factual reports of events, but they do contain genuine kernels of historical information. Along with archaeological evidence, they confirm Maya reports of the arrival in northern Yucatan of Mexicans with close ties to Tula and the Toltec sphere.

The deposed king of Tula himself presumably did not come to Yucatan, since the departure episode refers mainly to a later phase of Toltec history. Kukulcán-Quetzalcoatl in Maya histories is more a general designation or title than a personal name. It refers to leaders of more than one Mexican group. All histories link the Itzá to the Mexicans and their reign at Chichén Itzá. The Itzá were Maya, but foreign to northern Yucatan. According to the books of Chilam Balam, compendiums of Yucatec history and prophecy written during the colonial period, the Itzá were "the fatherless ones, the motherless ones," who "took the women of Ppole as their mothers" and "who speak our language brokenly."[6] The Chontal of the western frontier spoke a related but distinct Maya language, and would have had to develop local kinship ties by marrying into Yucatec families. They fit descriptions of the Itzá quite well.[7] Disparaging comments about their sinfulness and lewdness in Yucatec histories may refer to phallic cults introduced into Yucatan as part of the Late Classic Mexican influence. They also might imply no more than unfamiliar, and therefore "heathen," religious practices. The Toltecs themselves probably came from this same Gulf Coast zone, rather than directly from central Mexico. The Nonoalcas, Mexican neighbors of the Itzá along the western Maya frontier, were leading participants in the formation of Toltec civilization. The eastern Gulf Coast region remained an integral part of the Toltec world, an obvious intermediary in Tula's dealings with the Maya of Yucatan.

The chronology of the arrivals of these various groups of foreigners is very confusing. The Long Count went out of general use at the end of the Classic period. Late Maya traditional histories date events according to the Short Count, a repeating sequence of 13 katuns forming a cycle of about 256 years. The Maya concept of time, a blend of history and prophecy, made it appropriate to mention an event in connection with any katun of the correct name, not just at a single point in an elapsed time sequence. Yucatecan histories refer to a series of penetrations of Mexicans and Mexican-influenced Mayas from the west, not to a single group of Itzá led by Kukulcán. Archaeological evidence reinforces this historical picture, indicating a continuing Mexican-frontier Maya presence in western Yucatecan centers during the Late Classic period. At one point the Chilam Balam of Chumayel is straightforward, though not necessarily precise: "Three times it was, they say, that the foreigners arrived."[8]

Shortly before A.D. 1000, foreign pressures on northern Yucatan from the west, already several centuries old, intensified and took on a distinctly Toltec cast.[9] Many, but not all, historical accounts relate specifically to this episode. One influential interpretation of central Mexican history places the departure of Quetzalcoatl from Tula in A.D. 987, the very time of major Toltec impact on northern Yucatan. To assign the arrival of Kukulcán in Yucatan to the year 987 would be false precision. Accounts of the departure of Quetzalcoatl actually refer to a later period of Toltec history. In any case, Aztec dates for early Toltec events are mythical.

There is no question that a new dynasty established at Chichén Itzá about A.D. 1000 dominated northern Yucatan during the eleventh and twelfth centuries.[10] Nor is there any doubt that the new aristocracy had a strong foreign component, including both frontier Maya (Itzá) and Mexican (Toltec) elements.

Reliefs, murals, and embossed gold plaques at Chichén Itzá record some of the events that attended the new influx of foreigners. Scenes of combat between Mexicans and Mayas uniformly depict the Toltecs and their Itzá allies as victors. Maya warriors generally appear slain, in flight, as prisoners, or consigned to the sacrificial altar.

Chichén Itzá became the capital of the new Maya-Mexican dynasty, and a rebuilding program transformed it into an imposing civic center. Art and architecture reflect a new stylistic order superimposed on the old local tradition. New building types, designs, and decorative schemes came into vogue, but elements of the Puuc style persisted, as did traditional architectural techniques. The new public center of Chichén reflects foreign tastes and some new functional requirements imposed by the new rulers, but the work was surely carried out by local Yucatec craftsmen under the supervision of native architects. As time passed, processes of acculturation were at work on Toltec and Itzá aristocrats. They formed alliances with Yucatec families and developed a taste for local ways of doing things. Eleventh- and twelfth-century architecture, arts, and crafts all reflect the growth of a truly hybrid Maya-Mexican culture at Chichén Itzá. In the end, the local Maya tradition proved most durable and influential. The foreigners were largely assimilated into Yucatec societies. The Yucatan discovered by the Spaniards retained surprisingly few signs of the foreign impact.

The new civic heart of Chichén Itzá was an immense platform on which three great building complexes define a spacious plaza area. The monumental ball court to the east (Fig. 99) is the largest in all Mesoamerica. The I-shaped playing area is 150 meters long, with a small temple at either end. Tall platforms flank the main playing alley, with rings set high in the side walls (Fig. 100). Reliefs along the lower walls depict ball game ritual, including the sacrifice of losers by the victors. A temple looks down into the ball court from atop the east platform, with a lower chamber opening outside into the plaza.

The Castillo (Fig. 101), Chichén's most important temple and one of the few to follow the traditional high terraced pyramid design, stands at the south edge of the Great Plaza. Landa, who visited Chichén Itzá in the sixteenth century, says that this building was called Kukulcán. It probably was dedicated to the great Mexican god-hero, for feathered serpents are prominent in the decoration of the pyramid and the temple building. The feathered serpents that form the balustrades of the Castillo's northern stair (Fig. 102) are among the most remarkable Maya architectural ornaments. They are carved so that twice a year at the spring and autumn equinoxes, the late-afternoon sun brings them to life. As the afternoon advances, a shifting pattern of light and shadow

99. Great Ball Court, Chichén Itzá.

100. Great Ball Court, Chichén Itzá: view of playing area, with rings set high in the side walls. Temples stand atop the side platform and beyond the end court.

101. Castillo ("castle"), Chichén Itzá. This building is Chichén's most important temple, dedicated to Kukulcán.

102. Castillo, Chichén Itzá. The edges of the terraces cast shadows that form a diamond pattern along the feathered-serpent balustrade.

transforms the balustrades into images of slowly writhing diamondback rattlesnakes.

The final remodeling of the Castillo encased and preserved an earlier version of the Kukulcán temple built at the beginning of the Toltec period. A red-painted stone jaguar throne, with jade insets for eyes and spots and shell for teeth, still remained in the temple chamber along with a chacmool sculpture. The throne is identical to those of the Toltec lords portrayed in the murals of the Temple of the Chacmool, another building of the early Toltec period, later covered by the Temple of the Warriors.

The Temple of the Warriors (Fig. 103, Color Plate 5) is the most imposing building of the complex bordering the main plaza on the east. Behind a colonnade of square pillars, each adorned with Toltec warriors in relief, rises a low platform that supports the temple. Standard bearers guard the top of the stair (Fig. 104). A chacmool (Fig. 105) reclines before the main entrance. The serpent columns flanking the doorway once supported the lintel. The inner sanctum is complete with an altar borne by tiny Toltec warriors (Fig. 106). Long colonnaded halls furnished with benches border the large adjacent court—a hub of civic activity combining palace, administrative, and market functions. Nearby are two more ball courts and a sweat bath. Several low platforms within the Great Plaza itself never supported buildings (Fig. 107). One is a tzompantli, where the heads of sacrificial victims were displayed. Two others, according to Bishop Landa, were "stages... where they say that farces were represented, and comedies for the pleasure of the public."[11]

No doubt the plaza was the scene of many rites and festivals similar to the Chic Kaban ceremony, performed in later times at Maní in honor of Kukulcán:

On the 16th of Xul, all the priests and lords assembled in Mani, and with them a large multitude from the towns, who came already prepared by

103. Temple of the Warriors, Chichén Itzá.

104. Standard bearer, Temple of the Warriors,
Chichén Itzá.

105. Chacmool and serpent columns, Temple of the Warriors, Chichén Itzá.

106. Altar, Temple of the Warriors, Chichén Itzá. The Atlantean supports represent miniature Toltec warriors.

107. Venus platform, Chichén Itzá. This small platform, decorated with symbols of Kukulcán and the planet Venus, never supported a superstructure. It was probably a stage for public ritual performances. The causeway from the Great Plaza to the sacred cenote leads away from the Venus platform into the background.

their fasts and abstinences. On the evening of that day they went forth with a great procession of people, and with a large number of their comedians from the house of the lord, where they were assembled, and they went very quietly to the temple of Kukulcan, which they had previously properly adorned, and having arrived there, and making their prayers, they placed the banners on top of the temple, and they all spread out their idols below in the courtyard, . . . and having kindled new fire, they began to burn their incense in many places and to make offerings of food cooked without salt or pepper and of drinks made of their beans and the seeds of squashes. The lords and those who had fasted remained there without returning to their houses for five days and five nights in prayer, always burning copal [incense] and engaged in their offerings, and executing several sacred dances until the first day of Yaxkin [the following month]. The comedians went during these five days among the principal houses, playing their pieces and collected the gifts which were given to them, and they carried the whole of them to the temple where, when the five days were ended and past, they divided the gifts among the lords, priests and dancers, and they got together the banners and idols and returned to the house of the lord, and from there each one to his own house. They said and considered it as certain that Kukulcan came down from heaven on the last day of these (five days), and received their services, their vigils and offerings.[12]

North of Chichén's main plaza lies the sacred cenote (Fig. 108) from which Chichén Itzá ("mouth of the well of the Itzá") took its name. "From the court in front of these stages," reports Bishop Landa, "a wide and handsome causeway runs, as far as a well which is about two stones' throw off [300 meters]. Into this well they have had, and then had, the custom of throwing men alive as a sacrifice to the gods, in

THE WORLD OF THE ANCIENT MAYA

108. Sacred cenote, Chichén Itzá. The natural sink-hole was the scene of sacrificial ceremonies long after Chichén itself fell into eclipse.

times of drought, and they believed that they did not die though they never saw them again. They also threw into it a great many other things, like precious stones and things which they prized. And so if this country had possessed gold, it would be this well that would have the greater part of it, so great was the devotion which the Indians showed for it."[13]

Though the Maya did little metalwork, copper, gold, and gold-plated ornaments, bells, rings, masks, cups, figurines, and beautifully embossed plaques were among the offerings dredged from the cenote. Most of these metal objects were imported from Mexico, Honduras, and eastern Central America. Human bones confirm the cenote's role in sacrifice. These rites were both divinatory and propitiatory: they were meant to determine the disposition of the rain god and to placate him. According to the sixteenth-century Relación of Valladolid:

> In this cenote the lords and important men of all these provinces . . . were accustomed, having fasted for sixty days without raising their eyes in this time even to look upon their wives nor upon those who brought them food, and this they did as a preliminary to, upon reaching the mouth of that cenote, throwing into it at break of dawn some Indian women belonging to each of those lords, whom they had told to ask for a good year and all those things which seemed best to them (the lords). And thus, these Indian women having been thrown in without being bound, but flung down as from a cliff, they fell into the water striking it with great force. And at exactly midday the one who was to come out shouted for them to throw her a rope to take her out, and when she came above half dead they made great fires around her, censing her with copal. And when she came to, she said that there were many of their race below, men as well as women, who received her, and that when she raised her head to look at some one of them, they gave her severe blows on the neck so that she would keep her head bowed down, all of which occurred within the water in which they say there were many hollows and holes. And they replied to her whether they would have a good or bad year according to the questions which the Indian woman put. And if the demon was angry with one of the lords of those who threw in the Indian women, [no one asked] to be taken out on the point of noon.[14]

So sacred was this cenote that its cult still flourished hundreds of years after the decline of Chichén. Certainly ritual activity continued there when Bishop Landa visited Chichén in the sixteenth century. He wrote: "On the top close to the edge is a small building in which I found idols made in honor of all the principal buildings of the country, almost like the Pantheon at Rome. . . . And they held Cozumel and the well of Chichén Itzá in the same veneration as we have for pilgrimages to Jerusalem and Rome, and so they used to go (to visit these places) and to offer presents there. . . ."[15] Occasional objects of European origin dredged from the cenote suggest that it remained a pilgrimage center long after the conquest. The popular belief that only beautiful maidens were hurled into the cenote, after being deflowered by depraved priests, is pure Victorian embroidery. The most reliable early sources mention men, women, and children alike, and human bones taken from the cenote are indeed those of children and adults of both sexes. As the analyst who studied the bones remarked, "all of the individuals involved (or rather immersed) may have been virgins, but the osteological evidence does not permit a determination of this nice point."[16]

Except for the sacred cenote, the layout of Chichén's main plaza is strikingly like that of the civic heart of Tula, the Toltec capital. The Temple of the Warriors complex duplicates Tula's Pyramid B, a Quetzalcoatl temple with adjacent colonnaded halls. Even details of design, decoration, and associated sculpture (Fig. 109) are the same. Chichén's ties with Tula, however indirect they may have been, were strong enough to produce remarkably similar civic architecture at the core of each center. The relationship was not one of slavish copying of a metropolitan capital by a colonial outpost. The chief difference between the

109. Pyramid B, Tula. This building complex is the twin of Chichén's Temple of the Warriors.

two centers is that Chichén has by far the better architecture, and the buildings at Tula that most resemble those of Chichén were erected relatively late in its history. The relationship between the two great capitals was complex and involved the eastern Gulf Coast in an intermediary role. Each center reflects a complex amalgam of several cultural traditions. The Maya-Mexican culture of Chichén, though it owed much to central Mexican influence, had its own impact on the Toltecs.

Smaller complexes of public buildings surround the main plaza at Chichén, many of them linked to the civic core by causeways. One causeway leads south to a funerary temple called the High Priest's Grave: a smaller version of the Castillo containing the tomb of a great noble of the Toltec period. Nearby is the Caracol (Fig. 110), a round observatory probably first built in the Late Classic period. Windows opening off the spiral stair inside its dome define astronomical lines of sight. By analogy with contemporary Mesoamerican buildings, the round plan suggests that the Caracol was sacred to Kukulcán. Beyond, civic architecture stretches far to the south, where most of the public buildings of Late Classic Chichén were located. Many of them were remodeled and kept in service during the Toltec period.

Under Toltec-Itzá occupation, Chichén quickly rose to a position of political and economic supremacy on the peninsula. So thorough was its control that civic construction virtually ceased elsewhere in northern Yucatan. All other Late Classic centers went into eclipse. Many were actually abandoned. At Dzibilchaltún a simple village community survived, but with no sign of public works or monuments. No new civic centers rose to replace the old ones. Those communities with public buildings—Xcopte, on the northwest coast; the island of Cerritos, off

110. Caracol, Chichén Itzá. Windows opening out of the dome from the interior spiral stair were used for astronomical sightings.

the northwest coast; and a few others—look like outposts, established by Chichén as garrisons or commercial depots. No other Maya center anywhere rivaled Chichén Itzá in size or influence. Its economic and political contacts reached to the limits of the Maya world.

Chichén's actual control stretched far to the south, deep into the heart of Yucatan. Beyond, southern lowland communities did not maintain close connections with the north, though a few regional pottery styles indicate modest local spheres of communication.[17] There were no powerful political and economic centers. Most evidence suggests village societies with limited external contacts and no indications of powerful political hierarchies.

Chichén maintained its southern commercial ties mainly through maritime exchange networks that by-passed interior southern regions.[18] The lords of Chichén even had a special port facility near Ascención Bay where they launched trading ventures to Honduras, famous for cacao, feathers, and gold and other metals. In addition to local goods, Honduran markets could provide products that originated farther south and east, beyond the limits of Mesoamerica. In the Sula plain and in the Chamelecón Valley, scattered villages were all that remained of the settlement hierarchies of the Classic period. Naco, in the middle Chamelecón Valley, was still a small community with at

THE WORLD OF THE ANCIENT MAYA

most a few modest civic buildings. The region was involved in long-distance trade, but the great market centers that would later make it a hub of international commerce were not yet in evidence.

The Highlands

Chichén Itzá's connections also reached the Maya highlands, at least indirectly.[19] Ties with the Gulf Coast, already in evidence at the end of the Classic period, continued after A.D. 1000, as did influence from central Mexico via the Intermediate Zone. The southward and eastward diaspora of Nahua-speaking Pipil groups was another ongoing process. Central Mexican styles of arts and crafts became increasingly prominent in the Maya highlands and southern piedmont. Toltecs had an economic interest in the region, as a source of cacao and as a commercial link with areas farther east. Plumbate pottery, a finely glazed luxury ware manufactured in the Tajumulco region, was a popular import of Tula. Occasional Nicoya polychrome vessels from Costa Rica probably reached Tula via the Maya highlands. By the time of the conquest, highland Maya peoples showed many signs of Mexican impact, particularly in aristocratic status symbols and in the trappings of rulership.

As in Yucatan, highland Maya traditional histories often reflect, dimly, events and conditions of the eleventh and twelfth centuries. Several highland aristocracies explicitly claimed Toltec ancestry. References to leaders called Kukulcán or Gucumatz (Q'uq' Cumatz, "quetzal bird–snake" in Quiché and Cakchiquel) abound. Many of these claims may be fictional, reflecting local Maya rulers' attempts to bolster their claims to legitimacy, but highland Maya aristocracies were certainly Mexicanized. Some highland peoples probably even had hybrid Maya-Mexican ruling groups comparable to that of Chichén Itzá.

Much of this Toltec influence came to the highlands from the north, from the Gulf Coast and Toltec Yucatan, not directly from Tula. Nahua loan words in Quiché and other highland languages reflect the influence of Gulf Coast dialects, not of Nahuatl as it was spoken in central Mexico. Chichén Itzá itself may have been the primary center from which Toltec influence radiated to the southern regions of the Maya world. Chichén might also have been an intermediate provider of fine paste pottery to highland communities. Certainly there were economic links, for Chichén imported Plumbate pottery. Highland histories refer explicitly to Tula or Tollan, but this name had taken on a wider symbolic significance, connoting a semimythical place of past cultural grandeur, the font of Toltec sovereignty. It could easily designate Chichén Itzá, a new or surrogate Tula. The appellation Tulán Zuiva, Vucub Pec, Vucub Zivan (Tollan Zuiva, Seven Caves, Seven Ravines) in the Popol Vuh and other Quiché documents denotes the place of origin of the Quiché people or their gods. It is usually interpreted as a double reference to Tula and to another mythical birthplace homologous to the Chicomoztoc (Seven Caves) of central Mexican origin myths. Zuiva also appears as a place of origin in the traditional histories of northern Yucatan. Actually, the references may be to Chichén Itzá, for Uucil Abnal (Seven Hollows or Seven Bushy Places) was an ancient name for Chichén.

Quiché and Cakchiquel histories describe ceremonies in which the lord Nacxit invested highland Maya rulers with authority and sovereignty in his palace at Tollan. The Annals of the Cakchiquels explains:

> They came before Mevac and Nacxit, who was truly a great king. Then they entertained them, and the Ahauh Ahpop and Ahpop Qamahay [ah pop q'am haa] were chosen. Afterwards, they dressed them, they pierced their noses, and they gave them their offices.... And turning to all of them, the Lord Nacxit said: "Climb up to these columns of stone, enter into my house. I will give you sovereignty...." And thereupon they climbed up to the columns of stone. In this manner ended the granting of sovereignty to them in the presence of Nacxit, and they began to give shouts of joy.[20]

The Popul Vuh, the great book of Quiché tradition, has a fuller description:

> And then they said as they left,
> "We are going there to the sunrise,
> Whence our fathers came,"
>
> .   .   .
>
> Actually they crossed over the sea,
> And then they arrived there at the sunrise.
> They went to receive the lordship.
>
> .   .   .
>
> And when they arrived
> Before the lord,
> Nacxit was the name of the great lord,
> The sole judge
> Of a huge jurisdiction.
> And it was he who gave out the signs of authority,
> All the insignia.
> Then came the sign of the [ah pop, the ruler]
> And [ah pop q'am haa, the "Assistant Chief"]
> And then came the sign of the power
> And authority
> Of [ah pop]
> And [ah pop q'am ha]
> In the end Nacxit gave out
> The insignia of lordship.
> These are the names of them: Canopy,
> And Throne,
> Nose Bone
> And Earring,
> Jade Labret,
> And Gold Beads,
> Panther Claws
> And Jaguar Claws,
> Owl Skull
> And Deer,
> Armband of Precious Stones
> And Snail Shell Bracelet,

Bowing
And Bending,
Filled Teeth
And Inlay,
Parrot Feather Crest,
And Royal Crane Panache.
And so they took them all and came away;
Then they brought back across the sea
The Tula scripture,
The Scripture.[21]

Yucatecan chronicles link Nacxit with Kukulcán, both as a name for the god and culture hero and as a royal title.[22] Another early document reports that Guatemalan lords sent tokens of peace and friendship to the ruler of Chichén Itzá. These gifts may have been meant as tokens to acknowledge Chichén as the traditional source of their sovereignty.

Whether or not highland Maya rulers derived legitimacy from ties to Toltec Chichén, or even journeyed there for symbolic investiture, they were surely independent in day-to-day activity. Though historical traditions of their descendants portray them as powerful kings, Early Postclassic highland rulers controlled only small spheres of influence.[23] Their unimposing civic centers usually occupy hilltops or other easily defended localities. Some are fortified. Highland centers evidently had to cope with considerable local conflict, and perhaps with external military pressure as well. Zaculeu, typically situated on a plateau surrounded by deep ravines in the west-central highlands, was among the largest Early Postclassic highland centers.

In the western highlands, communities of the Late Classic period were already located on ridges and in other elevated, defensible situations. After A.D. 1000 this settlement pattern changed. Early Postclassic villages were oriented around new centers in broad valleys. In other respects, continuities between Late Classic and Early Postclassic societies are prominent, more so than in any other part of the Maya world. Western highland societies were relatively isolated and may have escaped many of the external pressures felt by their eastern neighbors. They did not continue to import fine paste luxury vessels, and rarely even acquired Plumbate pottery. Political and economic spheres remained quite local in scope, as the area underwent a process of regionalization. Cultural patterns at the time of the conquest do suggest that Toltecs or Mexicanized Mayas eventually had some impact on western highland peoples, but it must have been mild and indirect.

THE LATE POSTCLASSIC PERIOD (A.D. 1200–1525)

Chichén's great period lasted until the end of the twelfth century. Its hegemony in northern Yucatan came to an end as the result of a political upheaval engineered by Hunac Ceel, the lord of Mayapán.[24] Before this successful coup, Mayapán was a minor civic center of no particular distinction in the shadow of Chichén Itzá.

Mayapán is an excellent settlement site, for there are more than twenty cenotes in its immediate vicinity. A small community had grown up there during the Preclassic period.

Landa's report that Kukulcán founded Mayapán must refer to the late establishment of Toltec-Itzá leadership, perhaps a cadet line of Chichén's Maya-Mexican aristocracy.[25] Presently the Cocom family, allied with the Itzá and other Mexicanized frontier elements, established a dynasty that was to dominate Mayapán until its fall in the mid-fifteenth century. According to Landa, "After the departure of Kukulcan, the nobles agreed, in order that the government should endure, that the house of the Cocoms should have the chief power; because it was the most ancient or the richest family, or because at this time he who was at the head of it was a man of the greatest worth."[26] Landa's account of the Cocoms' accession by acclamation is suspect, since one of his principal informants, Juan Nachi Cocom, was a descendant of those estimable nobles. In any event, the Cocom family certainly did rise to a position of dominance at Mayapán.

In the late twelfth century the ruling Cocom was Hunac Ceel, whose magic and political machinations were to bring about the downfall of Chichén. Hunac Ceel was famous as a man of supernatural influence, having survived the plunge into Chichén's cenote to emerge with a prophecy favorable to himself. At the wedding festivities of the lord of Izamal, Hunac Ceel used a love charm concocted from the plumeria flower to inflame Chac Xib Chac, the ruler of Chichén Itzá, with a passion for the bride. Chac Xib Chac carried her off, adding insufferable insult to Izamal's long-standing grievance over the sacrifice of its youths to Chichén's serpent god. Hunac Ceel, with new allies reinforcing his Mexican mercenaries, orchestrated the sack of Chichén. The Itzá, abandoning their capital, fled south, ultimately to reestablish themselves at Tayasal, in the heart of the southern lowlands. The collapse of Tula and the breakup of the Toltec political sphere at roughly the same time no doubt sowed the seeds of political instability in Yucatan, contributing to the ease with which Hunac Ceel was able to destroy Chichén's hegemony.

After A.D. 1200, Mayapán replaced Chichén Itzá as the dominant force in northern Yucatan.[27] The Maya-Mexican heritage of Chichén Itzá is evident in the new order established at Mayapán, and the Cocoms maintained their alliances with Mexican and Mexicanized frontier peoples to the west, but foreign elements were never so prominent again. Mayapán's great period saw a renaissance of native Yucatecan noble lines and traditions. The book of Chilam Balam of Chumayel, an eighteenth-century compendium of traditional history, describes an "interrogation" administered in ritual language by a great chief. Those who respond correctly to the obscure questions and demands are confirmed as lords; those who lack the appropriate esoteric knowledge are to be tortured and put to death. The passage evidently describes a weeding out of foreign nobles as part of a renaissance of local aristocracies, for it concludes: "Thus are those of the lineage of Maya men established again in the Province of Yucatan."[28]

Early in the thirteenth century, Mayapán initiated an extensive re-building program. Its new status and power required new temples and colonnaded halls that served as palaces and administrative centers. Chichén's old civic buildings provided inspiration for the designers of the new Mayapán: the main temple, sacred to Kukulcán, echoed Chichén's Castillo in every major feature. The Caracol and the High Priest's Grave have their counterparts as well. Mayapán was planned as a new Chichén, but the execution did not measure up to the quality of the model. Mayapán's architecture is decadent, even slipshod, in comparison with Chichén's. Plaster replaced delicately carved stone, and corbeled vaults gave way to wooden roofs.

Specifically Mexican elements are relatively few, and some older Maya patterns reappear. Mayapán had no tzompantli, but at least twenty-five stelae were erected. Oddly, there is no ball court. The core of more than 120 civic buildings lies near the center of the settlement, immediately surrounded by elite residences. Farther out were ordinary houses. Other aspects of Mayapán's layout represent something of a departure from earlier Maya norms. Rough masonry walls define indi-vidual residential compounds, which are quite closely spaced. More than 4,000 buildings, mostly dwellings, were packed within the 4 square kilometers enclosed by the low stone wall surrounding the center. In its day, Mayapán must have seemed a confusing warren of buildings and alleyways, with none of the spaciousness of such earlier centers as Chichén and Uxmal.

The Cocom rulers of Mayapán imposed a new form of centralization on the politics and economy of northern Yucatan, perhaps to compen-sate for the fact that they lacked the prestige of the earlier Maya-Mexican aristocracy of Chichén Itzá. Governors administered sub-sidiary centers that controlled outlying provinces, but the titular lords themselves resided at Mayapán. According to Landa:

> They built houses for the lords only, dividing all the land among them, giving towns to each one, according to the antiquity of his lineage and his personal value.... [T]hey ordered that other houses should be construct-ed ... where each one of them could keep some servants, and to which the people from their towns could repair, when they came to the city on business. Each one then established in these houses his mayordomo, who bore for his badge of office a short and thick stick, and they called him *caluac*. He kept account with the towns and with those who ruled them; and to them was sent notice of what was needed in the house of their lord, such as birds, maize, honey, salt, fish, game, cloth and other things, and the *caluac* always went to the house of his lord, in order to see what was wanted and provided it immediately, since his house was, as it were, the office of his lord.... The lords appointed the governors, and if they were acceptable confirmed their sons in the offices.... All the lords were careful to respect, visit and to entertain Cocom, accompany-ing him, making feasts in his honor and repairing to him with important business....[29]

In effect, the Cocom ruler held his subsidiary lords hostage for the good behavior of their provinces. The thirteen important colonnaded halls in Mayapán's civic core may be the palaces and administrative offices of the lords of Mayapán's dependent provinces.

Mayapán's direct political and economic hegemony embraced all of northern Yucatan, but the Cocoms did not dominate so thoroughly or so directly as had the lords of Chichén Itzá.[30] Dependent communities emerged as minor civic centers. Even Dzibilchaltún, quite far down the settlement hierarchy, again constructed small-scale public buildings.

Economic ties with the western frontier, reflected by imported pottery, remained strong, as did social and political alliances. Landa reports that the Cocoms brought in Mexican mercenaries from the trade center of Xicalango, on the Laguna de Términos.[31] Exchange networks also linked Mayapán with areas far to the south and east. Obsidian and jade from the Maya highlands were high-volume imports, and occasional objects of hard volcanic or igneous stone came from there or from the Maya Mountains, in the east. Landa mentions that the only Cocom to escape slaughter in the overthrow of Mayapán happened to be abroad at the time on a trading venture in the Sula plain in Honduras.[32] Honduras, linked to the north through a series of exchange networks that stretched along the east coast, certainly provided Mayapán with tools and jewelry of gold, copper, and *tumbaga* (an alloy of the two metals). Honduran markets could also boast other Central American products alongside the cacao, feathers, and other perishable goods for which it became famous.[33]

The Cocoms maintained their hegemony over northern Yucatan until the mid-fifteenth century. Bishop Landa provides one account of the fall of Mayapán and the events that led up to it:

> Among the successors of the house of Cocom was a very haughty man, an imitator of Cocom, and he made another league with the men of Tabasco, and he introduced more Mexicans into the city, and he began to play the tyrant and to make slaves of the poorer people. On this account the nobles joined with the party of Tutul Xiu, who was a just statesman like his ancestors, and they conspired to put Cocom to death. And this they did, killing at the same time all his sons, except one who was absent. They sacked his house and took away the lands which he had in cacao and in other fruits, saying that they paid themselves for what he had taken from them.[34]

Again, Landa's version is not without bias, for Gaspar Antonio Chi, another principal informant, was the grandson of a Xiu ruler.[35] Still, there is little doubt that Cocom rule had grown increasingly onerous. Shortly before 1450 Mayapán was sacked, its buildings destroyed, its wall leveled.

Never again did a single center hold political or economic sway over all of northern Yucatan. Mayapán's sphere disintegrated into its constituent provinces (Map 4).[36] During the century between Mayapán's fall and the Spanish conquest, these states engaged in a bewildering series of conflicts and shifting alliances as they competed for local political and economic advantage. Western provinces maintained their traditionally close ties with the frontier region and with Mexican peoples. In Ah Canul, at least, the old political hierarchy dissolved entirely. The main centers, controlled mostly by men of the Canul family, generally acted in concert, but there was no paramount ruler.

The same situation obtained in east-central Yucatan, where the Cupul family controlled most of the towns. Chakán and Chikinchel were even less unified, with little more than casual alliances among the main towns. By contrast, Maní, the home province of the Tutul Xiu, retained the old political system. A halach uinic at least theoretically ruled the entire sphere through subordinate batabs in charge of the several minor centers. Neighboring Sotuta, the home of remnant Cocom groups, was ruled by a halach uinic who derived sovereignty from the old Mayapán dynasty. Landa followed their history:

> The son of Cocom who escaped death through absence on account of his trading in the land of Ulua, . . . when he heard of the death of his father and of the destruction of the city, returned very quickly and joined with his relations and vassals, and settled in a place which he called Tibolon. . . . And they built in those wooded places many more towns. From these Cocoms proceeded numerous families, and the province where this lord reigns is called Sotuta.[37]

Political and economic centralization survived in Chanpotón, Cehpech, Ah Kin Chel, Tazes, Cochuah, and Chetumal as well.

Eastern centers were oriented toward the flourishing maritime exchange networks that stretched along the coast, linking Yucatan with Honduras and Central America beyond. The island of Cozumel, just off the coast, was an important commercial and transshipment center with ties to Acalán in the west and to the Chetumal and Gulf of Honduras trading centers to the south.[38] The internal organization of Cozumel was physically decentralized, without a single dominant civic center. The island was also sacred to worshipers of Ix Chel, moon goddess and patroness of weaving, divination, medicine, and childbirth. Pilgrims came to Cozumel from all parts of Yucatan and beyond to consult the famous oracle in her shrine.

Tulum, which so impressed the men of the Grijalva expedition when they sighted it from the sea in 1518, was a major mainland port on the northeast coast.[39] Tulum stands on a bluff directly overlooking the sea (Color Plate 6). A wall pierced by arched gateways enclosed the community on the landward sides (Figs. 111, 112). Within the wall, the layout of public buildings and private houses suggests some attempt at community planning. Several buildings stand along what looks like a main avenue. Tulum's public buildings echo the architecture of such earlier, greater centers as Chichén Itzá in their serpent columns and other features, but the seemingly shoddy quality of the construction is much more reminiscent of Mayapán (Figs. 113, 114). Buildings are small, with thick plaster masking the irregular masonry. One building contained a stela with a Long Count date corresponding to A.D. 761. It was probably brought from nearby Tancah long after it was carved.

Modeled and painted plaster was the standard mode of architectural decoration. A stucco face on the corner of the upper facade of the Temple of the Frescoes (Fig. 115) recalls in spirit the mosaic deity masks of the old Puuc and central Yucatecan architectural styles. The most popular architectural ornament was an inverted relief figure, often set in a niche over the main doorway (Fig. 116). These "diving gods"

111. Enclosing wall, Tulum.

112. Gateway, Tulum. A corbeled arch forms this gate through the wall that encloses the center.

113. Castillo and adjacent buildings, Tulum. Tulum's buildings echo the architecture of earlier, greater centers, especially Mayapán.

114. Temple of the Frescoes, Tulum. Polychrome murals (see Fig. 117) adorn the inside walls.

115. Mask, Temple of the Frescoes, Tulum. This decoration recalls earlier styles of architectural ornamentation in western and central Yucatan.

116. Descending figure, Temple of the Diving God, Tulum. This inverted figure, common on Tulum's building facades, is actually a bee god.

actually represent the Ah Muzencabs, who were bee gods. They were particularly prominent in Ecab, where honey and wax were especially important in the regional economy. Murals painted on plaster wall facings (Fig. 117) were also quite popular at Tulum and at other contemporary centers along the east coast.[40] The content of the paintings and the associated hieroglyphs are uniformly Maya, but the execution reflects the strong influence of the Mixteca-Puebla style of central Mexico—reversing the pattern of the Cacaxtla murals. The adoption of this style at Tulum, Santa Rita, and other centers on the east coast indicates very strong, but not necessarily direct, ties with central Mexico. The maritime exchange networks that stretched around the coast of Yucatan could have brought Mexicans and Mexican ideas to the east from Xicalango and other Gulf Coast trade centers. One mural at Tulum, depicting Chac, the rain god, seated on a four-legged creature, may have been inspired by Spaniards on horseback. The noise and flash of their firearms suggested a connection with Chac, who brings thunder and lightning along with the rain. Cortés's horse, abandoned at Tayasal, was deified as Tizimin Chac, god of thunder and lightning. In Zinacantan the Earth Owner, Chac's modern equivalent, rides a deer.

Smaller communities and isolated watchtowers are located all along the east coast. Xelhá, Tancah, and other minor centers near Tulum were secondary ports within its orbit. Tancah, at least, shared Tulum's penchant for mural painting.

To the south lay the major commercial center of Chetumal, in Yucatan's main cacao-producing zone. A key port in the maritime exchange networks that linked Yucatan with the Gulf of Honduras, Chetumal

THE WORLD OF THE ANCIENT MAYA

117. Mural, Temple of the Frescoes, Tulum. The figure is the Maya goddess Ix Chel, but the style is heavily influenced by the Mixteca-Puebla school of central and southern Mexico.

was also at the eastern end of an overland trade route from western Yucatan. Cacao, gold, copper, and feathers were among the southern products imported for reshipment to the north. Salt, textiles, and other northern Yucatecan exports moved through Chetumal in the opposite direction. Mexicans, or at least Mexican ideas, also reached the Chetumal region by means of these networks. Santa Rita, nearby on Chetumal Bay, also has murals depicting Maya deities in a thoroughly Mexican style.

Active trade routes linked several independent peoples along an arc through the interior of the peninsula. Acalán, in the west, was the heartland of the Chontal-speaking Putún.[41] Acalán maintained close relations with Mexican peoples of the nearby frontier. Several Nahua-speaking communities existed as enclaves within Chontal country, and a few of Acalán's rulers even had Mexican names. Itzamkanac, Acalán's capital, was a major civic center with large temples and administrative buildings and many stone-walled houses. Putún nobles were great traders and took a leading role in the maritime commerce of coastal Yucatan. Chontal may even have become something of a lingua franca in port towns. At the same time, Putún economic connections stretched south and east through the Itzá region around Lake Petén Itzá and beyond to Nito, on the Gulf of Honduras.

By the mid-thirteenth century, a few communities in the interior of the southern lowlands had grown into substantial civic centers.[42] Topoxté, occupying a cluster of islands in Lake Yaxhá, controlled the surrounding region. Pottery basically continued local traditions, but the new popularity of effigy incense burners may have had its inspiration in the north. Topoxté's temples and low palace-administration buildings had beam-and-mortar roofs in place of vaults. They recall

NEW ORIENTATIONS: THE POSTCLASSIC MAYA   227

Mayapán and Tulum rather than the local architectural tradition of the Classic period. The basic population of the region did not change, but northern nobles may have established themselves as a foreign aristocracy, stimulating the renaissance of hierarchical political and economic organization dominated by powerful civic centers. If so, the emergence of Topoxté may reflect the arrival of a branch of the Itzá, who had fled south from the ruins of Chichén a generation or so earlier.

By the sixteenth century, the Itzá certainly dominated the region around Tayasal, another island capital in Lake Petén Itzá. Descriptions left by Cortés and other early Spanish visitors indicate that Tayasal was a civic center comparable to Topoxté, with temples, palaces, administrative buildings, and some two hundred houses. At the end of the seventeenth century, Tayasal, still independent, controlled a population of more than 20,000. Tayasal was an important link in transpeninsula trade, maintaining connections with the Putún to the northwest and with southeastern trade centers along the Gulf of Honduras. Canek, the ruler of Tayasal, even maintained an Itzá enclave on the east coast to grow cacao for him.

Nito, in Chol country on the Gulf of Honduras, was another major port in the commercial network linking Honduras and Yucatan.[43] Nito attracted merchants from as far away as Acalán, and the brother of the ruler of Itzamkanac ruled a large Putún enclave there. Nito's economic ties stretched northwest into the interior, north by sea to Chetumal and beyond, and south to Naco and the great commercial centers of the Sula plain, in northwestern Honduras.

A small community existed at Naco as early as Late Preclassic times. Naco grew slowly, but in the Late Postclassic period it became the most prominent commercial center in northwestern Honduras. Naco dominated the middle Chamelecón region, and extended its political and economic sphere well into the frontier region of the Sula plain. Naco's civic core contains temples, including a strange round structure capped by a plaster "emblem" (Fig. 118), aristocratic residences, and a ball court with stone rings. More humble dwellings cluster around the central precinct, extending for a considerable distance along both banks of the Río Naco. Early Spanish visitors estimated 2,000 houses and 10,000 people in Naco itself, without counting dependent villages.

Naco's commercial ties extended in every direction: north through the Sula plain to the Gulf of Honduras and Yucatan; west to the Maya highlands; south to the Lake Yojoa region; and beyond to the Pacific coast and Central America. Naco distributed regional products as well as long-distance imports. The Sula plain was one of Mesoamerica's premier cacao-producing zones. Several neighboring regions produced gold and copper tools and ornaments, and feathers were a famous Honduran export. Products of lower Central American metalworkers probably flowed through Naco, as did obsidian from highland Guatemala, and salt, textiles, and other goods exported from Yucatan.

Naco, on the fringe of the cultural potpourri of the eastern Maya frontier, was a cosmopolitan place. Its primary population was presumably Maya and the bulk of its Late Postclassic pottery indicates an affiliation with Maya groups of the eastern highlands. Vessels used by

118. "Emblem," Structure 4F-1, Naco. This unique plaster "cogwheel" emblem capped the summit of a round platform in Naco's civic center. Round structures elsewhere in Mesoamerica are associated with Kukulcán or Quetzalcoatl.

the people who lived in Naco's central precinct, however, represent a slightly different style suggesting ties with lowland regions to the north and west. Naco's nobles, like the Mexicanized aristocrats among the Quiché and their neighbors, may have claimed a cultural identity and heritage different from those of the populace at large. Early documents also hint at the possibility of a Nahua-speaking enclave, affiliated with Pipil groups to the south. There were certainly Náhua enclaves in central Honduras and along the north coast. Chetumal maintained commercial outposts in the Sula plain, and other northern centers may have done so as well. The Sula plain was a mosaic of enclaves of peoples of many cultural identities—Chol, Chortí, Yucatec, Jicaque, Lenca, Paya, and probably others—and Naco may have been similarly polyglot.

In the Maya highlands ceaseless conflict and shifting alliances among a remarkable array of peoples and polities characterized the Late Postclassic period. In the far west the Tzeltal, Tzotzil, and their neighbors comprised a series of independent local societies linked by a variety of social, political, and economic ties.[44] No great centers emerged to create large states or spheres of economic hegemony. Zinacantan, the Tzotzil center, among the most prominent western towns, controlled only a modest region. With access to abundant supplies of amber, quetzal feathers, animal pelts, and salt, Zinacantan was a prosperous commercial center. It was subject to constant pressure from the Chiapanecs to the west and south. Even the Aztecs made persistent attempts to control the area. They were largely unsuccessful, though they did finally establish a foothold at Zinacantan.

NEW ORIENTATIONS: THE POSTCLASSIC MAYA

Zaculeu, the Mam capital, controlled a larger area.[45] Long established in its elevated defensive location, Zaculeu became a powerful civic center in the Late Postclassic period. Nearly fifty buildings—temples, palaces, administrative buildings, "dance" platforms, and a small ball court—comprise the compact public core of Zaculeu (Figs. 119–121). Humble residences are scattered throughout the surrounding countryside. Though quite plain, Zaculeu's temples and colonnaded halls recall those of Mayapán and other late Yucatec centers. A few of the latest buildings may represent a garrison established by the Quiché, the conquest-minded eastern neighbors of the Mam.

In the central highlands local political and economic spheres grew and multiplied during the thirteenth and fourteenth centuries.[46] Shifting alliances and changing power relations were the order of the day. Local aristocracies absorbed Toltec ideas and symbols disseminated from Chichén Itzá in the preceding centuries. Some societies probably assimilated Mexican and northern Maya nobles as well. The result of this process of acculturation was a series of thoroughly Mexicanized

119. Structure 1, Zaculeu. This temple is the largest at Zaculeu.

THE WORLD OF THE ANCIENT MAYA

120. Stage, Zaculeu. This small platform, standing before Structure 1, never supported a building; it was probably the scene of ritual performances.

aristocracies that asserted Toltec ancestry. Many ruling lines based their claims to legitimacy on real or fictive connections with Tula or its surrogate, Chichén Itzá. More than one early leader bore the name or title Q'uq' Cumatz, the Quiché equivalent of Kukulcán. Elements of architecture, pottery, and arts and crafts continued to reflect Mexican

121. Ball court, Zaculeu. The I-shaped playing area, like the one at Iximché (see Fig. 122), is completely enclosed.

styles. Public buildings in the early Quiché civic centers, atop steep ridges and hills along the north edge of the Quiché basin, embody elements of Gulf Coast architectural styles. The many local groups comprising the Quiché and their close relatives were probably much alike at this time, for linquistic reconstructions suggest that Quiché, Cakchiquel, and Tzutuhil did not develop into distinct languages until about A.D. 1000.[47] Though traditional histories portray early rulers as great kings, this is largely a matter of descendants aggrandizing themselves by glorifying their ancestors. None of the early highland nobles controlled anything greater than a very localized sphere of influence.

The Quiché created the most powerful highland Maya state.[48] Utatlán, the Quiché capital at the time of the conquest, occupies six plateaus separated by deep ravines in the broad Quiché basin. Three distinct civic centers, each corresponding to one set of Quiché kinship groups, formed the heart of the composite community. Q'umaric Ah, eventually the preeminent civic precinct and home of the most powerful lineage, was founded about A.D. 1400. Presently it would boast an impressive array of temples, palaces, administrative buildings, and ball courts. Discrete architectural complexes, each with its own temples, palaces, and "council chambers," corresponded to the several noble lineages that lived there. Ordinary farmers, artisans, and landless "serfs" occupied outlying residential areas. During the fifteenth century Quiché society underwent radical changes as Utatlán's political and economic sphere expanded beyond the Quiché basin on all fronts. Control of lower, warmer valleys to the north and east secured access to precious stones, metals, feathers, and a variety of other lowland products. Thrusts to the southwest, into the broad, fertile highland basins and the cacao-producing piedmont beyond, provided a major economic boost to the Quiché state. Garrisons, often with scaled-down copies of Utatlán's civic buildings, marked Quiché penetration of neighboring territories. Utatlán probably maintained other types of enclaves outside the Quiché basin as well.

Eventually Quiché territorial expansion outstripped the evolution of administrative systems. Late in the fifteenth century the Cakchiquel broke away from the Quiché sphere and established an independent capital at Iximché, some 60 kilometers southwest of Utatlán.[49] The new civic center, with its temples, palaces, "council chambers," and ball courts, was very much in the Utatlán tradition, though more compact (Fig. 122, Color Plate 7). As at Utatlán, Mixteca-Puebla stylistic elements reflect the Mexican heritage claimed by the aristocracy as well as continuing ties with central Mexico. These connections could be quite direct at times. In 1510, Motecuzoma, the Aztec emperor, sent an ambassador to Iximché.

Following the Quiché pattern, the Cakchiquel quickly began their own expansion. A Cakchiquel garrison at Mixco Viejo marks an early thrust into the Motagua Valley. Here environments and natural resources complemented those of the Cakchiquel heartland, providing for greatly increased ecological diversity. Later expansion impinged mainly on Pokom territory to the east. The Tzutuhil around Lake Atit-

122. Ball court, Iximché. The I-shaped playing area, like the one at Zaculeu (see Fig. 121), is completely enclosed.

lán closed off Cakchiquel horizons to the west and south. The Tzutuhil felt some pressure from Cakchiquel competition for cacao-producing piedmont zones, but maintained control of an independent political and economic sphere.

To the east the situation was much the same as in the western highlands.[50] The Chortí and Pokom comprised a series of small regional spheres of influence with no very powerful centers. Pokom and Chortí groups mingled with Xinca, Lenca, Paya, Pipil, and other non-Maya peoples along the eastern frontier of the Maya world. Farther east, Maya populations gave way to Maya enclaves, and finally to solid blocks of people who did not share basic Mesoamerican cultural patterns.

CHAPTER NINE

PERSPECTIVES ON THE MAYA

The ancient Maya were the only fully literate native American people. They were the greatest scientists in the New World. Without the aid of the simplest optical instrument, Maya astronomers and chronologists created an astonishingly sophisticated calendar system. Maya peoples have produced some of the world's finest architecture, sculpture, painting, poetry, and epic literature. Hundreds of scholars have spent their careers trying to understand these achievements and their place in the Maya cultural tradition. Yet unanswered questions about the Maya and their history abound. Not one facet of Maya civilization is fully understood. Information on the Preclassic Maya world is naturally sketchy, but surprising gaps also mar reconstructions of later Maya societies. Along with archaeology, native traditional histories and early Spanish descriptions provide unusually full pictures of a few Maya societies at the period of the conquest. Even in these instances, available information is not uniform. It reflects politics and economics in detail, other aristocratic concerns less well, and many aspects of culture not at all. In some parts of the Maya world, the archaeological record is still entirely blank.

Even basic aspects of Maya civilization are puzzling. What were subsistence systems at the heart of Maya economies really like? Milpa farming, featuring maize, beans, and squash, was fundamental, but it was not standardized. What were the varied blends of accessory crops? How important were manioc and other root crops? What differences resulted from variations in soils, climates, scheduling, and the use of such techniques as terracing? Milpa farming was never the sole agricultural system. How important were ridged-field systems and other methods of intensive farming? To what extent did Maya farmers cultivate ramón, chicosapote, and other tree crops? What was the dietary importance of noncrop plants, fish, shellfish, and other wild foods?

Trade networks were vital to Maya societies. They distributed great quantities of raw materials and finished products. What perishable goods moved along these networks? How important was exchange of foods between communities and regions? By what social mechanisms did exchange operate? What balances of market and redistributive patterns characterized Maya economies? What roles did political leaders play in administering subsistence activities and commerce?

Extreme differences in wealth and social status developed within Maya societies during the Preclassic period. How sharply defined were social groups? How extensive was occupational specialization? To what extent did it coincide with social ranking? What mechanisms of social mobility were available to common folk?

Maya civic centers boasted impressive concentrations of monumental art and architecture. They were seats of great political and economic power. To what extent were they urban? Tikal, Dzibilchaltún, and several other great centers housed populations that numbered in the tens of thousands. At Mayapán and a few other late northern centers dense concentrations of dwellings clustered inside community walls. Maya centers certainly embodied many of the economic and political functions of true cities, but none had the urban form of Teotihuacán, with a huge dense population concentrated within a community laid out according to a rigid grid plan. Did the smaller and more dispersed populations of Maya centers enjoy different patterns of social relations? All of these questions, and many others, can be asked of every part of the Maya world in every period of its precolumbian history.

In part these gaps in understanding reflect an incomplete archaeological record. The accelerating pace of archaeological investigation constantly augments the available data. Improved archaeological techniques are contributing partial answers to some questions. Flotation procedures that can recover surprising quantities of plant remains even in tropical forests are becoming standard in Maya excavations. Archaeologists are asking new questions of Maya remains as they broaden their interests beyond the traditional preoccupation with temples, palaces, and monumental art.

As archaeologists and historians fill in more and more of the historical outline of the Maya cultural tradition, they can make better use of the more complete information about late Maya societies to understand earlier periods of Maya history. No culture is static and no group is a fossilized image of its ancestors, but societies are products of their histories. Every contribution to Maya culture history makes possible a better assessment of continuities in the Maya cultural tradition. Improved understanding of these continuities permits more informed use of analogy based on ethnographic, historical, and archaeological information.

Ethnographic analogy is the most obvious case. Today's Maya groups are functioning, integrated societies, not partial cultures reflecting an incomplete Maya pattern. Modern institutions must be understood in terms of their functional place in the contemporary social and environmental milieu *and* as historical products of more than four centuries of interaction between European and Maya cultural traditions. It is impossible to evaluate hypotheses about precolumbian equivalents of such modern institutions as the cargo system without this historical and functional context.

The same is true of analogies based on historical information from the time of the conquest. The interplay of political institutions, lineage organizations, social hierarchies, and religion in the operation of the Quiché state provides an apt general model for Classic Maya political organization. Full use of the Quiché pattern to create detailed testable hypotheses about earlier Maya societies requires a historical framework. What roles did Toltecs, Toltec-influenced northern Maya groups, and local highland societies have in the formation of the Quiché institutions that were functioning at the time of the conquest? What are the relations of each of these traditions to societies of the Classic period? In the same way, it is potentially misleading to base analogies on late Yucatecan societies without an understanding of the Toltec impact on northern Yucatan. In order to use data from the Classic period in reconstructing Preclassic societies, it is crucial to assess the impact of Teotihuacán on the Classic Maya as well as to understand the basic historical relations among the several regional traditions of development within the Maya world.

The fullest possible reconstruction of Maya culture history, region by region, is the essential framework for an understanding of the development of the Maya cultural tradition. Explanation—identifying and characterizing processes of culture change—is inseparable from historical reconstruction. Process *is* history. In the Maya world, history is also a catalog of variation on common themes. A regional perspective is essential.

The problem of explaining the decline that afflicted most of the Maya world at the end of the Classic period is a perfect example. Almost every conceivable factor has been advanced as the root cause: foreign invasion, peasant revolt, population decline, limited environmental potential, agricultural failure resulting from the exhaustion or erosion of the soil or from the invasion of grasses, earthquakes, hurricanes, disease.[1] Progressive improvement in the historical framework of the period has shown that the decline was not uniform and not even universal. It was not an event, but a series of processes that followed various courses, with timing and outcome varying from region to region. No simple explanation that relies on a single cause can possibly account for such varied phenomena. The best explanation points to foreign penetration and internal stresses as leading factors in a very complex set of chain reactions that eventually affected many related societies.

The rise of Maya civilization is an even more complex issue, embracing related developments throughout the Maya world during a period of many centuries. Single-cause explanations have the virtue of focusing attention on processes that may have been important in one or another region at some period, and they sometimes produce insights by presenting familiar information in new frames of reference, but no one factor alone can account for the emergence of Maya civilization.

Demographic factors loom large in explanations of prehistoric developments, and the rise of Maya civilization is no exception.[2] The problems inherent in arriving at reliable estimates of prehistoric populations make it difficult to verify or refute demographic hypotheses. Population profiles of early Maya communities are particularly impressionistic, but available data do suggest basic demographic trends. Not surprisingly, these data indicate considerable variation from region to region. There is a definite pattern of overall growth, but it was neither uniform nor continuous. The timing of population increases varies considerably in relation to the appearance of the characteristics of civilization in the several parts of the Maya world. Population growth certainly accompanied the emergence of Maya civilization, but the relationship is not necessarily direct. It may have been partial cause, effect, or a blend of the two.

The rise of Maya civilization has also been attributed to warfare, itself usually explained as a result of increasing populations.[3] Here, too, the archaeological evidence presents difficulties: distinguishing weapons from hunting implements and fortifications from massive constructions with other functions is not a straightforward task. A regional perspective weakens the warfare hypothesis. The Preclassic ditch and embankment at Becán were probably defensive, but there are very few indications of early conflict elsewhere. Tikal's earthworks may have been fortifications too, but there is no evidence that they were constructed in an early period.

Trade is a third popular causal factor. Maya commerce, involving durable goods easily recognized as imports, did leave clear archaeological traces. Exchange networks covered the Preclassic Maya world. One influential hypothesis attributes the initial development of key features of Maya civilization to an urgent and continuing need to procure vital resources.[4] Societies in the heart of the southern lowlands, lacking natural resources of obvious commercial value, supposedly developed specialized political leadership to procure salt, obsidian, and hard stone. These are valuable commodities, but the exotic stones were not essential to life. Local chert and limestone are inferior but adequate. The southern lowland core was not really without resources. Dozens of local tropical-forest products are potential trade goods, as are agricultural crops and manufactured commodities. Commerce need not be based on unique or even scarce commodities.[5] The ethnographic literature abounds with descriptions of societies that import items that could be procured or manufactured locally. There is no convincing evidence to show that any sector of the Maya world had a significantly greater need for special procurement institutions than any other. Exchange surely did have an important role in the evolution of Maya social and political institutions, but exchange alone can account neither for the form of those institutions nor for the order in which they appeared in the several regions of the Maya world.

Population growth, conflict, and especially exchange did contribute to the development of Maya civilization, but none is the sole or even the primary cause. A regional perspective on Maya culture history suggests that interaction among communities and regions was more important than any of these factors.[6] Exchange is only one facet of interaction. Enclaves, marriage alliances, pilgrimages, and attendance at special ceremonial events also linked Maya communities.

Information and ideas transmitted along such lines of communication played an important role in the development of Maya civilization. At roughly the same time, the several regions of the Maya world experienced varied but comparable processes of development that led from small, homogeneous villages to regional states dominated by great civic centers that were seats of powerful aristocracies. Interaction among regions allowed local developments to spread widely, often far beyond the areas immediately affected by the factors that stimulated them. Many causal factors contributed to the rise of Maya civilization, but all did not operate everywhere, or even in any one region. An institution developed in one region as a response to population growth and conflict might be adopted elsewhere, in regions of low population density, because it facilitated the acquisition of needed raw materials. Links among communities and regions are at least as important in explaining the rise of Maya civilization as are the immediate stimuli involved in the varied local developments.

Maya patterns of territorial organization fostered interaction. The cultural and linguistic landscape of the Maya world was not one of neatly bounded neighboring groups. As in the rest of Mesoamerica, people of contrasting cultural identity and linguistic affiliation mingled in complex mosaic arrangements. Enclaves—groups of people who lived and worked away from their own core territories, among people with different cultural traditions—were prominent everywhere.

Modern Maya communities commonly hold outlying pockets of farmland surrounded by fields that belong to neighboring communities. Many Maya farmers spend part of the year far from their home communities, working distant milpas in foreign territory. Outlying farm plots can form the nuclei of new communities. Chan Kom, in northern Yucatan, began as a cluster of houses and milpas that comprised an outlying part of the community of Ebtún, 50 kilometers away.[7] Most people returned there when agricultural activities were completed. Even the few people who lived at Chan Kom year round recognized the authority of Ebtún and retained their rights and obligations as members of that community. Gradually Chan Kom attracted more and more permanent residents, and eventually it became a community in its own right, with an independent political organization. Kinship links, common historical roots, and a host of social ties still marked Chan Kom as an enclave with ethnic ties to Ebtún.

Comparable enclaves dotted the precolumbian Maya world, along with others maintained to serve state political and economic ends.[8] Canek, ruler of Tayasal, told Cortés of his vassals on the coast who raised cacao for him. This enclave, probably located in the Nito region, was far beyond Tayasal's immediate sphere of political control. Tayasal and its dominions comprised an Itzá enclave in Chol country. The brother of Paxbolanacha, ruler of Acalán, governed a Chontal commercial enclave in the distant Chol trading port of Nito, on the Gulf of Honduras. Chetumal and other Yucatecan commercial centers maintained outposts in the Sula plain, at the base of the Gulf of Honduras. Xicalango, the great trading port on the Laguna de Términos, was a cosmopolitan community where Chontal, Yucatec, and other Maya traders mingled with Gulf Coast Mexicans. Even Aztec merchants from central Mexico maintained an enclave there.

The most obvious functions of enclaves are economic: they secure access to exotic raw materials, to environmental conditions needed to raise desired crops, to distant markets. The enclave pattern was a strategy of ecological diversification. Enclaves also fostered many kinds of interaction. Maya aristocracies depended on ties with other ruling groups—for formal confirmation of authority and sovereignty and transfer of their symbols, for exchange of esoteric religious and scientific information, for formation of marriage alliances. Enclaves were vital instruments of state activity. Maya merchants, like their Aztec counterparts, were probably prime sources of military intelligence. Political territories themselves probably often took the form of archipelagos, with many outlying parcels interspersed among islands of foreign territory. Tikal's interference in the affairs of Dos Pilas in the seventh century does not imply control of the intervening territory. The Aztec empire, Mesoamerica's greatest political entity, tolerated a hostile Tlaxcalan state within the heart of its central Mexican dominions.[9] Mesoamerican notions of normal territorial behavior did not emphasize exclusiveness. Block distributions of people of a single linguistic, cultural, or political affiliation were not the norm.

Cultural and linguistic contrasts are most extreme in frontier zones: between groups within the Maya world, between Maya and Mexican groups, and particularly between Maya and Central American peoples. The eastern frontier of the Maya world (and of Mesoamerica) was a mélange of enclaves, ranging from individual households to neighborhoods to entire communities. Foreign penetration of the Maya world involved the same territorial pattern. The enclave of colonial Teotihuacanos at Kaminaljuyú is the clearest example. Tikal probably housed a similar group from Kaminaljuyú. Recognizing concentrations of foreign elements as reflections of enclaves helps to put the issue of foreign impact on Maya societies in perspective. Teotihuacán maintained only a very limited presence in the Maya world. Most communities, especially in the lowlands, had only very indirect connections with Teotihuacán, through a few enclaves at such centers as Tikal and Kaminaljuyú. Even Kaminaljuyú's resident Mexicans may have had indirect ties with the central Mexican metropolis through a subsidiary province of Teotihuacán in the Intermediate Zone. On these grounds alone, the theory of a Teotihuacán stimulus for the rise of Maya civilization is decidedly weak. In any case, civilization emerged in the Maya world long before the onset of interaction with Teotihuacán. Later Mexican enclaves in the north had a much greater impact on the Maya world.

Ascertaining the nature of Maya frontiers and assessing the impact of Mexican peoples on the Maya world involve a larger issue: the relation between material culture and basic cultural identity. Language differences do not prevent interaction. Cultural frontiers are not barriers to the spread of objects, ideas, styles, or institutions. Intense interaction among the enclaves that comprise frontier zones actually fosters communication and the sharing of cultural patterns. Maya peoples in Yucatan and in the highlands shared styles of architecture, arts, and crafts with Aztecs, Mixtecs, and their central Mexican neighbors. Maya hieroglyphic inscriptions certainly indicate Maya speech, and the combination of Maya styles of architecture, art, and crafts surely marks Maya communities, but greater precision is elusive. Mexican traits sometimes mark foreign enclaves, but in other instances they reflect imported goods or foreign styles adopted by local craftsmen. Even with reams of historical data, it is impossible to separate Yucatec, Itzá, and Toltec components in the archaeological record of northern Yucatan. What contributions did Toltecs and Mexicanized northern Maya peoples make to the formation of the Quiché society found by the Spaniards? What were the roles of Maya and Zoque speakers in Izapan civilization? In Olmec civilization? What is the meaning of South American features in early Mesoamerican pottery?

Patterns of archaeological evidence in the Maya world—styles of architecture, art, and crafts; funerary customs; settlement systems and community layouts; traces of social, political, and economic institutions—must embody reflections of Maya identity. Understanding the relations between these patterns and the ethnic and linguistic variety that has always characterized the Maya world is the greatest challenge facing Maya archaeology today.

NOTES

Introduction

1. Stephens 1841:1:123–24.
2. Stephens 1841:1:103.
3. Childe 1951, 1954.
4. Wittfogel 1957.
5. Wittfogel 1972; Sanders and Price 1968.
6. Daniel 1968:142–43.
7. Vogt, ed., 1969; Wolf 1959.

1. Discovery of the Maya

1. MacNutt 1912:317; Sauer 1966:128–30.
2. Sauer 1966:166–68.
3. Tozzer, ed., 1941:236.
4. Crosby 1972:35–63; Stewart 1973:35–38.
5. Chamberlain 1953:53–57; Tozzer, ed., 1941:8–9, 233–39.
6. Closs 1976.
7. Chamberlain 1948:11–12.
8. Tozzer, ed., 1941:12.
9. Chamberlain 1948:13–14.
10. Roys 1957:147.
11. Pagden, trans. and ed., 1971.
12. Pagden, trans. and ed., 1971:359–61.
13. Pagden, trans. and ed., 1971:377, 519.
14. Kelly 1932.
15. Recinos and Goetz, trans., 1953:119–25.
16. Pagden, trans., 1975; Tozzer, ed., 1941.
17. Brunhouse 1973.
18. Stephens 1841, 1843; Von Hagen 1948, 1950.

19. Brunhouse 1975.
20. Wauchope 1962:20.
21. Kelley 1962b, 1976:3–7.
22. Gordon 1896.
23. Brunhouse 1971; Willey and Sabloff 1980.
24. Proskouriakoff 1960, 1961a.
25. Knorozov 1967.

2. The Maya World

1. Vogt, ed., 1969.
2. Kirchhoff 1943; Wolf 1959.
3. Borhegyi 1960; Kemrer 1968; Ritman 1968; Stern 1949.
4. Henderson 1977, 1978.
5. Parsons 1978.
6. Collier 1964; Stevens 1964; L. Stuart 1964; Tamayo and West 1964; Vivó Escoto 1964; Wagner 1964; West 1964a, 1964b.
7. Vogt 1969b, 1970.
8. Tozzer 1907:19–22.
9. Kaufman 1976.
10. Redfield 1941, 1950; Redfield and Villa Rojas 1934; Villa Rojas 1945, 1969b.
11. Villa Rojas 1969a.
12. Laughlin 1969a.
13. Lounsbury 1974:17.
14. Duby and Blom 1969; Tozzer 1907.
15. Healy 1974.
16. Laughlin 1969b; Villa Rojas 1969c; Vogt 1969a, 1969b, 1970.
17. Montagu 1969; Nash 1969; Wagley 1969.
18. Nash 1969; Wagley 1969.
19. Bunzel 1952; Nash 1958, 1969; Tax 1953; Tax and Hinshaw 1969.
20. Nash 1969; Reina 1966, 1969; Villa Rojas 1969a.
21. Nash 1969; Reina 1969; Wisdom 1940.

3. The Maya World on the Eve of the Spanish Conquest

1. Roys 1957, 1965, 1972; Roys, trans. and ed., 1967; Tozzer, ed., 1941.
2. Pagden, trans. and ed., 1971; Roys et al. 1940; Sabloff and Freidel 1975; Sabloff and Rathje 1975; Sabloff and Rathje, eds., 1975; Sabloff et al. 1974.
3. Chapman 1957.
4. Díaz 1916; Pagden, trans. and ed., 1971; Scholes and Roys 1968.
5. Simpson, trans. and ed., 1964:354.
6. Hellmuth 1977; Pagden, trans. and ed., 1971; J. E. S. Thompson 1951.
7. Henderson 1977, 1978; Henderson et al. 1979.
8. R. M. Adams 1961:359; Díaz 1912:305; Vogt 1969a:141–43.
9. Carmack 1973; Edmonson 1971; Fox 1978; Goetz and Morley, eds. and trans., 1950; Wallace and Carmack, eds., 1977.
10. Fox 1978; Guillemin 1967, 1977; Recinos and Goetz, trans., 1953.
11. Miles 1965b.
12. Miles 1957, 1965b.
13. Sharer 1974, 1978b.

4. The Maya Universe

1. Gossen 1974; Hunt 1977; Léon-Portilla 1973.
2. León-Portilla 1973; J. E. S. Thompson 1960.
3. Kelley 1976; Lounsbury 1978; Satterthwaite 1965; J. E. S. Thompson 1960.
4. Henderson 1974.
5. Caso 1965; Marcus 1976b.
6. LaFarge and Byers 1931; Lincoln 1942; Miles 1952.
7. Kelley 1976:3–33; Satterthwaite 1965:625–31; J. E. S. Thompson 1960:303–10.
8. M. Coe 1957, 1976; Marcus 1976b.
9. Hunt 1977; Kelley 1976:53–59; J. E. S. Thompson 1934, 1960.

10. Kelley 1976:61–105; Schellhas 1904; J. E. S. Thompson 1960, 1970:197–329.
11. Davies 1977.
12. Means 1917:72; Puleston 1979.
13. Kelley 1976.
14. Tozzer, ed., 1941:169.
15. Kelley 1962b.
16. J. E. S. Thompson 1960, 1965.
17. Kelley 1962b; Knorozov 1967.
18. Durbin 1969; Kelley 1976:178–80.
19. Berlin 1958; Kelley 1976:213–19.
20. Proskouriakoff 1960, 1961a.
21. Coggins 1979; Dutting 1979; Jones 1977; Kelley 1962a, 1976:214–43; Lounsbury 1974; Marcus 1976a; Mathews and Schele 1974; Proskouriakoff 1963b, 1964; Schele 1979.
22. Kelley 1965; Kubler 1974; Lounsbury 1976.
23. Proskouriakoff 1961b.

5. Origins

1. Aveleyra 1964; Willey 1971.
2. Lynch 1978.
3. Brown 1980; Gruhn and Bryan 1977.
4. Lynch 1978:462; NacNeish et al. 1980.
5. A system of land reclamation involving the conversion of swampy areas to highly productive garden plots. See Armillas 1971; M. Coe 1964; Denevan 1970.
6. M. Coe and Flannery 1964, 1967; Moseley 1975.
7. For example, Holmberg 1950.
8. Bray 1976; Flannery 1973.
9. Flannery 1968.
10. Byers 1967; MacNeish 1972; MacNeish et al. 1972.
11. MacNeish and Peterson 1962.
12. Brown 1980; MacNeish et al. 1980.
13. Voorhies 1976.
14. Kaufman 1976.
15. MacNeish 1972; MacNeish et al. 1972:341–504.
16. Brush 1965.
17. The end of the Early Preclassic period is set at 1400 B.C. so that the following Middle Preclassic period corresponds to the centuries when Olmec civilization flourished in Mesoamerica. Many traditional chronologies, developed before recent discoveries of early Olmec material, place the beginning of the Middle Preclassic after 1000 B.C., a time now known to be near the midpoint of Olmec history.
18. The radiocarbon dates from Cuello are often cited as evidence that a village had grown up there by 2500 B.C., if not before. While such an early date is quite possible, the radiocarbon evidence and the early pottery would also be consistent with a placement of 2000 B.C., or even somewhat later. See Hammond 1977a, 1977b; Hammond et al. 1979; Pring 1979.
19. M. Coe 1961; M. Coe and Flannery 1967; Green and Lowe 1967; Lowe 1975, 1977; Sedat and Sharer 1972; Voorhies 1976.
20. Davis 1975; Green and Lowe 1967; Lowe 1975.
21. M. Coe and Diehl 1980.
22. M. Coe 1960; Evans and Meggers 1966.
23. Willey 1971.
24. M. Coe 1968; Henderson 1979.
25. M. Coe and Diehl 1980.
26. Henderson 1979.
27. M. Coe 1968; Drucker et al. 1959.
28. Henderson 1979.
29. Baudez and Becquelin 1973; Ekholm 1973; Henderson 1979; Joesink-Mandeville and Meluzin 1976; Lowe 1977.
30. M. Coe 1977.
31. Quirarte 1976, 1977.
32. M. Coe 1968.
33. Campbell and Kaufman 1976; N. Thomas 1974.
34. Lowe 1977.

6. Foundations of Maya Civilization

1. Willey et al. 1967.
2. Hammond 1977a, 1977b; Hammond et al. 1979.
3. Gifford 1976; Willey et al. 1965.
4. A type of wall construction involving a clay or mud coating over a framework of poles.
5. R. E. W. Adams 1971; A. L. Smith 1972; Willey 1973a; Willey and Smith 1969.
6. J. Graham et al. 1972; Sabloff 1975; Willey 1970; Willey et al. 1975.
7. Rands 1969, 1977.
8. Sedat and Sharer 1972; Sharer and Sedat 1973; Willey 1977a.
9. Borhegyi 1965a, 1965b; Michels 1979; Michels, ed., 1979; Rands and Smith 1965; Sanders and Michels, eds., 1969.
10. Sharer 1978b.
11. W. Coe 1965; Culbert 1977.
12. Hammond 1977b; Hammond et al. 1979.
13. R. E. W. Adams 1971; Ball 1977a, 1977c; W. Coe 1965; Culbert 1977; Gifford 1976; Hammond 1977b, 1977c; Lowe 1977; Lowe and Mason 1965; Rands and Smith 1965; Sabloff 1975; Sharer 1978b; Willey et al. 1967.
14. Ball 1977c; Culbert 1977; Hammond 1977b, 1977c; Willey 1977a; Willey et al. 1965, 1975.
15. Andrews IV 1965a, 1965b; Ball 1977c.
16. W. Coe and M. Coe 1956.
17. Willey 1973a, 1977a; Willey et al. 1975.
18. Borhegyi 1965a, 1965b; Michels 1979; Michels, ed., 1979; Sanders and Michels, eds., 1977.
19. Most traditional chronologies recognize a Protoclassic period between the advent of the Floral Park pottery style in the southern Maya lowlands (about 50 B.C.) and the beginning of the Classic period (about A.D. 250). Because this new style was a regional phenomenon, not a reflection of cultural change throughout the Maya world or even of newly developed local cultural complexity, the Late Preclassic period is extended until A.D. 250.
20. R. E. W. Adams 1971; Ball 1977a, 1977c; W. Coe 1965; Culbert 1977; Gifford 1976; Hammond 1977c; Lowe 1977; Lowe and Mason 1965; Rands and Smith 1965; Sabloff 1975; Sharer 1978b; Willey et al. 1967.
21. Andrews IV 1965a, 1965b; Ball 1977c; W. Coe 1965; Culbert 1977; Hammond 1977c; Lowe 1977; Lowe and Mason 1965; Sharer 1978b.
22. Andrews V 1977a, 1977b; Borhegyi 1965a; Lowe and Mason 1965; Miles 1965a; Norman 1973, 1976.
23. Norman 1973, 1976; Quirarte 1976, 1977.
24. M. Coe 1957, 1976; J. Graham et al. 1978; Marcus 1976b; Miles 1965a; Parsons 1973; Sharer 1978b; Sharer and Sedat 1973.
25. Borhegyi 1965a, 1965b; Michels 1979; Michels, ed., 1979; Sanders and Michels, eds., 1969; Shook and Kidder 1952.
26. J. Graham et al. 1978; Miles 1965a.
27. W. Coe 1965; W. Coe and McGinn 1963; Culbert 1977; Ricketson and Ricketson 1937; A. L. Smith 1950, 1973.
28. Hammond 1977c; Willey 1973a, 1977a; Willey et al. 1965, 1975.
29. Hammond 1977c; Pring 1977b; Willey et al. 1967.
30. Rands and Smith 1965; Sharer 1978b; Sharer and Gifford 1970.
31. R. E. W. Adams 1971; Gifford 1976; Merwin and Vaillant 1932; Willey et al. 1965.
32. W. Coe 1965; Lowe 1977; Rands 1977; R. E. Smith 1955.
33. R. E. W. Adams 1977b; Ball 1977a, 1977c; Webster 1974.
34. Andrews IV 1965a, 1965b; Ball 1977b.
35. Joesink-Mandeville and Meluzin 1976; E. H. Thompson 1897.
36. Hammond 1977c; Puleston 1977.
37. Freidel 1979; Rathje 1971, 1977; Sanders 1977; Webster 1977; Willey 1977b.

7. Classic Maya Civilization

1. W. Coe 1965; Culbert 1974; A. L. Smith 1950, 1973; R. E. Smith 1955; Willey 1977b; Willey et al. 1967.
2. M. Coe 1976; Marcus 1976a, 1976b.
3. W. Coe 1967; Coggins 1979; Marcus 1976a; Shook and Kidder 1961.

4. Borhegyi 1965a; Hellmuth 1978; Kidder et al. 1946; Michels, ed., 1979; Millon 1967; Millon, ed., 1973; Sanders 1978; Sanders and Michels, eds., 1969, 1977.
5. W. Coe 1967; Marcus 1976a; Willey 1977b.
6. Willey 1974.
7. Miller 1978; Pendergast 1971; Pring 1977a; Willey et al. 1978.
8. Marcus 1976a; Willey et al. 1965.
9. Longyear 1952; Sharer 1978a; Willey and Leventhal 1979; Willey et al. 1978.
10. R. E. W. Adams 1971; J. Graham 1972; Marcus 1976a; Rands 1977; A. L. Smith 1972; Willey 1973a, 1977a.
11. Rands 1977.
12. R. E. W. Adams 1977b; Ball 1974b, 1977a; Webster 1974.
13. Andrews IV 1965a, 1965b; A. Andrews 1980; Ball 1977b; Marcus 1976a.
14. Andrews V 1977a, 1977b; Borhegyi 1965a, 1965b; Kidder et al. 1946; Michels 1979; Michels, ed., 1979; Millon 1967; Millon, ed., 1973; Rands and Smith 1965; Sanders 1978; Sanders and Michels, eds., 1969, 1977; Sharer 1978b; Sheets 1979; Shook and Kidder 1952.
15. Becquelin and Baudez 1979; Lowe 1977; Lowe and Mason 1965; Marcus 1976a; Willey et al. 1967.
16. Lounsbury 1978; J. E. S. Thompson 1960.
17. Borhegyi 1965b; Bullard 1960; Hammond 1974; Haviland 1966; Sanders 1973; Voorhies 1972; Willey 1956; Willey and Bullard 1965; Willey et al. 1965.
18. R. E. W. Adams 1974; Haviland 1965, 1969, 1970, 1972a, 1972b; Puleston 1974; Puleston and Callender 1967; Sanders 1973; J. E. S. Thompson 1971.
19. Ball and Eaton 1972; Bronson 1966; Cook 1972; U. Cowgill 1962; Dumond 1961; Folan et al. 1979; Harrison 1977; Harrison and Turner, eds., 1978; Netting 1977; Puleston 1971, 1977; Puleston and Puleston 1971; Reina and Hill 1980; Sanders 1973; Siemens and Puleston 1972; Stark et al. 1976; J. E. S. Thompson 1974; Turner 1974, 1979; Turner and Johnson 1979; West 1964a:376; Wilken 1971; Zier 1980.
20. R. E. W. Adams 1970; A. Andrews 1980; Asaro et al. 1978; Becker 1973a, 1973b; Hammond 1972; Hester and Heizer 1978; Hurtado and Jester 1978; Michels 1975; Nelson et al. 1977; Sheets 1975; Sidrys 1976; Sidrys et al. 1975; Tourtellot and Sabloff 1972; Voorhies 1973.
21. Haviland 1967, 1968, 1971, 1972c, 1977; R. E. W. Adams 1972; Marcus 1976a; Molloy and Rathje 1974; Willey and Shimkin 1973.
22. Vogt 1968.
23. R. E. W. Adams 1971, 1977a; Molloy and Rathje 1974.
24. Culbert, ed., 1973.
25. R. E. Smith 1955.
26. R. E. W. Adams et al. 1961; Carr and Hazard 1961; W. Coe 1967; Maler 1911; Shook et al. 1958; Tozzer 1911.
27. Marcus 1976a; I. Graham 1978, 1980; I. Graham and Von Euw 1975; Hammond 1975.
28. Kidder 1947; Ricketson and Ricketson 1937; A. L. Smith 1950, 1973; R. E. Smith 1955.
29. R. E. W. Adams 1971, 1977a; J. Graham 1972, 1973; Marcus 1976a; Sabloff 1975; A. L. Smith 1972; Willey 1973a; Willey et al. 1975.
30. Gordon 1896; Longyear 1952; Marcus 1976a; Molloy and Rathje 1974; Morley 1920; Willey and Leventhal 1979; Willey et al. 1978.
31. Ashmore, ed., 1979; Ashmore and Sharer 1978; Morley 1935; Sharer 1978a.
32. Henderson 1978; Henderson et al. 1979; Longyear 1952; Marcus 1976a; Morley 1920; Sharer 1978b; Stone 1941; Strong et al. 1938.
33. Carnegie Institution 1955; W. Coe 1959; I. Graham and Von Euw 1977, 1979; Maler 1901, 1903; Marcus 1976a; Proskouriakoff 1950, 1960, 1963b, 1964; Rands 1973, 1977.
34. G. Andrews 1967; Becquelin and Baudez 1979; Carlson 1976; Lounsbury 1974, 1976; Marcus 1976a; Mathews and Schele 1974; Rands 1969, 1973, 1974, 1977; Ruz 1952–58, 1973; Schele 1976, 1977, 1979.
35. Andrews IV 1965a, 1965b; Ball 1977b; Bolles 1977; Corson 1976; Kurjack 1974; Pollock 1980; Tozzer 1957.
36. Folan et al. 1979; Marcus 1976a; Thompson et al. 1932.
37. R. E. W. Adams 1977b; Andrews IV 1965a; Ball 1977a; Potter 1976.
38. Becquelin and Baudez 1979; Lowe and Mason 1965.
39. Borhegyi 1965a, 1965b; Dillon 1977; Rands and Smith 1965; Sharer 1978b.
40. Culbert, ed., 1973.
41. W. Coe 1967; Culbert, ed., 1973; Shook et al. 1958.
42. Marcus 1976a; Proskouriakoff 1950; Rands 1973.

43. R. E. W. Adams 1971, 1973; J. Graham 1972.
44. Ball 1974a; J. Graham 1973; Miller 1977; Sabloff 1970, 1973.
45. Ball 1974a; Miller 1977; J. E. S. Thompson 1970:3–47.
46. Caso 1967:166–86; Foncerrada 1978, 1979; López and Molina 1976.
47. Culbert, ed., 1973.
48. R. E. W. Adams 1977b; Andrews IV 1973; Ball 1977a.
49. Ashmore and Sharer 1978; Sharer 1978a; Willey 1973b; Willey and Leventhal 1979; Willey et al. 1978.
50. G. Cowgill 1979; Hamblin and Pitcher 1980; Hosler et al. 1977; Sharer 1977; Willey and Shimkin 1973.
51. Andrews IV 1973.
52. Lowe and Mason 1965.
53. Borhegyi 1965a; Campbell 1977; Davies 1977.

8. *New Orientations: The Postclassic Maya*

1. Davies 1977.
2. Edmonson 1971; Recinos and Goetz, trans., 1953; Roys, trans. and ed., 1967.
3. Baudez and Mathews 1979; Carnegie Institution 1955; M. Coe 1973, 1978.
4. Tozzer, ed., 1941:20–23.
5. Davies 1977.
6. Roys, trans. and ed., 1967:70, 164, 178.
7. Ball 1974a; Davies 1977; Miller 1977; Proskouriakoff 1965:494–95; J. E. S. Thompson 1970:3–47; Tozzer 1957:110–11.
8. Roys, trans. and ed., 1967:84.
9. Ball 1974a; Davies 1977; Jiménez Moreno 1941, 1966.
10. Andrews IV 1965a; Aveni 1977; Ball 1974a, 1977b; Davies 1977; Morris et al. 1931; Proskouriakoff 1974; Ruppert 1935; Tozzer, ed., 1941, 1957.
11. Tozzer, ed., 1941:179.
12. Tozzer, ed., 1941:158.
13. Tozzer, ed., 1941:179–82.
14. Tozzer, ed., 1941:181.
15. Tozzer, ed., 1941:109, 183.
16. Hooton 1940:273.
17. Bullard 1973.
18. Henderson 1977; Henderson et al. 1979; unpublished research by Anthony Wonderley.
19. Borhegyi 1965a, 1965b; Campbell 1977; Carmack 1968; Davies 1977; Diehl et al. 1974; Fox 1980; Rands and Smith 1965; Shepard 1948.
20. Recinos and Goetz, trans., 1953:64–65. The rulers' noses were pierced so that they could wear jewels in them as symbols of authority.
21. Edmonson 1971:215–18.
22. Davies 1977; Roys, trans. and ed., 1967:83, 169; Tozzer, ed., 1941:23, 33–34.
23. Borhegyi 1965a, 1965b; Fox 1978; Wallace and Carmack, eds., 1978; Woodbury and Trik 1953.
24. Pollock et al. 1962; Roys, trans. and ed., 1967; Tozzer, ed., 1941.
25. Tozzer, ed., 1941:23–26, 215.
26. Tozzer, ed., 1941:26.
27. Pollock et al. 1962; Proskouriakoff 1955.
28. Roys, trans. and ed., 1967:92.
29. Tozzer, ed., 1941:25–27.
30. Andrews IV 1965a, 1965b.
31. Tozzer, ed., 1941:32, 216.
32. Tozzer, ed., 1941:36–37, 39.
33. Henderson 1977.
34. Tozzer, ed., 1941:36–37.
35. Tozzer, ed., 1941:vii, 44–46.
36. Roys 1957, 1965, 1972.
37. Tozzer, ed., 1941:39.
38. Sabloff and Freidel 1975; Sabloff and Rathje 1975; Sabloff et al. 1974; Sabloff and Rathje, eds., 1975.
39. Lothrop 1924.

40. Fariss et al. 1975; Gann 1900; Miller 1973, 1975; Pagden, trans. and ed., 1971:377, 519; Sanders 1960; Vogt 1969b, 1970.
41. Díaz 1916; Pagden, trans. and ed., 1971; Scholes and Roys 1968.
42. Bullard 1970, 1973; Hellmuth 1977; Pagden, trans. and ed., 1971; J. E. S. Thompson 1951.
43. Díaz 1916; Henderson 1977, 1978; Henderson et al. 1979; Pagden, trans. and ed., 1971; Simpson, trans. and ed., 1965; unpublished research by Anthony Wonderley.
44. R. M. Adams 1961; Lowe and Mason 1965; Navarrete 1966.
45. Borhegyi 1965a, 1965b; Fox 1978; Woodbury and Trik 1953.
46. Carmack 1968; Fox 1978, 1980.
47. Campbell 1977; Kaufman 1976.
48. Carmack 1973; Edmonson 1971; Fox 1978; Goetz and Morley, eds. and trans., 1950; Wallace and Carmack, eds., 1977.
49. Fox 1978; Guillemin 1967, 1977; Recinos and Goetz, trans., 1953.
50. Miles 1957, 1965b; Sharer 1974, 1978b.

9. *Perspectives on the Maya*

1. G. Cowgill 1979; Culbert, ed., 1973; Hamblin and Pitcher 1980; Hosler et al. 1977; Sharer 1977; Willey and Shimkin 1973.
2. Sanders 1977.
3. Webster 1977.
4. Rathje 1971, 1977.
5. Voorhies 1973.
6. Freidel 1979.
7. Redfield 1950; Redfield and Villa Rojas 1934.
8. Henderson 1977, 1978. John Murra (1968, 1971) has described the enclave or archipelago pattern of territorial organization in the Andes.
9. Gibson 1952; Pagden, trans. and ed., 1971.

BIBLIOGRAPHY

ADAMS, RICHARD E. W. 1970. Suggested Classic period occupational specialization in the southern Maya lowlands. In William R. Bullard, Jr., ed., *Monographs and Papers in Maya Archaeology*, pp. 487–98. Harvard University, Peabody Museum of Archaeology and Ethnology, Papers, vol. 61.

———. 1971. *The Ceramics of Altar de Sacrificios*. Harvard University, Peabody Museum of Archaeology and Ethnology, Papers, vol. 63, no. 1.

———. 1972. Reply to Haviland. *American Antiquity* 37:140.

———. 1973. Maya collapse: transformation and termination in the ceramic sequence at Altar de Sacrificios. In T. Patrick Culbert, ed., *The Classic Maya Collapse*, pp. 133–63. Albuquerque: University of New Mexico Press.

———. 1974. A trial estimation of Classic Maya palace populations at Uaxactún. In Norman Hammond, ed., *Mesoamerican Archaeology: New Approaches*, pp. 285–96. Austin: University of Texas Press.

———. 1977a. Comments on the glyphic texts of the "Altar Vase." In Norman Hammond, ed., *Social Process in Maya Prehistory: Studies in Honour of Sir Eric Thompson*, pp. 409–20. New York: Academic Press.

———. 1977b. Río Bec archaeology and the rise of Maya civilization. In Richard E. W. Adams, ed., *The Origins of Maya Civilization*, pp. 77–99. Albuquerque: University of New Mexico Press.

———. et al. 1961. *Tikal Reports*, nos. 5–10. University of Pennsylvania, University Museum Monographs.

ADAMS, ROBERT M. 1961. Changing patterns of territorial organization in the central highlands of Chiapas, Mexico. *American Antiquity* 26:341–60.

ANDREWS, ANTHONY P. 1980. The salt trade of the Maya. *Archaeology* 33(4):24–33.

ANDREWS IV, E. WYLLYS. 1965a. Archaeology and pre-history in the northern Maya lowlands: an introduction. *Handbook of Middle American Indians* 2:288–330. Austin: University of Texas Press.

————. 1965b. Progress report on the 1960–1964 field seasons, National Geographic Society–Tulane University Dzibilchaltun Program. In *Archaeological Investigations on the Yucatan Peninsula*, pp. 23–67. Tulane University, Middle American Research Institute, Publication 31.

————. 1973. The development of Maya civilization after abandonment of the southern cities. In T. Patrick Culbert, ed., *The Classic Maya Collapse*, pp. 243–65. Albuquerque: University of New Mexico Press.

ANDREWS V, E. WYLLYS. 1977a. *The Archaeology of Quelepa, El Salvador.* Tulane University, Middle American Research Institute, Publication 42.

————. 1977b. The southeastern periphery of Mesoamerica: a view from eastern El Salvador. In Norman Hammond, ed., *Social Process in Maya Prehistory: Studies in Honour of Sir Eric Thompson*, pp. 113–34. New York: Academic Press.

ANDREWS, GEORGE F. 1967. *Comalcalco, Tabasco, Mexico: An Architectonic Survey of a Maya Ceremonial Center.* Eugene: University of Oregon.

ARMILLAS, PEDRO. 1971. Gardens on swamps. *Science* 174:653–61.

ASARO, F., H. V. MICHEL, R. SIDRYS, AND F. STROSS. 1978. High-precision chemical characterization of major obsidian sources in Guatemala. *American Antiquity* 43:436–43.

ASHMORE, WENDY, ed. 1979. *Quiriguá Reports*, vol. 1. University of Pennsylvania, University Museum Monographs.

————. AND ROBERT J. SHARER. 1978. Excavations at Quiriguá, Guatemala: the ascent of an elite Maya center. *Archaeology* 31(6):10–19.

AUSTIN, DONALD M., AND GORDON LOTHSON. 1969. Mound B-II-1 excavation. In William T. Sanders and Joseph W. Michels, eds., *The Pennsylvania State University Kaminaljuyú Project—1968 Season*, pt. 1, *The Exacavations*, pp. 99–136. Pennsylvania State University, Occasional Papers in Anthropology, no. 2.

AVELEYRA ARROYO DE ANDA, LUIS. 1964. The primitive hunters. *Handbook of Middle American Indians* 1:384–412. Austin: University of Texas Press.

AVENI, ANTHONY F. 1977. Concepts of positional astronomy employed in ancient Mesoamerican architecture. In Anthony F. Aveni, ed., *Native American Astronomy*, pp. 3–19. Austin: University of Texas Press.

BALL, JOSEPH W. 1974a. A coordinate approach to nothern Maya prehistory. *American Antiquity* 39:85–93.

BALL, JOSEPH W. 1974b. A Teotihuacán-style cache from the Maya lowlands. *Archaeology* 27(1):2–9.

————. 1977a. *Archaeological Ceramics of Becán, Campeche, Mexico.* Tulane University, Middle American Research Institute, Publication 43.

————. 1977b. An hypothetical outline of coastal Maya prehistory: 300 B.C.–A.D. 1200. In Norman Hammond, ed., *Social Process in Maya Prehistory: Studies in Honour of Sir Eric Thompson*, pp. 167–96. New York: Academic Press.

————. 1977c. The rise of the northern Maya chiefdoms: a socioprocessual analysis. In Richard E. W. Adams, ed., *The Origins of Maya Civilization*, pp. 101–32. Albuquerque: University of New Mexico Press.

————. AND JACK D. EATON. 1972. Marine resources and the prehistoric lowland Maya: a comment. *American Anthropologist* 74:772–76.

BAUDEZ, CLAUDE F., AND PIERRE BECQUELIN. 1973. *Archéologie de Los Naranjos, Honduras.* Mexico City: Mission Archéologique et Ethnologique Française au Méxique.

————. AND PETER MATHEWS. 1979. Capture and sacrifice at Palenque. In Merle Greene Robertson and Donald Call Jeffers, eds., *Tercera Mesa Redonda de Palenque*, pp. 31–40. Monterey, Calif.: Herald Printers.

BECKER, MARSHALL JOSEPH. 1973a. Archaeological evidence for occupational specialization among the Classic period Maya at Tikal, Guatemala. *American Antiquity* 38:396–406.

_____. 1973b. The evidence for complex exchange systems among the ancient Maya. *American Antiquity* 38:222–23.

BECQUELIN, PIERRE, AND CLAUDE F. BAUDEZ. 1979. *Toniná: Une Cité Maya du Chiapas (Méxique)*. Mexico: Mission Archéologique et Ethnologique Française au Méxique.

BERLIN, HEINRICH. 1958. El glifo "emblema" en las inscripciones mayas. *Journal de la Société des Américanistes* 47:111–19.

BOLLES, JOHN S. 1977. *Las Monjas: A Major Pre-Mexican Architectural Complex at Chichén Itzá*. Norman: University of Oklahoma Press.

BORHEGYI, STEPHAN F. 1960. America's ball game. *Natural History* 69:48–59.

_____. 1965a. Archaeological synthesis of the Guatemalan highlands. *Handbook of Middle American Indians* 2:3–58. Austin: University of Texas Press.

_____. 1965b. Settlement patterns of the Guatemalan highlands. *Handbook of Middle American Indians* 2:59–75. Austin: University of Texas Press.

BRAY, WARWICK. 1976. From predation to production: the nature of agricultural evolution in Mexico and Peru. In G. de G. Sieveking, T. H. Longworth, and K. E. Wilson, eds., *Problems in Economic and Social Archaeology*, pp. 73–95. London: Gerald Duckworth.

BRONSON, BENNET. 1966. Roots and the subsistence of the ancient Maya. *Southwestern Journal of Anthropology* 22:251–79.

BROWN, KENNETH L. 1980. A brief report on Paleoindian-Archaic occupation in the Quiché Basin, Guatemala. *American Antiquity* 45:313–24.

BRUNHOUSE, ROBERT L. 1971. *Sylvanus G. Morley and the World of the Ancient Mayas*. Norman: University of Oklahoma Press.

_____. 1973. *In Search of the Maya: The First Archaeologists*. Albuquerque: University of New Mexico Press.

_____. 1975. *Pursuit of the Ancient Maya: Some Archaeologists of Yesterday*. Albuquerque: University of New Mexico Press.

BRUSH, CHARLES. 1965. Pox pottery: earliest identified Mexican ceramic. *Science* 149:194–95.

BULLARD, WILLIAM R., JR. 1960. Maya settlement pattern in northeastern Petén, Guatemala. *American Antiquity* 25:355–72.

_____. 1970. Topoxté: a Postclassic Maya site in Petén, Guatemala. In William R. Bullard, Jr., ed., *Monographs and Papers in Maya Archaeology*, pp. 245–307. Harvard University, Peabody Museum of Archaeology and Ethnology, Papers, vol. 61.

_____. 1973. Postclassic culture in central Petén and adjacent British Honduras. In T. Patrick Culbert, ed., *The Classic Maya Collapse*, pp. 221–41. Albuquerque: University of New Mexico Press.

BUNZEL, RUTH. 1952. *Chichicastenango*. American Ethnological Society, Publication 22.

BYERS, DOUGLAS S., ed. 1967. *The Prehistory of the Tehuacán Valley*, vol. 1: *Environment and Subsistence*. Austin: University of Texas Press.

CAMPBELL, LYLE. 1977. *Quichean Linguistic Prehistory*. University of California Publications in Linguistics 81.

_____. AND TERRENCE KAUFMAN. 1976. A linguistic look at the Olmecs. *American Antiquity* 41:80–89.

CARLSON, JOHN B. 1976. Astronomical investigations and site orientation influences at Palenque. In Merle Greene Robertson, ed., *The Art, Iconography and Dynastic History of Palenque, Part III*, pp. 107–22. Pebble Beach, Calif.: Robert Louis Stevenson School.

CARMACK, ROBERT M. 1968. Toltec influence on the Postclassic culture history of highland Guatemala. In *Archaeological Studies of Middle America*, pp. 42–92. Tulane University, Middle American Research Institute, Publication 26.

_____. 1973. *Quichean Civilization: The Ethnohistoric, Ethnographic, and Archaeological Sources*. Berkeley: University of California Press.

Carnegie Institution of Washington. 1955. *Ancient Maya Paintings of Bonampak, Mexico.* Supplementary Publication 46.

CARR, ROBERT F., AND JAMES E. HAZARD. 1961. Map of the ruins of Tikal, El Petén, Guatemala. *Tikal Report,* no. 11. University of Pennsylvania, University Museum Monographs.

CASO, ALFONSO. 1965. Zapotec writing and calendar. *Handbook of Middle American Indians* 3:931–47. Austin: University of Texas Press.

———. 1967. *Los Calendarios Prehispánicos.* Universidad Nacional Autónoma de México, Instituto de Investigaciones Históricas, Serie Cultura Nahuatl, Monografías 6.

CHAMBERLAIN, ROBERT S. 1948. *The Conquest and Colonization of Yucatan, 1517–1550.* Carnegie Institution of Washington, Publication 582.

———. 1953. *The Conquest and Colonization of Honduras, 1502–1550* (reprinted ed., 1966). New York: Octagon Books.

CHAPMAN, ANNE M. 1957. Port of trade enclaves in Aztec and Maya civilizations. In Karl Polanyi, Conrad M. Arensberg, and Harry W. Pearson, eds., *Trade and Market in the Early Empires,* pp. 114–53. Glencoe, Ill.: Free Press.

CHILDE, V. GORDON. 1951. *Man Makes Himself.* New York: New American Library.

———. 1954. *What Happened in History.* Rev. ed. Baltimore: Penguin Books.

CLOSS, MICHAEL P. 1976. New information on the European discovery of Yucatan and the correlation of the Maya and Christian calendars. *American Antiquity* 41:192–95.

Codex Dresdensis. 1975. Graz: Akademische Druck- u. Verlagsanstalt.

Codex Tro-Cortesianus (Codex Madrid). 1967. Graz: Akademische Druck- u. Verlagsanstalt.

COE, MICHAEL D. 1957. Cycle 7 monuments in Middle America: a reconsideration. *American Anthropologist* 59:597–611.

———. 1960. Archaeological linkages with North and South America at La Victoria, Guatemala. *American Anthropologist* 62:363–93.

———. 1961. *La Victoria: An Early Site on the Pacific Coast of Guatemala.* Harvard University, Peabody Museum of Archaeology and Ethnology, Papers, vol. 53.

———. 1964. The chinampas of Mexico. *Scientific American* 211(1):90–98.

———. 1966. *The Maya.* London: Thames & Hudson.

———. 1968. *America's First Civilization.* New York: American Heritage Publishing Company.

———. 1973. *The Maya Scribe and His World.* New York: Grolier Club.

———. 1976. Early steps in the evolution of Maya writing. In H. B. Nicholson, ed., *Origins of Religious Art and Iconography in Preclassic Mesoamerica.* Los Angeles: UCLA Latin American Center.

———. 1977. Olmec and Maya: a study in relationships. In Richard E. W. Adams, ed., *The Origins of Maya Civilization,* pp. 183–95. Albuquerque: University of New Mexico Press.

———. 1978. *Lords of the Underworld: Masterpieces of Classic Maya Ceramics.* Princeton University, The Art Museum.

——— AND RICHARD A. DIEHL. 1980. *In the Land of the Olmec.* 2 vols. Austin: University of Texas Press.

——— AND KENT V. FLANNERY. 1964. Microenvironments and Mesoamerican prehistory. *Science* 143:650–54.

——— AND ———. 1967. *Early Cultures and Human Ecology in South Coastal Guatemala.* Smithsonian Institution, Contributions to Anthropology, no. 3.

COE, WILLIAM R. 1959. *Piedras Negras Archaeology: Artifacts, Caches, and Burials.* University of Pennsylvania, University Museum Monographs.

———. 1965. Tikal, Guatemala, and emergent Maya civilization. *Science* 147:1401–19.

———. 1967. *Tikal: A Handbook of the Ancient Maya Ruins.* Philadelphia: University of Pennsylvania, The University Museum.

———— AND MICHAEL D. COE. 1956. Excavations at Nohoch Ek, British Honduras. *American Antiquity* 21:370–82.

———— AND JOHN J. McGINN. 1963. Tikal: The North Acropolis and an early tomb. *Expedition* 5 (2):25–32.

COGGINS, CLEMENCY. 1979. A new order and the role of the calendar: some characteristics of the Middle Classic period at Tikal. In Norman Hammond and Gordon R. Willey, eds., *Maya Archaeology and Ethnohistory*, pp. 38–50. Austin: University of Texas Press.

COLLIER, ALBERT. 1964. The American Mediterranean. *Handbook of Middle American Indians* 1:122–42. Austin: University of Texas Press.

COOK, SHERBURNE F. 1972. *Prehistoric Demography*. Addison-Wesley Module in Anthropology no. 16.

CORSON, CHRISTOPHER. 1976. *Maya Anthropomorphic Figurines from Jaina Island, Campeche*. Ballena Press Studies in Mesoamerican Art, Archaeology and Ethnohistory, no. 1.

COWGILL, GEORGE L. 1979. Teotihuacán, internal militaristic competition, and the fall of the Classic Maya. In Norman Hammond and Gordon R. Willey, eds., *Maya Archaeology and Ethnohistory*, pp. 51–62. Austin: University of Texas Press.

COWGILL, URSULA M. 1962. An agricultural study of the southern Maya lowlands. *American Anthropologist* 64:273–86.

CROSBY, ALFRED W. 1972. *The Columbian Exchange: Biological and Cultural Consequences of 1492*. Westport, Conn.: Greenwood Press.

CULBERT, T. PATRICK. 1973. The Maya downfall at Tikal. In T. Patrick Culbert, ed., *The Classic Maya Collapse*, pp. 63–92. Albuquerque: University of New Mexico Press.

————. 1974. *The Lost Civilization: The Story of the Classic Maya*. New York: Harper & Row.

————. 1977. Early Maya development at Tikal, Guatemala. In Richard E. W. Adams, ed., *The Origins of Maya Civilization*, pp. 27–43. Albuquerque: University of New Mexico Press.

————, ed. 1973. *The Classic Maya Collapse*. Albuquerque: University of New Mexico Press.

DANIEL, GLYN. 1968. *The First Civilizations: The Archaeology of Their Origins*. New York: Thomas Y. Crowell.

DAVIES, NIGEL. 1977. *The Toltecs: Until the Fall of Tula*. Norman: University of Oklahoma Press.

DAVIS, DAVE D. 1975. Patterns of Early Formative subsistence in southern Mesoamerica. *Man* 10:41–59.

DENEVAN, WILLIAM M. 1970. Aboriginal drained-field cultivation in the Americas. *Science* 169:647–54.

DIAZ DEL CASTILLO, BERNAL. 1912, 1916. *The True History of the Conquest of New Spain*. Vols. 4 and 5. Trans. A. P. Maudslay. London: Hakluyt Society.

DIEHL, RICHARD A., R. LOMAS, AND J. T. WYNN. 1974. Toltec trade with Central America: new light and evidence. *Archaeology* 27:182–87.

DILLON, BRIAN D. 1977. *Salinas de los Nueve Cerros, Guatemala: Preliminary Archaeological Investigations*. Ballena Press Studies in Mesoamerican Art, Archaeology and Ethnohistory, no. 2.

DRUCKER, PHILIP, ROBERT F. HEIZER, AND ROBERT J. SQUIER. 1959. *Excavations at La Venta, Tabasco, 1955*. Smithsonian Institution, Bureau of American Ethnology, Bulletin 170.

DUBY, GERTRUDE, AND FRANS BLOM. 1969. The Lacandón. *Handbook of Middle American Indians* 7:276–97. Austin: University of Texas Press.

DUMOND, DONALD E. 1961. Swidden agriculture and the rise of Maya civilization. *Southwestern Journal of Anthropology* 17:301–16.

DURBIN, MARSHALL. 1969. *An Interpretation of Bishop Diego de Landa's Maya Alphabet*. Tulane University, Middle American Research Institute, Philological and Documentary Studies, vol. 2, no. 4.

DUTTING, DIETER. 1979. Birth, inauguration and death in the inscriptions of Palenque, Chiapas, Mexico. In Merle Greene Robertson and Donald Call Jeffers, eds. *Tercera Mesa Redonda de Palenque*, pp. 183–214. Monterey, Calif.: Herald Printers.

EDMONSON, MUNRO S. 1971. *The Book of Counsel: The Popol Vuh of the Quiché Maya of Guatemala.* Tulane University, Middle American Research Institute, Publication 35.

EKHOLM, SUSANNA M. 1973. *The Olmec Rock Carving at Xoc, Chiapas, Mexico.* New World Archaeological Foundation Papers, no. 32.

EVANS, CLIFFORD, AND BETTY J. MEGGERS. 1966. Mesoamerica and Ecuador. *Handbook of Middle American Indians.* 4:243–64.

FARISS, NANCY M., ARTHUR G. MILLER, AND ARLEN F. CHASE. 1975. Late Maya mural paintings from Quintana Roo, Mexico. *Journal of Field Archaeology* 2:5–10.

FLANNERY, KENT V. 1968. Archaeological systems theory and early Mesoamerica. In Betty J. Meggers, ed., *Anthropological Archaeology in the Americas*, pp. 67–87. Anthropological Society of Washington.

———. 1973. The origins of agriculture. *Annual Review of Anthropology* 2:271–310.

FOLAN, WILLIAM J., LARAINE A. FLETCHER, AND ELLEN R. KINTZ. 1979. Fruit, fiber, bark, and resin: social organization of a Maya urban center. *Science* 204:697–701.

FONCERRADA DE MOLINA, MARTA. 1978. The Cacaxtla murals: an example of cultural contact? *Ibero-Amerikanisches Archiv* 4(2):141–60.

———. 1979. La pintura mural de Cacaxtla. *Actes du XLIIe Congrès International des Américanistes* 7:321–35.

FOX, JOHN W. 1978. *Quiché Conquest: Centralism and Regionalism in Highland Guatemalan State Development.* Albuquerque: University of New Mexico Press.

———. 1980. Lowland to highland Mexicanization processes in southern Mesoamerica. *American Antiquity* 45:43–54.

FREIDEL, DAVID A. 1979. Culture areas and interaction spheres: contrasting approaches to the emergence of civilization in the Maya lowlands. *American Antiquity* 44:36–54.

GANN, THOMAS. 1900. *Mounds in Northern Honduras.* Smithsonian Institution, Nineteenth Annual Report, pt. 2, pp. 655–92.

GIBSON, CHARLES. 1952. *Tlaxcala in the Sixteenth Century.* New Haven: Yale University Press.

GIFFORD, JAMES C. 1976. *Prehistoric Pottery Analysis and the Ceramics of Barton Ramie in the Belize Valley.* Harvard University, Peabody Museum of Archaeology and Ethnology, Memoirs, vol. 18.

GOETZ, DELIA, AND SYLVANUS G. MORLEY, eds. and trans. 1950. *Popol Vuh: The Sacred Book of the Ancient Quiché Maya.* Norman: University of Oklahoma Press.

GORDON, GEORGE B. 1896. *Prehistoric Ruins of Copán, Honduras.* Harvard University, Peabody Museum of American Archaeology and Ethnology, Memoirs, vol. 1, no. 1.

GOSSEN, GARY H. 1974. *Chamulas in the World of the Sun: Time and Space in a Maya Oral Tradition.* Cambridge: Harvard University Press.

GRAHAM, IAN. 1978. *Corpus of Maya Hieroglyphic Inscriptions*, vol. 2, pt. 2. Cambridge: Harvard University, Peabody Museum of Archaeology and Ethnology.

———. 1980. *Corpus of Maya Hieroglyphic Inscriptions*, vol. 2, pt. 3. Cambridge: Harvard University, Peabody Museum of Archaeology and Ethnology.

———. AND ERIC VON EUW. 1975. *Corpus of Maya Hieroglyphic Inscriptions*, vol. 2, pt. 1. Cambridge: Harvard University, Peabody Museum of Archaeology and Ethnology.

——— AND ———. 1977. *Corpus of Maya Hieroglyphic Inscriptions*, vol. 3, pt. 1.

Cambridge: Harvard University, Peabody Museum of Archaeology and Ethnology.

——— AND ———. 1979. *Corpus of Maya Hieroglyphic Inscriptions*, vol. 3, pt. 2. Cambridge: Harvard University, Peabody Museum of Archaeology and Ethnology.

GRAHAM, JOHN A. 1972. *The Hieroglyphic Inscriptions and Monumental Art of Altar de Sacrificios*. Harvard University, Peabody Museum of Archaeology and Ethnology, Papers, vol. 64, no. 2.

———. 1973. Aspects of non-Classic presences in the inscriptions and sculptural art of Seibal. In T. Patrick Culbert, ed., *The Classic Maya Collapse*, pp. 207–19. Albuquerque: University of New Mexico Press.

———, ROBERT F. HEIZER, AND EDWIN M. SHOOK. 1978. Abaj Takalik 1976: exploratory investigations. *University of California, Archaeological Research Facility, Contributions* 36:85–109.

———, THOMAS R. HESTER, AND ROBERT N. JACK. 1972. Sources for the obsidian at the ruins of Seibal, Petén, Guatemala. *University of California, Archaeological Research Facility, Contributions* 16:111–16.

GREEN, DEE F., AND GARETH W. LOWE. 1967. *Altamira and Padre Piedra: Early Preclassic Sites in Chiapas, Mexico*. New World Archaeological Foundation Papers, no. 20.

GRUHN, RUTH, AND ALAN L. BRYAN. 1977. Los Tapiales: A Paleoindian campsite in the Guatemalan highlands. *American Philosophical Society, Proceedings* 121(3):235–73.

GUILLEMIN, GEORGES F. 1967. The ancient Cakchiquel capital of Iximché. *Expedition* 9(2):22–35.

———. 1977. Urbanism and hierarchy at Iximché. In Norman Hammond, ed., *Social Process in Maya Prehistory: Studies in Honour of Sir Eric Thompson*, pp. 227–64. New York: Academic Press.

HAMBLIN, ROBERT L., AND BRIAN L. PITCHER. 1980. The Classic Maya collapse: testing class conflict hypotheses. *American Antiquity* 45:246–67.

HAMMOND, NORMAN. 1972. Obsidian trade routes in the Maya area. *Science* 178:1092–93.

———. 1974. The distribution of Late Classic Maya major ceremonial centers in the Central Area. In Norman Hammond, ed., *Mesoamerican Archaeology: New Approaches*, pp. 313–34. Austin: University of Texas Press.

———. 1975. *Lubaantún: A Classic Maya Realm*. Harvard University, Peabody Museum of Archaeology and Ethnology, Monographs, no. 2.

———. 1977a. The earliest Maya. *Scientific American* 236(3):116–33.

———. 1977b. The Early Formative in the Maya lowlands. In Norman Hammond, ed., *Social Process in Maya Prehistory: Studies in Honour of Sir Eric Thompson*, pp. 77–101. New York: Academic Press.

———. 1977c. Ex oriente lux: a view from Belize. In Richard E. W. Adams, ed., *The Origins of Maya Civilization*, pp. 45–76. Albuquerque: University of New Mexico Press.

———, DUNCAN PRING, RICHARD WILK, SARA DONAGHEY, FRANK P. SAUL, ELIZABETH S. WING, ARLENE V. MILLER, AND LAWRENCE H. FELDMAN. 1979. The earliest lowland Maya: definition of the Swasey phase. *American Antiquity* 44:92–110.

HARRISON, PETER D. 1977. The rise of the *bajos* and the fall of the Maya. In Norman Hammond, ed., *Social Process in Maya Prehistory: Studies in Honour of Sir Eric Thompson*, pp. 469–508. New York: Academic Press.

——— AND B. L. TURNER II, eds. 1978. *Pre-Hispanic Maya Agriculture*. Albuquerque: University of New Mexico Press.

HAVILAND, WILLIAM A. 1965. Prehistoric settlement at Tikal, Guatemala. *Expedition* 7(3):15–23.

———. 1966. Maya settlement patterns: a critical review. In *Archaeological Studies in Middle America*, pp. 21–47. Tulane University, Middle American Research Institute, Publication 26.

―――. 1967. Stature at Tikal, Guatemala: implications for ancient Maya demography and social organization. *American Antiquity* 32:316–25.

―――. 1968. *Ancient lowland Maya social organization.* In *Archaeological Studies in Middle America,* pp. 93–117. Tulane University, Middle American Research Institute, Publication 26.

―――. 1969. A new population estimate for Tikal, Guatemala. *American Antiquity* 34:429–33.

―――. 1970. Tikal, Guatemala, and Mesoamerican urbanism. *World Archaeology* 2:186–97.

―――. 1971. Entombment, authority, and descent at Altar de Sacrificios, Guatemala. *American Antiquity* 36:102–5.

―――. 1972a. Estimates of Maya population: comments on Thompson's comments. *American Antiquity* 37:261–62.

―――. 1972b. Family size, prehistoric population estimates, and the ancient Maya. *American Antiquity* 37:135–39.

―――. 1972c. A new look at Classic Maya social organization at Tikal. *Cerámica de Cultura Maya et al.* 8:1–16.

―――. 1977. Dynastic genealogies from Tikal, Guatemala: implications for descent and political organization. *American Antiquity* 42:61–67.

HEALY, PAUL F. 1974. The Cuyamel caves: Preclassic sites in northeast Honduras. *American Antiquity* 39:435–47.

HELLMUTH, NICHOLAS. 1977. Cholti-Lacandón (Chiapas) and Petén-Ytzá agriculture, settlement pattern and population. In Norman Hammond, ed., *Social Process in Maya Prehistory: Studies in Honour of Sir Eric Thompson,* pp. 421–48. New York: Academic Press.

―――. 1978. Teotihuacán art in the Escuintla, Guatemala region. In Esther Pasztory, ed., *Middle Classic Mesoamerica: A.D. 400–700,* pp. 71–85. New York: Columbia University Press.

HENDERSON, JOHN S. 1974. Origin of the 260-day cycle in Mesoamerica. *Science* 185–542.

―――. 1977. The Valle de Naco: ethnohistory and archaeology in northwestern Honduras. *Ethnohistory* 24:363–77.

―――. 1978. El noroeste de Honduras y la frontera oriental maya. *Yaxkin* 2:241–53.

―――. 1979. *Atopula, Guerrero, and Olmec Horizons in Mesoamerica.* Yale University Publications in Anthropology 77.

―――, ILENE STERNS, ANTHONY WONDERLEY, AND PATRICIA A. URBAN. 1979. Archaeological investigations in the Valle de Naco, northwestern Honduras: a preliminary report. *Journal of Field Archaeology* 6:169–92.

HESTER, THOMAS R. AND ROBERT F. HEIZER. 1978. An introductory bibliography for Mesoamerican obsidian studies. In Thomas R. Hester, ed., *Archaeological Studies of Mesoamerican Obsidian,* pp. 200–210. Ballena Press Studies in Mesoamerican Art, Archaeology and Ethnohistory, no. 3.

HOLMBERG, ALAN R. 1950. *Nomads of the Long Bow: The Sirionó of Eastern Bolivia.* Smithsonian Institution, Institute of Social Anthropology, Publication 10.

HOOTON, EARNEST A. 1940. Skeletons from the Cenote of Sacrifice at Chichén Itzá. In *The Maya and Their Neighbors,* pp. 272–80. New York: D. Appleton-Century.

HOSLER, DOROTHY, JEREMY A. SABLOFF, AND DALE RUNGE. 1977. Simulation model development: a case study of the Classic Maya collapse. In Norman Hammond, ed., *Social Process in Maya Prehistory: Studies in Honour of Sir Eric Thompson,* pp. 553–90. New York: Academic Press.

HUNT, EVA. 1977. *The Transformation of the Hummingbird: Cultural Roots of a Zinacantecan Mythical Poem.* Ithaca: Cornell University Press.

HURTADO DE MENDOZA, LUIS AND WILLIAM A. JESTER. 1978. Obsidian sources in Guatemala: a regional approach. *American Antiquity* 43:424–35.

JIMÉNEZ MORENO, WIGBERTO. 1941. Tula y los toltecas según las fuentes históricas. *Revista Mexicana de Estudios Antropológicos* 5:79–83.

_____. 1966. Los imperios prehispánicos de Mesoamérica. *Revista Mexicana de Estudios Antropológicos* 20:179–95.

JOESINK-MANDEVILLE, L. R. V., AND SYLVIA MELUZIN. 1976. Olmec-Maya relationships: Olmec influence in Yucatan. In H. B. Nicholson, ed., *Origins of Religious Art and Iconography in Preclassic Mesoamerica*, pp. 87–105. Los Angeles: UCLA Latin American Center.

JONES, CHRISTOPHER. 1977. Inauguration dates of three Late Classic rulers of Tikal, Guatemala. *American Antiquity* 42:28–60.

KAUFMAN, TERRENCE. 1976. Archaeological and linguistic correlations in Mayaland and associated areas of Meso-America. *World Archaeology* 8(1):101–18.

KELLEY, DAVID H. 1962a. Glyphic evidence for a dynastic sequence at Quiriguá, Guatemala. *American Antiquity* 27:323–35.

_____. 1962b. A history of the decipherment of the Maya script. *Anthropological Linguistics* 4(8):1–48.

_____. 1965. The birth of the gods at Palenque. *Estudios de Cultura Maya* 5:93–134.

_____. 1976. *Deciphering the Maya Script.* Austin: University of Texas Press.

KELLY, JOHN E. 1932. *Pedro de Alvarado: Conquistador.* Port Washington, N.Y.: Kennikat Press.

KEMRER, MEADE F. 1968. A re-examination of the ball-game in pre-Columbian Mesoamerica. *Cerámica de Cultura Maya et al.* 5:1–26.

KIDDER, ALFRED V. 1947. *The Artifacts of Uaxactún, Guatemala.* Carnegie Institution of Washington, Publication 576.

_____, JESSE D. JENNINGS, AND EDWIN M. SHOOK. 1946. *Excavations at Kaminaljuyú, Guatemala.* Carnegie Institution of Washington, Publication 561.

KIRCHHOFF, PAUL. 1943. Mesoamerica: its geographic limits, ethnic composition, and cultural characteristics. In John A. Graham, ed., *Ancient Mesoamerica: Selected Readings* (1966), pp. 1–14. Palo Alto, Calif.: Peek Publications.

KNOROZOV, YURII V. 1967. *Selected Chapters from the Writing of the Maya Indians.* Trans. Sophie Coe. Harvard University, Peabody Museum of Archaeology and Ethnology, Russian Translation Series, vol. 4.

KUBLER, GEORGE. 1974. Mythological ancestries in Classic Maya inscriptions. In Merle Greene Robertson, ed., *Primera Mesa Redonda de Palenque, Part II*, pp. 23–43. Pebble Beach, Calif.: Robert Louis Stevenson School.

KURJACK, EDWARD B. 1974. *Prehistoric Lowland Maya Community and Social Organization: A Case Study at Dzibilchaltún, Yucatan, Mexico.* Tulane University, Middle American Research Institute, Publication 38.

LA FARGE, OLIVER, AND DOUGLAS S. BYERS. 1931. *The Year Bearer's People.* Tulane University, Middle American Research Institute, Publication 3.

LAUGHLIN, ROBERT M. 1969a. The Huastec. *Handbook of Middle American Indians* 7:298–311. Austin: University of Texas Press.

_____. 1969b. The Tzotzil. *Handbook of Middle American Indians* 7:152–94. Austin: University of Texas Press.

LEÓN-PORTILLA, MIGUEL. 1973. *Time and Reality in the Thought of the Maya.* Boston: Beacon Press.

LINCOLN, J. STEWART. 1942. *The Maya Calendar of the Ixil of Guatemala.* Carnegie Institution of Washington, Contributions to American Anthropology and History, 38.

LONGYEAR, JOHN M. III. 1952. *Copán Ceramics: A Study of Southeastern Maya Pottery.* Carnegie Institution of Washington, Publication 597.

LÓPEZ, DIANA, AND DANIEL MOLINA. 1976. Los murales de Cacaxtla. *Instituto Nacional de Antropología e Historia, Boletín* 16:3–8.

LOTHROP, SAMUEL K. 1924. *Tulum: An Archaeological Study of the East Coast of Yucatan.* Carnegie Institution of Washington, Publication 335.

LOUNSBURY, FLOYD G. 1974. The inscription of the sarcophagus lid at Palenque. In Merle Greene Robertson, ed., *Primera Mesa Redonda de Palenque, Part II*, pp. 5–19. Pebble Beach, Calif.: Robert Louis Stevenson School.

———. 1976. A rationale for the initial date of the Temple of the Cross at Palenque. In Merle Greene Robertson, ed., *The Art, Iconography and Dynastic History of Palenque, Part III*, pp. 211-24. Pebble Beach, Calif.: Robert Louis Stevenson School.

———. 1978. Maya numeration, computation, and calendrical astonomy. *Dictionary of Scientific Biography*, vol. 15, suppl. 1, pp. 759-818.

LOWE, GARETH W. 1975. *The Early Preclassic Barra Phase of Altamira, Chiapas: A Review with New Data*. New World Archaeological Foundation Papers, no. 38.

———. 1977. The Mixe-Zoque as competing neighbors of the early lowland Maya. In Richard E. W. Adams, ed., *The Origins of Maya Civilization*, pp. 197-248. Albuquerque: University of New Mexico Press.

——— AND J. ALDEN MASON. 1965. Archaeological survey of the Chiapas coast, highlands, and upper Grijalva Basin. *Handbook of Middle American Indians* 2:195-236. Austin: University of Texas Press.

LYNCH, THOMAS F. 1978. The South American Paleo-Indians. In Jesse D. Jennings, ed., *Ancient Native Americans*, pp. 455-89. San Francisco: W. H. Freeman.

MACNEISH, RICHARD S. 1972. The evolution of community patterns in the Tehuacán Valley of Mexico and speculations about the cultural processes. In Peter J. Ucko, Ruth Tringham, and G. W. Dimbleby, eds., *Man, Settlement and Urbanism*, pp. 67-93. London: Gerald Duckworth.

———, MELVIN L. FOWLER, ANGEL GARCIA COOK, FREDERICK A. PETERSON, ANTOINETTE NELKEN-TERNER, AND JAMES A. NEELY. 1972. *The Prehistory of the Tehuacán Valley*, vol. 5: *Excavations and Reconnaissance*. Austin: University of Texas Press.

——— AND FREDERICK A. PETERSON. 1962. *The Santa Marta Rock Shelter, Ocozocoautla, Chiapas, Mexico*. New World Archaeological Foundation Papers, no. 14.

———, S. JEFFREY K. WILKERSON, AND ANTOINETTE NELKEN-TERNER. 1980. *First Annual Report of the Belize Archaic Archaeological Reconnaissance*. Andover, Mass.: Robert S. Peabody Foundation for Archaeology.

MACNUTT, FRANCIS A. 1912. *De Orbe Novo: The Eight Decades of Peter Martyr d'Anghiera*, vol. 1. New York: G. P. Putman's Sons.

MALER, TEOBERT. 1901. *Researches in the Central Portion of the Usumacintla Valley*. Harvard University, Peabody Museum of American Archaeology and Ethnology, Memoirs, vol. 2, no. 1.

———. 1903. *Researches in the Central Portion of the Usumacintla Valley*. Harvard University, Peabody Museum of American Archaeology and Ethnology, Memoirs, vol. 2, no. 2.

———. 1911. *Explorations in the Department of Petén, Guatemala: Tikal*. Harvard University, Peabody Museum of American Archaeology and Ethnology, Memoirs, vol. 5, no. 1.

MARCUS, JOYCE. 1976a. *Emblem and State in the Classic Maya Lowlands: An Epigraphic Approach to Territorial Organization*. Washington: Dumbarton Oaks.

———. 1976b. The origins of Mesoamerican writing. *Annual Review of Anthropology* 5:35-67.

MATHEWS, PETER, AND LINDA SCHELE. 1974. Lords of Palenque—the glyphic evidence. In Merle Greene Robertson, ed., *Primera Mesa Redonda de Palenque, Part I*, pp. 63-76. Pebble Beach, Calif.: Robert Louis Stevenson School.

MEANS, PHILIP A. 1917. *History of the Spanish Conquest of Yucatan and of the Itzás*. Harvard University, Peabody Museum of American Archaeology and Ethnology, Papers, vol. 7.

MERWIN, RAYMOND E., AND GEORGE C. VAILLANT. 1932. *The Ruins of Holmul, Guatemala*. Harvard University, Peabody Museum of American Archaeology and Ethnology, Memoirs, vol. 8, no. 2.

MICHELS, JOSEPH W. 1975. El Chayal, Guatemala: a chronological and behavioral reassessment. *American Antiquity* 40:103-6.

_____. 1979. *The Kaminaljuyú Chiefdom.* State College: Pennsylvania State University Press.

_____, ed. 1979. *Settlement Pattern Excavations at Kaminaljuyú, Guatemala.* State College: Pennsylvania State University Press.

MILES, S. W. 1952. An analysis of modern Middle American calendars. In Sol Tax, ed., *Acculturation in the Americas: Proceedings and Selected Papers of the 29th International Congress of Americanists,* pp. 273–84. Chicago: University of Chicago Press.

_____. 1957. *The Sixteenth-Century Pokom-Maya: A Documentary Analysis of Social Structure and Archaeological Setting.* American Philosophical Society, Transactions, n.s. 47, pt. 4.

_____. 1965a. Sculpture of the Guatemala-Chiapas highlands and Pacific slopes, and associated hieroglyphs. *Handbook of Middle American Indians* 2:237–75. Austin: University of Texas Press.

_____. 1965b. Summary of preconquest ethnology of the Guatemala-Chiapas highlands and Pacific slopes. *Handbook of Middle American Indians* 2:276–87. Austin: University of Texas Press.

MILLER, ARTHUR G. 1973. Archaeological investigations of the Quintana Roo mural project: a preliminary report of the 1973 season. In John A. Graham, ed., *Studies in Ancient Mesoamerica,* pp. 137–48. University of California, Archaeological Research Facility, Contributions, vol. 18.

_____. 1975. Archaeological investigations at Tulum and Tancah, Quintana Roo, Mexico: a progress report of the 1974 season. In John A. Graham, ed., *Studies in Ancient Mesoamerica II,* pp. 10–16. University of California, Archaeological Research Facility, Contributions, vol. 27.

_____. 1977. Captains of the Itzá: unpublished mural evidence from Chichén Itzá. In Norman Hammond, ed., *Social Process in Maya Prehistory: Studies in Honour of Sir Eric Thompson,* pp. 197–225. New York: Academic Press.

_____. 1978. A brief outline of the artistic evidence for Classic period cultural contact between Maya lowlands and central Mexican highlands. In Esther Pasztory, ed., *Middle Classic Mesoamerica: A.D. 400–700,* pp. 63–70. New York: Columbia University Press.

MILLON, RENÉ. 1967. Teotihuacán. *Scientific American* 216(6):38–48.

_____, ed. 1973. *Urbanization at Teotihuacán, Mexico,* vol. 1: *The Teotihuacán Map,* pts. 1 and 2. Austin: University of Texas Press.

MOLLOY, JOHN P., AND WILLIAM L. RATHJE. 1974. Sexploitation among the Late Classic Maya. In Norman Hammond, ed., *Mesoamerican Archaeology: New Approaches,* pp. 431–44. Austin: University of Texas Press.

MONTAGU, ROBERTA. 1969. The Tojolabal. *Handbook of Middle American Indians* 7:226–29. Austin: University of Texas Press.

MORLEY, SYLVANUS G. 1920. *The Inscriptions at Copán.* Carnegie Institution of Washington, Publication 219.

_____. 1935. *Guide Book to the Ruins of Quiriguá.* Carnegie Institution of Washington.

MORRIS, EARL H., JEAN CHARLOT, AND ANN AXTELL MORRIS. 1931. *The Temple of the Warriors at Chichén Itzá, Yucatan.* Carnegie Institution of Washington, Publication 406.

MOSELEY, MICHAEL E. 1975. *The Maritime Foundations of Andean Civilization.* Menlo Park, Calif.: Cummings.

MURRA, JOHN V. 1968. An Aymará Kingdom in 1567. *Ethnohistory* 15:115–51.

_____. 1971. El "control vertical" de un máximo de pisos ecológicos en la economía de las sociedades andinas. In *Visita de la Provincia de León de Huanuco (1562),* vol. 2, pp. 429–76. Huanuco: Universidad Hermilio Valdizan.

NASH, MANNING. 1958. *Machine Age Maya: The Industrialization of a Guatemalan Community.* American Anthropological Association, Memoir 87.

_____. 1969. Guatemalan highlands. *Handbook of Middle American Indians* 7:30–45. Austin: University of Texas Press.

NAVARRETE, CARLOS. 1966. *The Chiapanec History and Culture.* New World Archaeological Foundation Papers, no. 21.

NELSON, FRED W., KIRK K. NIELSON, NOLAN F. MANGELSON, MAX W. HILL, AND RAY T. MATHENY. 1977. Preliminary studies of the trace element composition of obsidian artifacts from northern Campeche, Mexico. *American Antiquity* 42:209–25.

NETTING, ROBERT McC. 1977. Maya subsistence: mythologies, analogies, possibilities. In Richard E. W. Adams, ed., *The Origins of Maya Civilization,* pp. 299–333. Albuquerque: University of New Mexico Press.

NORMAN, V. GARTH. 1973, 1976. *Izapa Sculpture.* New World Archaeological Foundation Papers, no. 30.

PAGDEN, A. R., trans. and ed. 1971. *Hernán Cortés: Letters from Mexico.* New York: Grossman.

———, trans. 1975. *The Maya: Diego de Landa's Account of the Affairs of Yucatan.* Chicago: J. Philip O'Hara.

PARSONS, LEE A. 1973. Iconographic notes on a new Izapan stela from Abaj Takalik, Guatemala. *Atti del XL Congresso Internazionale degli Americanisti* 1:203–12.

———. 1978. The peripheral coastal lowlands and the Middle Classic period. In Esther Pasztory, ed., *Middle Classic Mesoamerica: A.D. 400–700,* pp. 25–34. New York: Columbia University Press.

PENDERGAST, DAVID M. 1971. Evidence of early Teotihuacán–lowland Maya contact at Altún Ha. *American Antiquity* 36:455–60.

PIÑA CHÁN, ROMÁN. 1955. *Chalcatzingo, Morelos.* Instituto Nacional de Antropología e Historia (Mexico), Dirección de Monumentos Prehispánicos, report no. 4.

POLLOCK, HARRY E. D. 1980. *The Puuc: An Architectural Survey of the Hill Country of Yucatan and Northern Campeche, Mexico.* Harvard University: Peabody Museum of Archaeology and Ethnology, Memoirs, vol. 19.

———, RALPH L. ROYS, TATIANA PROSKOURIAKOFF, AND A. LEDYARD SMITH. 1962. *Mayapán, Yucatan, Mexico.* Carnegie Institution of Washington, Publication 619.

POTTER, DAVID F. 1976. Prehispanic architecture and sculpture in central Yucatan. *American Antiquity* 41:430–48.

PRING, DUNCAN C. 1977a. The dating of Teotihuacán contact at Altún Ha: the new evidence. *American Antiquity* 42:626–28.

———. 1977b. Influence or intrusion? The "Protoclassic" in the Maya lowlands. In Norman Hammond, ed., *Social Process in Maya Prehistory: Studies in Honour of Sir Eric Thompson,* pp. 135–65. New York: Academic Press.

———. 1979. The Swasey complex of northern Belize: a definition and discussion. In John A. Graham, ed., *Studies in Ancient Mesoamerica, IV,* pp. 215–29. University of California, Archaeological Research Facility, Contributions, vol. 41.

PROSKOURIAKOFF, TATIANA. 1950. *A Study of Classic Maya Sculpture.* Carnegie Institution of Washington, Publication 593.

———. 1955. The death of a civilization. Reprinted in *Cities: Their Origin, Growth and Human Impact,* pp. 93–97. San Francisco: W. H. Freeman.

———. 1960. Historical implications of a pattern of dates at Piedras Negras, Guatemala. *American Antiquity* 25:454–75.

———. 1961a. The lords of the Maya realm. *Expedition* 4(1):14–21.

———. 1961b. Portraits of women in Maya art. In Samuel K. Lothrop et al., *Essays in Pre-Columbian Art and Archaeology,* pp. 81–99. Cambridge: Harvard University Press.

———. 1963a. *An Album of Maya Architecture.* Norman: University of Oklahoma Press.

———. 1963b. Historical data in the inscriptions of Yaxchilán, pt. 1. *Estudios de Cultura Maya* 3:149–67.

———. 1964. Historical data in the inscriptions of Yaxchilán, pt. 2. *Estudios de Cultura Maya* 4:177–201.

————. 1965. Sculpture and major arts of the Maya lowlands. *Handbook of Middle American Indians* 2:469–97. Austin: University of Texas Press.

————. 1974. *Jades from the Cenote of Sacrifice, Chichén Itzá, Yucatan.* Harvard University, Peabody Museum of Archaeology and Ethnology, Memoirs, vol. 10, no. 1.

PULESTON, DENNIS E. 1971. An experimental approach to the function of Classic Maya chultuns. *American Antiquity* 36:322–35.

————. 1974. Intersite areas in the vicinity of Tikal and Uaxactún. In Norman Hammond, ed., *Mesoamerican Archaeology: New Approaches,* pp. 303–11. Austin: University of Texas Press.

————. 1977. The art and archaeology of hydraulic agriculture in the Maya lowlands. In Norman Hammond, ed., *Social Process in Maya Prehistory: Essays in Honour of Sir Eric Thompson,* pp. 449–67. New York: Academic Press.

————. 1979. An epistemological pathology and the collapse, or Why the Maya kept the Short Count. In Norman Hammond and Gordon R. Willey, eds., *Maya Archaeology and Ethnohistory,* pp. 63–71. Austin: University of Texas Press.

———— AND D. W. CALLENDER, JR. 1967. Defensive earthworks at Tikal. *Expedition* 9(3):40–48.

———— AND OLGA S. PULESTON. 1971. An ecological approach to the origins of Maya civilization. *Archaeology* 24:330–37.

QUIRARTE, JACINTO. 1976. The relationship of Izapan-style art to Olmec and Maya art: a review. In H. B. Nicholson, ed., *Origins of Religious Art and Iconography in Preclassic Mesoamerica,* pp. 73–86. Los Angeles: UCLA Latin American Center.

————. 1977. Early art styles of Mesoamerica and Early Classic Maya art. In Richard E. W. Adams, ed., *The Origins of Maya Civilization,* pp. 249–83. Albuquerque: University of New Mexico Press.

RALPH, ELIZABETH K., H. N. MICHAEL, AND M. C. HAN. 1973. Radiocarbon dates and reality. *MASCA Newsletter* 9(1):1–20.

RANDS, ROBERT L. 1969. *Mayan Ecology and Trade: 1967–1968.* Southern Illinois University, University Museum, Research Records, Mesoamerican Studies, no. 2.

————. 1973. The Classic Maya collapse: Usumacinta zone and the northwestern periphery. In T. Patrick Culbert, ed., *The Classic Maya Collapse,* pp. 165–205. Albuquerque: University of New Mexico Press.

————. 1974. A chronological framework for Palenque. In Merle Greene Robertson, ed., *Primera Mesa Redonda de Palenque, Part I,* pp. 35–39. Pebble Beach, Calif.: Robert Louis Stevenson School.

————. 1977. The rise of Classic Maya civilization in the northwestern zone: isolation and integration. In Richard E. W. Adams, ed., *The Origins of Maya Civilization,* pp. 159–80. Albuquerque: University of New Mexico Press.

———— AND ROBERT E. SMITH. 1965. Pottery of the Guatemalan highlands. *Handbook of Middle American Indians* 2:95–145. Austin: University of Texas Press.

RATHJE, WILLIAM L. 1971. The origin and development of lowland Classic Maya civilization. *American Antiquity* 36:275–85.

————. 1977. The Tikal connection. In Richard E. W. Adams, ed., *The Origins of Maya Civilization,* pp. 373–82. Albuquerque: University of New Mexico Press.

RECINOS, ADRIAN, AND DELIA GOETZ, trans. 1953. *The Annals of the Cakchiquels.* Norman: University of Oklahoma Press.

REDFIELD, ROBERT. 1941. *The Folk Culture of Yucatan.* Chicago: University of Chicago Press.

————. 1950. *A Village That Chose Progress: Chan Kom Revisited.* Chicago: University of Chicago Press.

———— AND ALFONSO VILLA ROJAS. 1934. *Chan Kom: A Maya Village.* Carnegie Institution of Washington, Publication 448.

REINA, RUBEN E. 1966. *The Law of the Saints.* New York: Bobbs-Merrill.

―――. 1969. Eastern Guatemalan highlands: the Pokomames and Chorti. *Handbook of Middle American Indians* 7:101–32. Austin: University of Texas Press.

―――― AND ROBERT M. HILL II. 1980. Lowland Maya subsistence: notes from ethnohistory and ethnography. *American Antiquity* 45:74–79.

RICKETSON, OLIVER G., JR., AND EDITH BAYLES RICKETSON. 1937. *Uaxactún, Guatemala: Group E, 1926–1931.* Carnegie Institution of Washington, Publication 477.

RITMAN, LAWRENCE H. 1968. The rubber ball-game of Mesoamerica. *Cerámica de Cultura Maya et al.* 5:27–57.

ROBERTSON, MERLE GREENE, ROBERT L. RANDS, AND JOHN A. GRAHAM. 1972. *Maya Sculpture from the Southern Lowlands, the Highlands and the Pacific Piedmont.* Berkeley: Lederer, Street & Zeus.

ROYS, RALPH L. 1957. *Political Geography of the Yucatan Maya.* Carnegie Institution of Washington, Publication 613.

―――. 1965. Lowland Maya native society at Spanish contact. *Handbook of Middle American Indians* 3:659–78. Austin: University of Texas Press.

―――. 1972. *The Indian Background of Colonial Yucatan.* New ed. Norman: University of Oklahoma Press.

――――, FRANCE V. SCHOLES, AND E. B. ADAMS. 1940. *Report and Census of the Indians of Cozumel, 1570.* Carnegie Institution of Washington, Contributions to American Anthropology and History, no. 30.

――――, trans. and ed. 1967. *The Book of Chilam Balam of Chumayel.* New ed. Norman: University of Oklahoma Press.

RUPPERT, KARL. 1935. *The Caracol at Chichén Itzá, Yucatan, Mexico.* Carnegie Institution of Washington, Publication 454.

RUZ LHUILLER, ALBERTO. 1952–58. Exploraciones arqueológicas en Palenque: 1949–1956. *Instituto Nacional de Antropología e Historia, Anales* 4(32):49-60, 5(33):25–65, 6(34):79–110, 10(39):69–299.

―――. 1973. *El Templo de las Inscripciones.* Instituto Nacional de Antropología e Historia (Mexico), Colección Científica, no. 7.

SABLOFF, JEREMY A. 1970. Type descriptions of the Fine Paste ceramics of the Bayal Boca complex, Seibal, Petén, Guatemala. In William R. Bullard, Jr., ed., *Monographs and Papers in Maya Archaeology,* pp. 357–404. Harvard University, Peabody Museum of Archaeology and Ethnology, Papers, vol. 61.

―――. 1973. Continuity and disruption during Terminal Late Classic times at Seibal: ceramic and other evidence. In T. Patrick Culbert, ed., *The Classic Maya Collapse,* pp. 107–31. Albuquerque: University of New Mexico Press.

―――. 1975. *Excavations at Seibal: Ceramics.* Harvard University, Peabody Museum of Archaeology and Ethnology, Memoirs, vol. 13, no. 2.

―――― AND DAVID A. FREIDEL. 1975. A model of a pre-Columbian trading center. In Jeremy A. Sabloff and C. C. Lamberg-Karlovsky, eds., *Ancient Civilization and Trade,* pp. 369–408. Albuquerque: University of New Mexico Press.

―――― AND WILLIAM L. RATHJE. 1975. The rise of a Maya merchant class. *Scientific American* 233(4):72–82.

――――, WILLIAM L. RATHJE, DAVID A. FREIDEL, J. G. CONNER, AND PAULA L. W. SABLOFF. 1974. Trade and power in Postclassic Yucatan: initial observations. In Norman Hammond, ed., *Mesoamerican Archaeology: New Approaches,* pp. 397–416. Austin: University of Texas Press.

―――― AND WILLIAM L. RATHJE, eds. 1975. *A Study of Changing Pre-Columbian Commercial Systems: The 1972–1973 Seasons at Cozumel, Mexico.* Harvard University, Peabody Museum of Archaeology and Ethnology, Monographs, no. 3.

SANDERS, WILLIAM T. 1960. *Prehistoric Ceramics and Settlement Patterns in Quintana Roo, Mexico.* Carnegie Institution of Washington, Contributions to American Anthropology and History, no. 60.

―――. 1973. The cultural ecology of the lowland Maya: a reevaluation. In T.

Patrick Culbert, ed., *The Classic Maya Collapse*, pp. 325–65. Albuquerque: University of New Mexico Press.

———. 1977. Environmental heterogeneity and the evolution of lowland Maya civilization. In Richard E. W. Adams, ed., *The Origins of Maya Civilization*, pp 287–97. Albuquerque: University of New Mexico Press.

———. 1978. Ethnographic analogy and the Teotihuacán horizon style. In Esther Pasztory, ed., *Middle Classic Mesoamerica: A.D. 400–700*, pp. 35–44. New York: Columbia University Press.

——— AND BARBARA J. PRICE. 1968. *Mesoamerica: The Evolution of a Civilization*. New York: Random House.

——— AND JOSEPH W. MICHELS, eds. 1969. *The Pennsylvania State University Kaminaljuyú Project—1968 Season*, pt. 1: *The Excavations*. Pennsylvania State University, Occasional Papers in Anthropology, no. 2.

——— AND ———, eds. 1977. *Teotihuacán and Kaminaljuyú: A Study in Prehistoric Culture Contact*. State College: Pennsylvania State University Press.

SATTERTHWAITE, LINTON. 1965. Calendrics of the Maya lowlands. *Handbook of Middle American Indians* 3:603–31. Austin: University of Texas Press.

SAUER, CARL ORTWIN. 1966. *The Early Spanish Main*. Berkeley: University of California Press.

SCHELE, LINDA. 1976. Accession iconography of Chan-Bahlum in the group of the Cross at Palenque. In Merle Greene Robertson, ed., *The Art, Iconography and Dynastic History of Palenque, Part III*, pp. 9–34. Pebble Beach, Calif.: Robert Louis Stevenson School.

———. 1977. Palenque: the house of the dying sun. In Anthony F. Aveni, ed., *Native American Astronomy*, pp. 42–56. Austin: University of Texas Press.

———. 1979. Genealogical documentation on the tri-figure panels at Palenque. In Merle Greene Robertson and Donald Call Jeffers, eds., *Tercera Mesa Redonda de Palenque*, pp. 41–70. Monterey, Calif.: Herald Printers.

SCHELLHAS, PAUL. 1904. *Representation of Deities of the Maya Manuscripts*. Harvard University, Peabody Museum of American Archaeology and Ethnology, Papers, vol. 4, no. 1.

SCHOLES, FRANCE V., AND RALPH L. ROYS. 1968. *The Maya Chontal Indians of Acalán-Tixchel: A Contribution to the History and Ethnography of the Yucatan Peninsula*. New ed. Norman: University of Oklahoma Press.

SEDAT, DAVID W., AND ROBERT J. SHARER. 1972. Archaeological investigations in the northern Maya highlands: new data on the Maya Preclassic. In John A. Graham, ed., *Studies in the Archaeology of Mexico and Guatemala*, pp. 23–35. University of California, Archaeological Research Facility, Contributions, vol. 16.

SHARER, ROBERT J. 1974. The prehistory of the southeastern Maya periphery. *Current Anthropology* 15:165–87.

———. 1977. The Maya collapse revisited: internal and external perspectives. In Norman Hammond, ed., *Social Process in Maya Prehistory: Studies in Honour of Sir Eric Thompson*, pp. 532–52. New York: Academic Press.

———. 1978a. Archaeology and history at Quiriguá, Guatemala. *Journal of Field Archaeology* 5:51–70.

———. 1978b. *The Prehistory of Chalchuapa, El Salvador*. 3 vols. Philadelphia: University of Pennsylvania Press.

——— AND JAMES C. GIFFORD. 1970. Preclassic ceramics from Chalchuapa, El Salvador, and their relationships with the Maya lowlands. *American Antiquity* 35:441–62.

——— AND DAVID W. SEDAT. 1973. Monument 1, El Portón, Guatemala, and the development of Maya calendrical and writing systems. In John A. Graham, ed., *Studies in Ancient Mesoamerica*, pp. 177–94. University of California, Archaeological Research Facility, Contributions, vol. 18.

SHEETS, PAYSON D. 1975. A reassessment of the precolumbian obsidian industry of El Chayal, Guatemala. *American Antiquity* 40:98–103.

————. 1979. Maya recovery from volcanic disasters: Ilopango and Cerén. *Archaeology* 32(3):32–42.

SHEPARD, ANNA O. 1948. *Plumbate: A Mesoamerican Trade Ware.* Carnegie Institution of Washington, Publication 573.

SHOOK, EDWIN M., WILLIAM R. COE, VIVIAN L. BROMAN, AND LINTON SATTERTHWAITE. 1958. *Tikal Reports,* nos. 1–4. University of Pennsylvania, University Museum Monographs.

———— AND ALFRED V. KIDDER. 1952. *Mound E-III-3, Kaminaljuyú, Guatemala.* Carnegie Institution of Washington, Contributions to American Anthropology and History, no. 53.

———— AND ALFRED KIDDER II. 1961. The painted tomb at Tikal. *Expedition* 4(1):2–7.

SIDRYS, RAYMOND V. 1976. Classic Maya obsidian trade. *American Antiquity* 41:449–64.

————, JOHN ANDRESEN, AND DEREK MARCUCCI. 1975. Obsidian sources in the Maya area. *Journal of New World Archaeology* 1(5):1–13.

SIEMENS, ALFRED H., AND DENNIS E. PULESTON. 1972. Ridged fields and associated features in southern Campeche: new perspectives on the lowland Maya. *American Antiquity* 37:228–39.

SIMPSON, LESLEY BYRD, trans. and ed. 1964. *Cortés: The Life of the Conqueror by His Secretary, Francisco López de Gómara.* Berkeley: University of California Press.

SMITH, A. LEDYARD. 1950. *Uaxactún, Guatemala: Excavations of 1931–1937.* Carnegie Institution of Washington, Publication 588.

————. 1972. *Excavations at Altar de Sacrificios: Architecture, Settlement, Burials, and Caches.* Harvard University, Peabody Museum of Archaeology and Ethnology, Papers, vol. 62, no. 2.

————. 1973. *Uaxactún: A Pioneering Excavation in Guatemala.* Addison-Wesley Module in Anthropology no. 40.

SMITH, ROBERT E. 1955. *Ceramic Sequence at Uaxactún, Guatemala.* Tulane University, Middle American Research Institute, Publication 20.

SPINDEN, HERBERT J. 1913. *A Study of Maya Art.* Harvard University, Peabody Museum of American Archaeology and Ethnology, Memoirs, vol. 6.

STARK, BARBARA L., ALFRED H. SIEMENS, AND DENNIS E. PULESTON. 1976. Comments on southern Campeche Maya canals. *American Antiquity* 41:381–84.

STEPHENS, JOHN LLOYD. 1841. *Incidents of Travel in Central America, Chiapas, and Yucatan.* 2 vols. Reprint ed. 1949. New Brunswick: Rutgers University Press.

————. 1843. *Incidents of Travel in Yucatan.* 2 vols. Reprint ed. 1963. New York: Dover.

STERN, THEODORE. 1949. *The Rubber-Ball Games of the Americas.* American Ethnological Society Monographs, no. 17.

STEVENS, RAYFRED L. 1964. The soils of Middle America and their relation to Indian peoples and cultures. *Handbook of Middle American Indians* 1:265–315. Austin: University of Texas Press.

STEWART, T. D. 1973. *The People of America.* New York: Charles Scribner's Sons.

STONE, DORIS Z. 1941. *Archaeology of the North Coast of Honduras.* Harvard University, Peabody Museum of Archaeology and Ethnology, Memoirs, vol. 9, no. 1.

STRONG, WILLIAM DUNCAN, ALFRED KIDDER II, AND A. J. DREXEL PAUL, JR. 1938. *Preliminary Report on the Smithsonian Institution–Harvard University Archeological Expedition to Northwestern Honduras, 1936.* Smithsonian Miscellaneous Collections, vol. 97, no. 1.

STUART, GEORGE E. 1975. The Maya: riddle of the glyphs. *National Geographic* 148:768–91.

STUART, L. C. 1964. Fauna of Middle America. *Handbook of Middle American Indians* 1:316–62. Austin: University of Texas Press.

TAMAYO, JORGE L., AND ROBERT C. WEST. 1964. The hydrography of Middle

America. *Handbook of Middle American Indians* 1:84–121. Austin: University of Texas Press.

Tax, Sol. 1953. *Penny Capitalism: A Guatemalan Indian Economy.* Smithsonian Institution, Institute of Social Anthropology, Publication 16.

———— and Robert Hinshaw. 1969. The Maya of the midwestern highlands. *Handbook of Middle American Indians* 7:69–100. Austin: University of Texas Press.

Thomas, Cyrus. 1904. Mayan calendar systems, II. *Smithsonian Institution, Bureau of American Ethnology, Twenty-Second Annual Report, 1900–1901,* pt. 1, pp. 197–305.

Thomas, Norman D. 1974. *The Linguistic, Geographic, and Demographic Position of the Zoque of Southern Mexico.* New World Archaeological Foundation Papers, no. 36.

Thompson, Edward H. 1897. *Cave of Loltún, Yucatan.* Harvard University, Peabody Museum of American Archaeology and Ethnology, Memoirs, vol. 1, no. 2.

Thompson, J. Eric S. 1934. *Sky Bearers, Colors and Directions in Maya and Mexican Religion.* Carnegie Institution of Washington, Contributions to American Anthropology and History, no. 10.

————. 1951. The Itzá of Tayasal, Petén. In *Homenaje al Dr. Alfonso Caso,* pp. 389–400. Mexico: Nuevo Mundo.

————. 1960. *Maya Hieroglyphic Writing: An Introduction.* New ed. Norman: University of Oklahoma Press.

————. 1965. Maya hieroglyphic writing. *Handbook of Middle American Indians* 3:632–58. Austin: University of Texas Press.

————. 1970. *Maya History and Religion.* Norman: University of Oklahoma Press.

————. 1971. Estimates of Maya population: deranging factors. *American Antiquity* 36:214–216.

————. 1974. "Canals" of the Río Candelaria basin, Campeche, Mexico. In Norman Hammond, ed., *Mesoamerican Archaeology: New Approaches,* pp. 297–302. Austin: University of Texas Press.

————, H. E. D. Pollock, and J. Charlot. 1932. *A Preliminary Study of the Ruins of Cobá, Quintana Roo, Mexico.* Carnegie Institution of Washington, Publication 424.

Tourtellot, Gair, and Jeremy A. Sabloff. 1972. Exchange sytems among the ancient Maya. *American Antiquity* 37:126–35.

Tozzer, Alfred M. 1907. *A Comparative Study of the Mayas and the Lacandones.* New York: Archaeological Institute of America.

————. 1911. *A Preliminary Study of the Prehistoric Ruins of Tikal, Guatemala.* Harvard University, Peabody Museum of American Archaeology and Ethnology, Memoirs, vol. 5, no. 2.

————. 1957. *Chichén Itzá and Its Cenote of Sacrifice: A Comparative Study of Contemporaneous Maya and Toltec.* Harvard University, Peabody Museum of Archaeology and Ethnology, Memoirs, vols. 11, 12.

————, ed. 1941. *Landa's "Relación de las Cosas de Yucatán."* Harvard University, Peabody Museum of Archaeology and Ethnology, Papers, vol. 18.

Turner, B. L. II. 1974. Prehistoric intensive agriculture in the Maya lowlands. *Science* 185:118–24.

————. 1979. Prehispanic terracing in the central Maya lowlands: problems of agricultural intensification. In Norman Hammond and Gordon R. Willey, eds., *Maya Archaeology and Ethnohistory,* pp. 103–115. Austin: University of Texas Press.

———— and William C. Johnson. 1979. A Maya dam in the Copán valley, Honduras. *American Antiquity* 44:299–305.

Villa Rojas, Alfonso. 1945. *The Maya of East Central Quintana Roo.* Carnegie Institution of Washington, Publication 559.

————. 1969a. Maya lowlands: the Chontal, Chol, and Kekchi. *Handbook of Middle American Indians* 7:230–43. Austin: University of Texas Press.

————. 1969b. The Maya of Yucatan. *Handbook of Middle American Indians* 7:244–75. Austin: University of Texas Press.

————. 1969c. The Tzeltal. *Handbook of Middle American Indians* 7:195–225. Austin: University of Texas Press.

VIVÓ ESCOTO, JORGE A. 1964. Weather and climate of Mexico and Central America. *Handbook of Middle American Indians* 1:187–215. Austin: University of Texas Press.

VOGT, EVON Z. 1968. Some aspects of Zinacantan settlement patterns and ceremonial organization. In K. C. Chang, ed., *Settlement Archaeology*, pp. 154–73. Palo Alto: National Press Books.

————. 1969a. Chiapas highlands. *Handbook of Middle American Indians* 7:133–51. Austin: University of Texas Press.

————. 1969b. *Zinacantan: A Maya Community in the Highlands of Chiapas.* Cambridge: Harvard University Press.

————. 1970. *The Zinacantecos of Mexico: A Modern Maya Way of Life.* New York: Holt, Rinehart & Winston.

————, ed. 1969. *Handbook of Middle American Indians* 7:21–311. Austin: University of Texas Press.

VON HAGEN, VICTOR W. 1948. *Maya Explorer: John Lloyd Stephens and the Lost Cities of Central America and Yucatan.* Norman: University of Oklahoma Press.

————. 1950. *Frederick Catherwood, Archt.* New York: Oxford University Press.

VOORHIES, BARBARA. 1972. Settlement patterns in two regions of the southern Maya lowlands. *American Antiquity* 37:115–26.

————. 1973. Possible social factors in the exchange system of the prehistoric Maya. *American Antiquity* 38:486–89.

————. 1976. *The Chantuto People: An Archaic Period Society of the Chiapas Littoral, Mexico.* New World Archaeological Foundation Papers, no. 41.

WAGLEY, CHARLES. 1969. The Maya of northwestern Guatemala. *Handbook of Middle American Indians* 7:46–68. Austin: University of Texas Press.

WAGNER, PHILIP L. 1964. Natural vegetation of Middle America. *Handbook of Middle American Indians* 1:216–64. Austin: University of Texas Press.

WALLACE, DWIGHT T., AND ROBERT M. CARMACK, eds. 1977. *Archaeology and Ethnohistory of the Central Quiché.* State University of New York at Albany, Institute for Mesoamerican Studies, Publication 1.

WAUCHOPE, ROBERT. 1962. *Lost Tribes and Sunken Continents: Myth and Method in the Study of American Indians.* Chicago: University of Chicago Press.

WEBSTER, DAVID L. 1974. The fortifications of Becán, Campeche, Mexico. In *Archaeological Investigations on the Yucatan Peninsula*, pp. 123–27. Tulane University, Middle American Research Institute, Publication 31.

————. 1977. Warfare and the evolution of Maya civilization. In Richard E. W. Adams, ed., *The Origins of Maya Civilization*, pp. 335–72. Albuquerque: University of New Mexico Press.

WEST, ROBERT C. 1964a. The natural regions of Middle America. *Handbook of Middle American Indians* 1:363–83. Austin: University of Texas Press.

————. 1964b. Surface configuration and associated geology of Middle America. *Handbook of Middle American Indians* 1:33–83. Austin: University of Texas Press.

WILKEN, GENE C. 1971. Food-producing systems available to the ancient Maya. *American Antiquity* 36:432–48.

WILLEY, GORDON R. 1956. Problems concerning prehistoric settlement patterns in the Maya lowlands. In Gordon R. Willey, ed., *Prehistoric Settlement Patterns in the New World*, pp. 107–14. Viking Fund Publications in Anthropology, no. 23.

————. 1970. Type descriptions of the ceramics of the Real Xe complex, Seibal, Petén, Guatemala. In William R. Bullard, Jr., ed., *Monographs and Papers in*

Maya Archaeology, pp. 313–55. Harvard University, Peabody Museum of Archaeology and Ethnology, Papers, vol. 61.

————. 1971. *An Introduction to American Archaeology,* vol. 2: *South America.* Englewood Cliffs: Prentice-Hall.

————. 1973a. *The Altar de Sacrificios Excavations: General Summary and Conclusions.* Harvard University, Peabody Museum of Archaeology and Ethnology, Papers, vol. 64, no. 3.

————. 1973b. Certain aspects of the Late Classic to Postclassic periods in the Belize Valley. In T. Patrick Culbert, ed., *The Classic Maya Collapse,* pp. 93–106. Albuquerque: University of New Mexico Press.

————. 1974. The Classic Maya hiatus: a "rehearsal" for the collapse? In Norman Hammond, ed., *Mesoamerican Archaeology: New Approaches,* pp. 417–30. Austin: University of Texas Press.

————. 1977a. The rise of Classic Maya civilization: a Pasión Valley perspective. In Richard E. W. Adams, ed., *The Origins of Maya Civilization,* pp. 133–57. Albuquerque: University of New Mexico Press.

————. 1977b. The rise of Maya civilization: a summary view. In Richard E. W. Adams, ed., *The Origins of Maya Civilization,* pp. 383–423. Albuquerque: University of New Mexico Press.

———— AND WILLIAM R. BULLARD, JR. 1965. Prehistoric settlement patterns in the Maya lowlands. *Handbook of Middle American Indians* 2:360–77. Austin: University of Texas Press.

————, ————, JOHN B. GLASS, AND JAMES C. GIFFORD. 1965. *Prehistoric Maya Settlements in the Belize Valley.* Harvard University, Peabody Museum of Archaeology and Ethnology, Papers, vol. 54.

————, T. PATRICK CULBERT, AND RICHARD E. W. ADAMS. 1967. Maya lowland ceramics: a report from the 1965 Guatemala City conference. *American Antiquity* 32:289–315.

———— AND RICHARD M. LEVENTHAL. 1979. Prehistoric settlement at Copán. In Norman Hammond and Gordon R. Willey, eds., *Maya Archaeology and Ethnohistory,* pp. 75–102. Austin: University of Texas Press.

————, ————, AND WILLIAM L. FASH, JR. 1978. Maya settlement in the Copán Valley. *Archaeology* 31(4):32–43.

———— AND JEREMY A. SABLOFF. 1980. *A History of American Archaeology.* 2d ed. San Francisco: W. H. Freeman.

———— AND DEMITRI B. SHIMKIN. 1973. The Maya collapse: a summary view. In T. Patrick Culbert, ed., *The Classic Maya Collapse,* pp. 457–501. Albuquerque: University of New Mexico Press.

———— AND A. LEDYARD SMITH. 1969. *The Ruins of Altar de Sacrificios, Department of Petén, Guatemala: An Introduction.* Harvard University, Peabody Museum of Archaeology and Ethnology, Papers, vol. 62, no. 1.

————, ————, GAIR TOURTELLOT III, AND IAN GRAHAM. 1975. *Excavations at Seibal: Introduction. The Site and Its Setting.* Harvard University, Peabody Museum of Archaeology and Ethnology, Memoirs, vol. 13, no. 1.

WISDOM, CHARLES. 1940. *The Chorti Indians of Guatemala.* Chicago: University of Chicago Press.

WITTFOGEL, KARL A. 1957. *Oriental Despotism: A Comparative Study of Total Power.* New Haven: Yale University Press.

————. 1972. The hydraulic approach to pre-Spanish Mesoamerica. In Frederick Johnson, ed., *The Prehistory of the Tehuacán Valley,* vol. 4: *Chronology and Irrigation,* pp. 59–80. Austin: University of Texas Press.

WOLF, ERIC R. 1959. *Sons of the Shaking Earth.* Chicago: University of Chicago Press.

WOODBURY, RICHARD B., AND AUBREY TRIK. 1953. *The Ruins of Zaculeu, Guatemala.* 2 vols. Richmond: William Byrd Press.

ZIER, CHRISTIAN J. 1980. A Classic-period Maya agricultural field in western El Salvador. *Journal of Field Archaeology* 7:65–74.

INDEX

THE WORLD OF
THE ANCIENT MAYA

Composed by The Composing Room of Michigan, Inc.
in 10 point VIP Palatino, 2 points leaded,
with display lines in Palatino.
Printed offset by Vail-Ballou Press
on Warren's Patina Coated Matte, 70 pound basis.
Bound by Vail-Ballou Press.
Color plates printed by
Kingsport Press.